SHAKESPEARE *FOR* WRITERS

SHAKESPEARE

FOR WRITERS

BOOK 1

Protagonist, Plot, Antagonist

Maggi Kramm

DEDICATION

For the late Professor Tom Clayton, who generously shared his deep knowledge of Shakespeare with countless students, colleagues, and other audiences on both sides of the Atlantic. He channeled the inexhaustible spirit and brilliance he found in his beloved Shakespeare.

Contents

Error! No text of specified style in document.

INTRODUCTION

The Shakespeare for Writers Series

It's been 400 years since Shakespeare's death, and there's so much we don't know about him as a writer. Why did he become an in-house playwright, instead of dedicating himself to writing poetry for a select few, as it seems he wished to do as a young man? Did heartbreak over a love triangle cause Shakespeare to pour out his soul in his sonnets, or did he simply imagine the scenario for literary material? Did he really mean for *Hamlet* to run four hours in performance? If so, how did his audiences feel about that?

We have uncovered no production notes, diaries, essays, or even love letters attributed to him, let alone advice to other writers on his craft. Aside from a handful of signatures on legal documents, and perhaps three pages of the collaboratively written play, *Sir Thomas More*, we have nothing for sure in his own handwriting.

But he did leave us around 38 plays and more than 150 poems. From these, along with research on the period, we can infer a lot about how he worked as a writer. We can offer plausible answers to questions such as:

- What makes the plot of *Hamlet* structurally solid and reliably exhilarating?
- How does Shakespeare create a Cleopatra so variable and fascinating that this protagonist does justice to the historical figure?
- Why does Shakespeare recycle so many ideas from other sources, and how does he manage to improve on them?

From the works themselves we can extract some of his writing techniques. We can highlight what he does well in solving writing challenges, and see what he discards or develops over time.

What Is This Series About?

Shakespeare for Writers is a three-part series of books describing Shakespeare's writing techniques and the logic behind his choices. These techniques are illustrated with plentiful examples from his works. From time to time, we will speculate on his views of the craft of writing and examine what he says about creative inspiration.

This first book analyzes how Shakespeare constructs his protagonists, plots, and antagonists. The two later books explore specialized topics, such as how he uses literary devices to paint his scenes and to achieve a particular mood, how he shapes his beginnings and endings, what he gains by adding subplots or foil characters, and how he builds momentum.

Who Is This Series For?

Shakespeare for Writers is for writers and others who want to analyze the mechanics of Shakespeare's writing. It is for those interested in seeing what Shakespeare was aiming for in making certain choices—which components he typically includes in his plots, for instance, or the traits his protagonists and antagonists often display as well as the kinds of journeys he takes them on.

The examples draw primarily from his plays—from the most famous, such as *Hamlet, Othello, Macbeth, Richard III,* and *Much Ado About Nothing,* to the lesser known ones, such as *Pericles, Coriolanus,* and *All's Well That Ends Well.*

Although these texts were meant for stage production, Shakespeare's specific writing challenges and solutions can find parallel application in writing of many kinds. For instance, hooking an audience's interest at the beginning is a handy skill whether you're writing a newsletter or a novel. His indelible use of language and deft strokes of character building can inspire writers of nearly all genres: prose or poetry, film scripts, novels, short fiction, or nonfiction.

What Is This Series Not?

Although we will reflect along the way on what Shakespeare does exceptionally well, these books do not aim to be literary criticism. They focus instead on his practice of writing.

This is also not a writing manual. The books will not tell *you* how to write. Although we will examine Shakespeare's technical choices, there will be no advice on how to apply these to your own writing, let alone how to "write like Shakespeare." Aside from that being an unrealistically high bar, it is better to write like yourself. Shakespeare used a lot of sources in preparing his own works, but he absorbed what he read, took inspiration from it, and transformed whatever he borrowed. That is the job of a writer who wants to learn from others.

And besides, times have changed. Would Shakespeare write for film instead of the stage today? Or novels? Or take lucrative speech-writing or advertising work and write poetry on the side? Who knows? He was a product of his time, and that time will never come again. Shakespeare ended up as a playwright (as well as actor, manager, investor, and poet as his schedule permitted). So much about the business of writing—its audiences, its markets, even its media—has changed beyond what he'd recognize.

But Shakespeare was efficient and pragmatic in his approach to writing. This series will not explain how to apply his techniques, but Shakespeare's nuts-and-bolts approach to writing will become more apparent. By analyzing the way his works are constructed, the reader will perceive the critical thinking he engaged in, how he reflected on and learned from other writers. His example may inspire you to bring a more perceptive eye to whatever models you are drawn to and to reexamine the structural features of your own writing.

How Is This Series Organized, and How to Use It?

Shakespeare, not surprisingly, excelled in techniques ranging from the most basic to the most virtuosic. We'll cover many of these throughout this series.

- **Book 1** addresses some fundamental elements of writing: how he constructs his major characters (protagonist and antagonist) and builds his plots. Athough these are basic topics, this covers a lot of what makes Shakespeare so effective as a writer. In the opening chapter, we also touch on questions of how he learned to be a writer and who and what inspired him. For many readers, this book will provide illustration enough of Shakespeare's approach to his craft.
- For those who want to continue, **Book 2** addresses more specialized writing topics, such as his use of descriptive language to conjure up the scene and mood, and how he begins and ends his works. It reviews techniques he uses to keep momentum going and characteristics of what we are calling his language of love.
- **Book 3** explores techniques that are more advanced, including how he builds pace and sharpens focus in his work. It examines in some detail his use of theme and variation through his subplots, foil characters, and other elements in his works. And Book 3 reviews his astonishing range of wordplay and literary devices. It concludes on a speculative note, with a look at what Shakespeare thought about the nature of inspiration.

Each chapter concludes with definitions of special terms, if any, and a Takeaway for Writers section that summarizes key practical points. An Extras section provides longer passages from Shakespeare or other writers discussed in the chapter, so you can study examples in a fuller excerpt.

Many of the chapter topics in this series will sound familiar to experienced authors and students of writing alike. They reflect some of the traditional building blocks of creative and nonfiction writing. Other chapters, such as those on theme and variations, literary devices, and focus, might be less well known. It's fine to skip ahead to the chapters and topics that most interest you. But because the chapters introduce historical and literary background along the way, reading in sequence will have some advantages.

How Much Shakespeare Do You Need to Know?

Your only prerequisite is an interest in Shakespeare and in the craft of writing. The more experience you have with his works, the better. But these books are geared to readers with only a passing familiarity with Shakespeare. If you are unfamiliar with specific plays, the excerpts and summaries in the chapters should speak for themselves. There are also nearly endless resources available online or in print to help clarify Shakespeare's plots, characters, and language. See the end of this book for recommendations.

It's normal to find Shakespeare's writing challenging. He composed in an often dense and complex style, and by now his language is 400 years old. But keep in mind that you do not need to follow every word to appreciate what Shakespeare is getting at.

Reading Shakespeare's works for the first time might feel like you are encountering a tidal wave of words, many of them archaic. Some of his language was no doubt dense even to his own audiences. Even so, there is a core of meaning and beauty that can usually get through to us.

Partly this is because Shakespeare often builds in useful redundancy—that is, he says much the same thing more than once but in different ways. Shakespeare is not a man of few words. It was through words that he constructed the backdrops and lighting for his stories, making the audience see the early morning sun peeking out over distant hills, and become enthralled to Cleopatra's beauty even when performed by an adolescent male actor.

Let the words flow through you, even if you don't comprehend them all. You don't need to understand all of his words to be touched by what Shakespeare is saying. Probably the most challenging part is that Shakespeare requires an attentive mindset, a willingness to dive deeply. He is not superficially easy, but he rewards the effort.

Shakespeare learned and progressed in his art by studying others. That is what this series aims to help you do. It casts a spotlight on how he constructed his works, why he made some choices over others, and illustrates ways in which he absorbed existing ideas and reimagined them in original ways. *Shakespeare for Writers* highlights approaches Shakespeare used that can serve as inspiration for writers today, just as many other writers served as inspiration to Shakespeare in his day.

CHAPTER 1: HOW SHAKESPEARE LEARNED TO WRITE

W e can conclude a lot about how Shakespeare learned to write and what influenced him as an artist. We're on shakier ground if we claim to know how he became a *great* writer. Greatness was a subject that fascinated Shakespeare, though, and he explores it throughout his works. In the comedy *Twelfth Night*, he identifies three pathways: "Some are born great, some achieve greatness, and some have greatness thrust upon 'em." He's referring here to social greatness—to the power that comes from high rank—but it can apply to genius as well.

Was Shakespeare thinking of himself at all? Was he born great? Did he achieve greatness through hard work? Or was it thrust upon him by virtue of being in the right place at the right time? If Shakespeare asked these questions about himself, he likely couldn't answer them any more than we can.

But he did proceed as if his career were in his own hands. We know that he worked hard to exploit whatever natural gifts he had and whatever opportunities fell his way. The words didn't just descend from on high. He developed as a writer at first by closely studying and emulating others. As he gained more confidence, he innovated and found his own paths. He soon became the writer that his peers emulated, "The glass of fashion and the mould of form," as Ophelia says of Hamlet. But he never ceased his habit of gleaning ideas and inspiration from others.

In turn, he has become for us one of the best models a writer could ask for. Much has changed in the intervening centuries: our tastes, culture, and media types have evolved to a point he'd probably find bewildering. But bridging this gap of time and culture is a communicator so effective that he is still one of the most read, performed, and admired writers today, some 400 years after his death.

He has a lot to teach us as writers. In this book we will focus mainly on the traces he left behind, his plays in particular. We will identify technically what he did, and why these skills are so effective.

1

But in this opening chapter, we begin with Shakespeare himself—his background, his influences, the risks he took, the efforts he made, his strokes of good luck and bad. From these we can speculate on how he took a hand in his own development as a writer.

While genius is a mystery, writing is based on skills that can be learned, and these can be advanced by seeing how others did it.

This chapter will outline some ways he was influenced in learning the nuts and bolts of his own writing. Those who want to get straight to the techniques and examples should skip ahead to Chapter 2.

How Shakespeare Learned to Write

We know a lot about the life of Shakespeare compared to other writers of his era. There is little direct evidence about his youth, and there are major gaps in his biography. Still, scholars have unearthed nearly as much about him as about any of his contemporaries.

Though we cannot account for what made him a genius, we can plausibly describe much of what contributed to Shakespeare's growth as a writer. We can describe the circumstances in which he grew into his inherent talents, the influences that surrounded him and that he sought out. We can glean a lot from what his writing itself shows and what others said about him. Piecing these together, we can infer a great deal about his journey as a writer.

He Learned Early How to Write by Imitating Good Models

Shakespeare had an auspicious start simply in having been born when and where he was. He was the eldest son of a prosperous glove-maker in Stratford. His family's standing entitled the boy to a good education at Stratford-upon-Avon's grammar school. Students typically attended till the age of 14 or 15. Had he been a girl, or a poor farmer's son, grammar school would have been out of reach.

His grammar school was a lot different from ours today. Its curriculum would have hammered into the students a classical training in languages and rhetoric in addition to subjects such as history and geography. Shakespeare was exposed early on to Latin classics, the Bible, possibly ancient Greek writers. The boys may have performed scenes from Roman drama as part of their studies, and read the Latin poet Ovid's marvelous mythic stories in *Metamorphoses*. We know this collection of comic and tragic stories captured Shakespeare's lifelong affection, for he would ransack it for plots, characters, and various stylistic models throughout his career.

2

Day in, day out, William would have learned to think and write through traditional methods. Students would read great works; translate them; and then imitate them in their own words.

These methods encouraged the youngster to read closely and explicate what he read, and to express himself with rhetorical strategies established by the classical writers. With Latin, and some Greek, he would have the building blocks to craft new vocabulary, as he eventually did when writing became his profession.

Although his time in grammar school was brief, his studies connected him with thousands of years of literature and common references that would bring him in contact with authors past and present, from home and abroad.

Perhaps he wasn't a model student. He often parodies schoolmasters and pedants, and usually connects students' attitude to school as one of drudgery. One of the seven stages of man, says Jacques in *As You Like It*, is "the whining schoolboy, with his satchel / And shining morning face, creeping like snail / Unwillingly to school" (2.7).

Yet there's no question Shakespeare became a deep and careful reader, and his early literary training was critical. The works he read as a child and adolescent show up throughout his later output.

He Observed Life around Him

No doubt he was a happy truant when given the chance. There was plenty in and around his hometown to explore and endless delights for the senses.

John Milton, who was himself a learned scholar, would praise Shakespeare a generation later as "Fancy's child" who "Warble[d] his native wood-notes wild" ("L'Allegro" 133-34). For Milton, in other words, he was a natural talent, like a bird who sings from instinct. This might sound like a back-handed compliment, but Milton is just appreciating the vivid, unbookish way Shakespeare expresses himself, as if he is inspired by nature, not imitating other writers.

Stratford Countryside and Town

William would have heard his share of wood-notes wild as he explored the nearby countryside. There he would find rolling hills, forests, and streams; he could wander from farm to village. Shakespeare would have learned the names of flowers and the habits of animals, the threats of storm and drought, and any number of natural phenomena that he incorporates in his writing. In *As You Like It*, a cheerful character speaks of the forest as an education in itself, where he "Finds tongues in trees, books in the running brooks, / Sermons in stones, and good in

3

everything" (2.1). In *A Midsummer Night's Dream*, a sensuous world is evoked through an array of fragrant plants:

> I know a bank where the wild thyme blows,
> Where oxlips and the nodding violet grows,
> Quite over-canopied with luscious woodbine,
> With sweet musk-roses and with eglantine. (2.1)

His mother, Mary Arden, was literate; she likely read to him and first taught him his letters. Around the winter's hearth he would have heard tales of the magic that fairies spin and the tricks to be wary of from sprites like Robin Goodfellow, aka Puck. As an imaginative child he might have encountered these creatures himself during his ramblings; certainly, they will take on reality in his writing.

It's likely he saw his first theater performances as a boy when traveling players passed through towns like Stratford and enacted religious-themed plays and comical interludes. Their arrival would be a major event, bringing not just entertainment, but news and gossip from the world beyond.

But to a curious child, life in this market town would be an education in itself. He could observe its merchants and clients in action; watch as well-off gentry came to order his father's gloves, and heard the clamor and bargaining of those who bought and sold in the weekly market.

Over the years, his father served in elected roles for the town, including as alderman. William would have been privy to the stories of those in dire straits, as his father had the authority to direct alms to impoverished families or provide for orphans. Some sights would have been disturbing, such as when beggars were whipped to chase them from the town, or when other transgressors, such as those who committed adultery or scolded their husbands, were placed in stocks for public shaming. He would hear whisperings of domestic scandals and religious divisions, especially of the papists who clung the old religion and worse, plotted to restore a Catholic monarch on the throne. During his youth, the town endured near-famine in lean years and bouts of pestilence, leading to the horrors that both bring. Stratford would have been a stage itself for a boy fascinated by the drama of everyday existence.

Connecting to the Natural World

Whether this was a talent he developed in youth, or later in life, Shakespeare had an affinity with the natural world, and he observed it with an uncannily sensitive eye. The images and innate drama of nature would seep into his writing.

In Sonnet 73, he conveys what it is like to observe a person reaching the end of life—the sadness and beauty of the spectacle. The speaker likens this state to three natural phenomena:

1. Trees in the autumn, "When yellow leaves, or none, or few, do hang / Upon those boughs which shake against the cold, / Bare ruin'd choirs, where late the sweet birds sang." This person once hosted the lively song of birds, but now the branches are bare—or at most, retain some yellow leaves, which shake in the cold.

2. Twilight, moments after "sunset fadeth in the west"; this is soon taken away by black night, which is "Death's second self, that seals up all in rest."

3. The glowing of a fire, whose ashes are like one's youth and whose embers are the bed upon which one will die. Life is "Consum'd with that which it was nourish'd by": there is still a glowing light, but the wood, which nourished its life, is being consumed.

Shakespeare probably wrote this sonnet well before turning forty years old. It displays fine skills of observation along with a sympathetic nature. He didn't need to experience old age himself to catch its essence. He writes of what it will feel like to see someone at the end of their lifetime—their decreasing vibrancy, the fading and eventually complete darkness that awaits them. And he expresses it by finding an equivalence between the natural world and the human state. To write like this requires a mind that not only sees, but deeply resonates with, the world around them.

He Had Reasons for Trying His Luck Elsewhere

In addition to the drama he found in the town and countryside around him, he would in time find plenty of it in his own domestic life. His father John became deeply in debt by the time William was 15. Records even show that the elder Shakespeare skipped compulsory church services; this was one way of avoiding the bailiff, who would wait outside the church to arrest offenders.

Then William, at the precocious age of 18, married Anne Hathaway, eight years his senior. Some six months later Anne gave birth to Susanna, and within two more years, the twins Hamnet and Judith.

We don't know what occupation William followed at this time. But with his father's finances in distress, and a growing family to provide for, it made sense for the young man to leave home and loved ones for opportunities elsewhere.

Some scholars speculate he joined up with one of the touring companies that passed through Stratford. If so, he might have begun learning his craft in the provinces. But we simply don't know where he was or what he was doing during his early 20s. All we can say is that sometime after the birth of his twins in 1585 and before 1592 he ended up in London.

He Broadened His Horizons

And what a London he found. Cosmopolitan and sophisticated, London was the largest and fastest-growing city in Europe. The country as a whole was thriving. In 1588, England escaped invasion by the Spanish when a storm wrecked the invading armada. The English felt saved by Providence. While Sir Walter Raleigh and his fellow explorers were expanding knowledge of the globe, scientists and theorists were expanding other domains, from anatomy to astronomy. Trade brought waves of exotic imports and foreign influences into the country, increasing awareness of the world beyond their island.

A Blossoming Literary and Theater World

Most pertinent for Shakespeare, Londoners showed an appetite for words and communication in any genre. There was a growing market in poetry, plays, travel narratives, and ephemera such as ballads, pamphlets, and gossipy fare. Whether they were literate or not, the citizens of London were *hearing* language that was often crafted to high standards. This extended from the pulpit to the stage to the street performers. It was an aurally adept audience.

The Church attracted brilliant and poetic thinkers, such as John Donne, to the profession, and sermons were long and intellectually demanding,. For some Londoners, the hour-long addresses given by their parish clergy were not enough. They would flock by the thousands to the courtyard of Paul's Cross to hear special sermons, while "many laypeople regularly crossed parish boundaries to hear sermons by their favourite preachers, a practice known as 'sermon-gadding'" (Hunt 14).

The ability to write poetry and elegant prose was valued among the aristocracy. Queen Elizabeth herself wrote verse and found time to translate the classics. Even the Bible was treated as an opportunity for scholarly and literary magnificence thanks to James I's commission of a new English translation; the King James Bible remains a cultural landmark to this day (begun in 1604 but not published until the end of Shakespeare's career in 1611).

Both of the monarchs Shakespeare lived under—Elizabeth I and James I—were patrons of the arts, with a special fondness for performances. The theater was attracting some of the most brilliant and daring talents. And theater—both the public ones that catered to a wide swath of society, and the more exclusive private ones—became a central cultural force.

Shakespeare is rightly credited with enriching English vocabulary immeasurably. But from the start of his career, Shakespeare found an audience primed for innovations. The English language had already entered a golden age, spurred in part by the printing press, the influx of ideas and art from foreign lands, and impressive home-grown talent.

It's difficult to imagine Shakespeare in a more inspiring atmosphere or that he could achieve what he did at any other time or place.

He Got His Foot in the Door and Took His Knocks

In one way or another, Shakespeare clearly soaked in what London had to offer. He would write about vice and virtue with indelible vividness in a range of contexts, from bawdy houses to convents, from court councils to battlefields.

But history is discreet about any scrapes the young man from the provinces might have gotten into. In fact, the trail goes cold in 1585 in Stratford and doesn't pick up again until 1592, when Shakespeare is about 28 years old.

His Early Career, and an Early Critic

We have an embittered London rival to thank for the clues. Robert Greene is dictating a pamphlet called "A Groats-Worth of Wit" from his deathbed. In it he shares his final words of wisdom and warns his fellow university-educated playwrights about:

> an upstart crow, beautified with our feathers, that with his Tygers heart wrapt in a Players hide supposes he is as well able to bombast out a blank verse as the best of you; and, being an absolute Johannes Factotum, is in his own conceit the only Shake-scene in a country. (*Riverside* 588)

The "Tygers heart wrapt in a Players hide" directly echoes a line from Shakespeare's *Henry VI, Part 3,* and with the coinage "Shake-scene," it's obvious who Greene's target is.

We can be grateful to him for his sour grapes, since they shed light on what the younger man has been up to. The Shake-scene has been a player (actor), a writer of blank verse (unrhymed iambic pentameter), and a presumptuous filcher of others' material.

Greene isn't wholly wrong here. Shakespeare did borrow plots and other elements from both old and new sources. But the young writer was hardly alone in this period in literary scavenging, and he would continue this practice unapologetically the rest of his career. Did Shakespeare "bombast out" his blank verse — pad it out with hyperbole, as the phrase implies? This, too, has some justice: there are sections in his earliest works, the *Henry VI* history plays, that are rather overwrought.

But what seems to have rankled Greene the most was that a grammar-school boy was attempting to compete with the university graduates. The upstart provincial didn't know his place.

Shakespeare must have found this public criticism embarrassing, not to mention bad for business. A few months after Greene's death, Henry Chettle, the pamphlet's publisher, issued an apology saying he was "as sorry as if the original fault had been my fault." Chettle mentions he received complaints and has since met the subject of the criticism, the result being "myself have seen his demeanor no less civil than he [is] excellent in the quality he professes." Others who know him better, Chettle says, have affirmed to him Shakespeare's "uprightness of dealing, which argues his honesty," as well as his "grace in writing, which approves his Art."

Chettle is not be alone in his more generous appraisal of Shakespeare. Later accounts also draw a picture of Shakespeare as an honest dealer and a graceful and fluent wordsmith. But here at the start of his writing career, we can see from the comments by Greene and Chettle that Shakespeare found early admirers and that he'd gotten a bit bruised along the way in London's competitive literary world.

He Collaborated and Learned His Trade Thoroughly

We don't know who gave Shakespeare his initial break as an actor or writer, but early on he made some excellent connections. By the early 1590s, he had joined forces with the talented Burbage family. James Burbage was a builder and impresario, constructing the first purpose-built open-air theater in London, which was called simply the Theatre. James' son Richard would become the most popular actor in London, premiering Shakespeare's famous heroic roles, such as Romeo, Hamlet, Othello, Macbeth, and Lear. Another son, Cuthbert, handled the business side of things.

The Burbages were the nucleus of a new troupe that operated as a collective. It was financed and managed by "sharers," who invested large sums in return for their share of profits, and who oversaw every angle of the business. Shakespeare was one of the eight original "sharers," so his duties, at least nominally, entailed scheduling the repertoire, buying new plays, training new actors, outlaying money for costumes and props, monitoring the ledger, and deciding when and where the company should go on tour. He was also acting on a regular basis, and, of course he was writing them plays, for which he'd be paid extra.

Greene was right that Shakespeare was a Johannes Factotum, a jack of all trades. As a sharer, he had to be. And his writing tasks would have been varied, especially as a novice. Scholars think he was probably tasked at first with literary grunt work—patching up old plays to fit current tastes and adding new speeches as needed. He would have graduated to collaborating with more experienced playwrights. There were many fine rivals, perhaps even collaborators, he would learn from, the greatest of whom was Christopher Marlowe. After proving himself, he would write entire plays on his own. Before long he was popular enough that his works were being pirated, with or without his name on the title page. Shakespeare's works in print were making publishers money, even if the writer saw none of it.

He Adapted to Circumstances

Shakespeare's acting company became so esteemed that the Lord Chamberlain, a prominent official, became their patron, and they performed occasionally for Elizabeth I herself. After her death in 1603, they garnered the protection of her successor James I, earning them the new name, the King's Men.

But even these illustrious protectors couldn't spare them from threats to their livelihood. Outbreaks of the plague were common, and theaters would be shut down for long stretches. During a long closure in 1592–93, the company likely toured the provinces to support themselves. But if they did, Shakespeare seems to have stayed behind, because during this period he immersed himself in writing long-form poetry. He published a semi-comic romantic poem *Venus and Adonis* and then the tragic *Rape of Lucrece*. The works show the enormous literary strides he made during his hiatus from the stage. The verse form he selected was far more intricately structured than the blank verse of most of his plays. For Shakespeare, it would have been like an elite athlete honing a particular skill set in off-season.

He dedicated both works to a young aristocrat, the Earl of Southampton, apparently in the hopes of eliciting his patronage. Whether this worked or not, we don't know. But when the theaters reopened, Shakespeare resumed acting and writing for the stage. This is when he really hit his stride with his early great works *A Comedy of Errors, Romeo and Juliet,* and *A Midsummer Night's Dream.*

In 1598 financial catastrophe loomed again. The lease on the Theatre's land expired, and the owner not only refused to renew the lease, but claimed the building reverted to him. The Chamberlain's Men were obliged to search for a new home. They acquired a property south of the Thames River, just outside London's jurisdiction. After some skullduggery in which they absconded with lumber from their old theater, the company built their new playhouse, the Globe. Even with the repurposed oak beams, this new state-of-the-art theater required a tremendous outlay of money, as well as faith that audiences would follow them to Southwark.

All risks and profits were shared by the partners. In this case, the gamble paid off—in no small part because Shakespeare's plays and Richard Burbage's acting were becoming the hottest draw in town. With this arrangement, Shakespeare enjoyed more financial benefits and artistic freedom than many of his contemporaries who wrote their plays on a freelance basis.

For many years the company tried to get leave to perform in Blackfriars, an indoor private theater space they acquired in 1596. Not until 1608, rather late in Shakespeare's career, were they finally able to stage works there. Shakespeare's final works show him adapting to the possibilities this new space gave him, particularly by including more scenic effects.

He Exploited His Opportunities

His playgoers, especially at the public theaters, were a mixed bunch in terms of social class and education. But they were avid and demanding audiences, vocal in their approval and disapproval. For an actor-turned-writer, it was an ideal learning situation. In speaking his own and other playwrights' lines, he learned through trial and error how to make an audience pay attention.

As he performed, he traced out for himself the potentials of a stage space. The upper story of the tiring house could become Juliet's balcony, and the trap door in the stage floor could be where the Ghost in *Hamlet* emerges as if from purgatory. When his Richard III or Iago confides their villainy, or Hamlet unburdens his distress in soliloquies, Shakespeare would envisage them at farthest point downstage on the thrust platform, so the actors could connect more intimately with the audience.

The new Globe stage in 1599 would certainly have been designed with his input. Shakespeare knew his theater literally from the ground up.

Beyond this familiarity with his playing environment, his talented peers inspired him, and he them. *Hamlet* would not be the monumental work it is if Shakespeare not seen in Richard Burbage the capacity to depict mercurial tonal shifts and intellectual profundity. And in the early 1600s, we see Shakespeare's Fool characters shift toward a more witty and mordant complexity; this coincided with the arrival of the comedian Robert Armin, who apparently specialized in this kind of humor.

Shakespeare wrote to their strengths, and through the scripts we can infer just how capable his actors were. No doubt he learned a lot from the great talent around him.

His day job as an actor must have also spilled over into his writing. He and his company performed plays in repertory, which meant that Shakespeare needed to have numerous parts ready to perform at short notice. To be an actor meant developing an impressive memory stuffed with hundreds, if not thousands, of lines.

When he wrote, the words of other writers would be swirling at some level of his brain. One illustration of this is cited by Darren Freebury-Jones, who noticed that specific phrases from a particular character in Ben Jonson's *Every Man in His Humour* made their way into Shakespeare's works. These Jonsonian phrases appear in *Othello, Hamlet,* and *Twelfth Night*—plays that Shakespeare composed about the time his company was performing Jonson's play. This suggests to Freebury-Jones that Shakespeare acted this role and that "Shakespeare was, perhaps unconsciously, remembering his own lines." The words he spoke during the day flowed through his pen back in his lodgings.

It's a small example, but points to the permeability between Shakespeare's acting life and his writing.

He Knew His Own Strengths and Followed His Instincts

His tight-knit theater company provided him with the chance to take risks that the freelance playwrights likely couldn't afford. Shakespeare's troupe would survive if a play or two fell flat. That security surely suited Shakespeare; we can see from his frequent innovations in genre and style that he didn't care to repeat himself much. When he shifts gears, it may be to capitalize on emerging trends—as when he turned his hand to domestic dramas, which had become popular around the turn of the seventeenth century. But often he is making the new inroads himself.

He may have had the occasional flop. There are several plays that leave no trace during his lifetime—no pirated copies, no allusions to them in diaries, ledgers, or other writing. We only know about them because they show up in the 1623 First Folio. This was the volume that compiled, posthumously, all of Shakespeare's works for the first time. Was *Troilus and Cressida*, for example, ever performed in his lifetime? We can date its composition, on various grounds, to a period when Shakespeare's works took on a darker tone, with sometimes unlikeable protagonists and challenging themes. Collectively, these works are often called "problem plays." Perhaps *Troilus and Cressida* was just ahead of its time, for it has found appreciative audiences in recent centuries. But we hear nothing about it in its own day.

Flops or not, he forged ahead. Some of his finest works, such as *Macbeth* and *King Lear*, are the results of his willingness to explore extremely difficult, psychologically complex stories, well beyond what had yet been seen on London's stages.

He seems to have known his own strengths and, at times, opted not to follow the trends. We see this in his decision not to write masques. These were early musical-dance extravaganzas—spectacles in which the music, dance, and special effects were usually more prominent than the language. They were very popular with King James and his courtiers, and Shakespeare would have been well renumerated had he written one (eight times what a play would bring, according to James Shapiro). The craze for this style came when Shakespeare was at the peak of his profession, but he apparently decided the genre was not a good match for him strengths.

> That Shakespeare never accepted such a commission tells us as much about him as a writer as the plays he left behind. There was a price to be paid for writing masques, which were shamelessly sycophantic and propagandistic, compromises he didn't care to make. He must have also recognized that it was an elite and evanescent art form that didn't suit his interests or his talents. (Shapiro 4–5)

Instead, during the heyday of the masques, he wrote a series of masterpieces in a span of about eighteen months: *King Lear*, *Macbeth*, and *Antony and Cleopatra*. Posterity thanks him for not succumbing to the masque trend, or we might not have had those landmark works.

He Read Widely and Borrowed Judiciously

We know that Shakespeare relied on a wide range of sources when composing his own works, because we those sources left traces in his writing. High-brow to low-brow, ancient to contemporary, English to continental—he surveyed it all. He knew the works of his fellow London playwrights and poets, of course, and ephemeral works such as ballads and political pamphlets. He mined the same historical tomes or story collections again and again for plot ideas. But he also kept up on new currents of all kinds, from theology to the art of fencing to medicine. He read eclectically throughout his career.

Often he uses multiple sources for one work, and the mix may sound incongruous. In *The Tempest,* for example, he starts with a ripped-from-the-headlines travelogue about the New World. But Shakespeare incorporates reflections (*pensées*) by the French philosopher Michel Montaigne, who describes "savages" as more humane than civilized society. And he revisits an old favorite resource, Ovid's *Metamorphoses,* for descriptions about magic.

What made him think to bring all these together in one story? We can't reconstruct how he started this writing process. But it's plausible that Shakespeare had the nucleus of a story in mind first—the basic plot—and as he considered how to flesh it out, certain images or themes would emerge, and these reminded him of books he had read earlier, which he would then chase down and review. It's probable Shakespeare had several books ready to consult when he wrote because of how closely he will reproduce some of their language.

At times, Shakespeare borrows more than just ideas or descriptions; he adapts a scene almost wholesale. It's instructive to see what he chooses, though, and how he invariably improves on it.

Example of Borrowing and Improving: Plutarch's "Coriolanus"

A good example comes in his late tragedy *Coriolanus*. In it, an arrogant Roman military hero, Coriolanus, scorns the plebians, and they, in turn, run him out of Rome. For his story, Shakespeare closely follows Plutarch's biography of the Roman general, which he found in Sir Thomas North's fine 1579 translation. Out of this account, Shakespeare structures his dramatic plot, crafts lengthy verse dialogue from suggestions in North's prose, but he also invents or conflates characters and events. And he probes the characters' emotional universe even more deeply than Plutarch does.

In one key scene, Shakespeare hews closely to his source, but makes very effective changes. This comes about midway through the play. Coriolanus, now banished from Rome, seeks an alliance with Tullus Aufidius, the leader of the enemy Volscians. Here is how North's translation presents the meeting, in which Coriolanus has disguised (muffled) his appearance:

> Tullus rose presently from the board, and coming towards him, asked him what he was, and wherefore he came. Then Martius [Coriolanus] unmuffled

himself, and after he had paused awhile, making no answer, he said unto him:

"If thou knowest me not yet, Tullus, and, seeing me, dost not perhaps believe me to be the man I am indeed, I must of necessity bewray myself to be that I am. I am Caius Martius, who hath done to thyself particularly, and to all the Volsces generally, great hurt and mischief, which I cannot deny for my surname of Coriolanus that I bear." (337)

In a lengthy passage, Coriolanus then offers to fight for the Volsces so that he may revenge himself against the Romans or to let Aufidius take his life.

Tullus hearing what he said, was a marvellous glad man, and taking him by the hand, he said unto him: "Stand up, O Martius, and be of good cheer, for in proffering thyself unto us, thou doest us great honour...." (338)

This passage clearly arrested Shakespeare. We know this not just because he ends up using North's exact phrases in many places. He finds that Plutarch has already found a way to shape this encounter dramatically. Instead of dryly reciting that Coriolanus conspired with his old enemy, Plutarch adds suspense by describing how Coriolanus approaches him in disguise and hesitates to reveal himself. "Why not incorporate that?" Shakespeare thought.

But he decides to go further by imagining the event from Aufidius' perspective and developing Aufidius' emotional response.

Here is how Shakespeare reworks the scene; passages in bold show the repetition and emphasis that Shakespeare uses to develop Aufidius' emotional reaction:

AUFIDIUS Whence com'st thou? What wouldst thou? **Thy name?**
Why speak'st not? Speak, man: what's thy name?
CORIOLANUS *[Unmuffling.]* If, Tullus,
Not yet thou know'st me, and seeing me, dost not
Think me for the man I am, necessity
Commands me name myself.
AUFIDIUS   **What is thy name?**
CORIOLANUS A name unmusical to the Volscians' ears,
And harsh in sound to thine.
AUFIDIUS   **Say, what's thy name?**
Thou hast a grim appearance, and thy face
Bears a command in 't. Though thy tackle's torn,
Thou show'st a noble vessel. **What's thy name?**
CORIOLANUS Prepare thy brow to frown. Know'st thou me yet?

14

AUFIDIUS **I know thee not. Thy name?**
CORIOLANUS My name is Caius Martius, who hath done
To thee particularly, and to all the Volsces,
Great hurt and mischief; thereto witness may
My surname Coriolanus....

Coriolanus continues at length, offering to fight with the Volscians against Rome or let Aufidius kill him. But Shakespeare gives Aufidius a very distinctive response toward his enemy:

AUFIDIUS   O Martius, Martius!
Each word thou hast spoke hath weeded from my heart
A root of ancient envy....
I lov'd the maid I married; never man
Sigh'd truer breath; but that I see thee here,
Thou noble thing, more dances my rapt heart
Than when I first my wedded mistress saw
Bestride my threshold. (4.5)

Notice how even more exciting Shakespeare has made this scene. He stretches out the tension by having Aufidius repeatedly demand Coriolanus to name himself, which Coriolanus hesitates to say. Why the hesitation? It helps the audience appreciate the gravity of what Coriolanus is doing: he in putting himself in his enemy's hands and betraying his own city.

Shakespeare's version also suggests now that Aufidius is powerfully intrigued by this stranger. Perhaps he guesses the truth, but can't believe his own eyes?

When Coriolanus offers his life to show his sincerity, Aufidius responds rapturously: he is more thrilled to see Coriolanus now than he did his wife even on their wedding day. This reaction goes beyond what Plutarch suggests. Shakespeare's Aufidius is putting Coriolanus on a pedestal; he's practically star-struck.

The newly hatched alliance will have tragic consequences later for Coriolanus. In this scene we can see that Shakespeare has also been thinking ahead: he plants a seed to justify why Aufidius will later react so furiously, like a jilted lover, when Coriolanus shows mercy to Rome.

From this example, we can paint a picture of Shakespeare at his desk. He identifies a key moment in one of his source texts, and re-reads it as he reflects how to adapt it. He imagines what each of the main characters are feeling at this juncture, not just the hero, and reflects on how he could highlight their conflicting desires. He appraises how the scene fits into the rest of the story—how to expand on the moment so it becomes the critical turning point of the plot and how it will pay off at the end.

And only after considering the scene from these angles of character and plot does he pick up his pen. Perhaps he glances at the source text from time to time, or else North's phrases made a strong imprint on him, because many of North's exact expressions are fluently interspersed with his own. And in this way Shakespeare has taken something already well written and exploited it for even more drama.

He Wrote Quickly and Revised Little

Londoners had an enormous appetite for new plays. As his company's main playwright, Shakespeare managed to generate new works at an impressive rate. For nearly 20 years, he averaged two new scripts a year—and what complex scripts they were. This was in addition to his other professional duties.

How did he achieve such focus? What was it like when he wrote? He didn't directly explain it, but we have some indirect clues. In *A Midsummer Night's Dream*, Duke Theseus describes the poet in action:

> The poet's eye, in a fine frenzy rolling,
> Doth glance from heaven to earth, from earth to heaven;
> And as imagination bodies forth
> The forms of things unknown, the poet's pen
> Turns them to shapes, and gives to aery nothing
> A local habitation and a name. (5.1)

Theseus likens poets (a term also used for playwrights) to lunatics and lovers. What they all have in common is seeing things that aren't "real." But unlike the lunatic and lover, the poet can make these imaginary forms knowable to others, and, in some sense, give them a reality by the power of their pen. To accomplish that, the poet will enter a heightened state in which they glance back and forth between earth and heaven: between what is real—the world around us—and that which is beyond—more beautiful, or life as it might be.

It's tempting to think Shakespeare is describing this from personal experience, even as a glimpse of how he felt at peak moments during the writing process.

Testimony from Those Who Knew Him

We have a few more clues about his nature as a writer. It appears he wrote quickly, with little need (or perhaps time) to revise. We owe this picture, in large part, to the testimony of John Heminge and Henry Condell, actors in his company who knew him for many years. After his death, they sifted through the available versions of his scripts, half of which had not yet been printed, to compile the first complete works, called the First Folio (1623). In their preface, they testified to Shakespeare's fluent pen. They affirmed that "His mind and hand went together, and what he thought, he uttered [on the page] with that easiness that we have scarce received from him a blot in his papers" (*Riverside* 63).

Ben Jonson, a perfectionist as well as friend and rival of Shakespeare, provides support for this notion, albeit in a backhanded way. Jonson noted, "I remember, the players have often mentioned it as an honour to Shakespeare that in his writing (whatsoever he penned) he never blotted out a line. My answer hath been, would he had blotted a thousand. Which they thought a malevolent speech...." (*Riverside* 1846).

In other words, according to those who worked closely with him, Shakespeare didn't delete much and didn't litter his margins with afterthoughts. Yet his works are complex and integrated. The nineteenth-century poet and critic Samuel Taylor Coleridge called them "organic"—they are so well composed that they seem like living entities. Jonson himself was a chronic reviser, and thought Shakespeare would be even better had he done likewise.

It's true that some inconsistencies do creep into the texts, errors that a careful reviser would catch. A minor character's name might change halfway through a play, as if Shakespeare decided midstream on a new name and didn't think to go back and revise the speech-headings. He doesn't show what becomes of the Fool in *King Lear*, which seems like an oversight. We do have a few of his plays in very different versions, *Hamlet*, for instance. So it may be that after initial performances, Shakespeare—or others—did, in fact, revise extensively. Perhaps the initial performances were disappointing, or playing conditions changed. But what Heminge and Condell emphasize is how quickly and decisively Shakespeare wrote the manuscripts they found, even if they got reworked in later years.

Was the pressure to write efficiently a benefit to him? Very possibly. But no matter what, the mostly complete first drafts speak to an incredible degree of concentration on Shakespeare's part as he wrote.

He Withdrew for Deep Study

In Shakespeare's London, many families, consisting of multiple generations, tended to live together in close quarters. It might not have been easy for him to find a quiet place to write. One of the few civil records pertaining to Shakespeare's time in London gives us a glimpse of his personal living situation in the early

1600s. We learn from the proceedings of a lawsuit, in which Shakespeare gives testimony, that he rented rooms from a prosperous family of headdress-makers. Shakespeare's own wife and children remained in Stratford and he had no roommates. So, these private rooms must have been a haven from London's noises and crowds.

For a variety of reasons, the hero of *The Tempest*, Prospero, is often seen as Shakespeare's alter ego. Shakespeare composed this work shortly before he retired from the stage to return home to Stratford. In Prospero we can perhaps find a clue to the conditions Shakespeare needed for his own practice of literary magic.

Early in the play, we learn Prospero's backstory: as the Duke of Milan, he had neglected worldly affairs in favor of deep study. He was "all dedicated / To closeness and the bettering of my mind. / .... Me (poor man) my library / Was dukedom large enough" (1.2).

Prospero's scheming brother had taken advantage of this, seizing power and setting Prospero and his young daughter adrift on a ship. They landed on an uncharted island, but fortunately, the kindly counselor Gonzago had done Prospero a good turn: "Knowing I lov'd my books, he furnished me / From mine own library with volumes that / I prize above my dukedom."

On this island for twelve years, Prospero continues his habits of withdrawing to study. As his daughter Miranda, now grown-up, explains to her suitor, "My father / Is hard at study.... / He's safe for these three hours" (3.1).

Prospero's powers are formidable: "Graves at my command / Have waked their sleepers, oped, and let 'em forth / By my so potent art" (5.1), he declares. He exercises his will over the strange creatures on the isle, including the spirit Ariel and the carnal man-monster Caliban. He commands the elements to do his bidding and conjures up masques and music. In short, Prospero masters the art of making others perform as he wishes.

The source of Prospero's magic is tied repeatedly to his books. As Caliban claims to his fellow renegades,

> Remember
> First to possess his books, for without them
> He's but a sot [idiot], as I am; nor hath not
> One spirit to command: they all do hate him
> As rootedly as I. Burn but his books. (3.2)

Although Caliban isn't a neutral observer, his speech underlines the connection Shakespeare makes several times between books and creative powers. To perfect his art, Prospero must master his environment both in terms of body (Caliban) and spirit (Ariel), and for this he needs his books and the opportunity for deep study.

The poet in his London retreat would have felt no less the need for self-discipline — writing takes a lot of mental concentration and physical self-restraint. And that poet, trying to make the famous dead, such as Henry V and Cleopatra, come back to life, might have felt like a sot without his books.

The comparison between Prospero and Shakespeare goes only so far. Shakespeare had *not* neglected worldly ends. He was retiring to Stratford rich and respected, with investments in land, property, and commodities. But he might well have considered his two decades in London as an exile from his home and loved ones. During this period, his children were growing up; his wife was getting her first gray hairs. His 11-year-old son died, as did both of his parents, and his elder daughter got married. He probably managed to visit regularly, especially when the theaters were closed during Lent, since Stratford was just 3 or 4 days' commute away. His work, though, would have kept him in London most of the time. Confined to his private rooms for long stretches to write, this life might have felt to him like banishment.

Yet it was during this period, with much help from his books, that he learned to master his art. In the quiet of his study, with resources at his elbow, he achieved a concentration that allowed him to write in the fluent manner he did. Even a magician has to work hard to maintain his powers. They do not just drop from the heavens.

He Respected His Profession and His Power

If he had had his choice to write anything, would he have been a playwright? To judge from the sonnets, no.

In Sonnet 111, Shakespeare — or at least his narrator — claims to feel sullied by his career. He laments that he must make his living in a "public" way, which he says coarsens his manners. The speaker entreats his friend, possibly a patron, to chide Fortune for him —

> The guilty goddess of my harmful deeds,
> That did not better for my life provide
> Than public means which public manners breeds.
> Thence comes it that my name receives a brand,
> And almost thence my nature is subdu'd
> To what it works in, like the dyer's hand....

The environment seeps into his nature like a dye, he says. He laments that Fortune didn't give him means to avoid this career. She is the cause of his coarse displays on the public stage (his "harmful deeds" leading to a blemished reputation).

Writing for the public theaters was not necessarily seen as unsavory work, but in many quarters, it was not prestigious either, while acting was often compared to trickery and deceit.

Shakespeare's few long poems and his 154 sonnets were evidently meant for a more exclusive readership. The sonnets were first circulated in manuscript copies, earning him praise among the cognoscenti, such as Sir Francis Meres, who declared in 1598: "the sweet witty soul of Ovid lives in mellifluous and honey-tongued Shakespeare."

It would be only natural if Shakespeare wondered what heights he could attain if he had the means to compose only for more discriminating audiences, as did Sir Philip Sidney, the great poet and wealthy aristocrat.

Shakespeare may have felt demeaned at times by selling his wares to common audiences. Or perhaps this was just a stance he adopted for the more refined readers of his sonnets.

To judge from the plays, in any case, Shakespeare deeply admired actors and the world of the theater. He knew he achieved mastery there as a playwright, and that he, with his fellow players, wielded some clout.

In the scene in which Hamlet speaks with the traveling actors, Hamlet warns Polonius that performers "are the abstract and brief chronicles of the time: after your death you were better have a bad epitaph than their ill report while you live" (3.2). In other words, what actors say can make or mar your reputation, so show them respect.

There's a chasm between what Sonnet 111's narrator says—that he's been tarnished by his public milieu—and this claim of how much power an actor wields.

Hamlet continues in his advice to the Players, expressing his views about aesthetics and the power of art. As a statement of what art can achieve, it is indeed ambitious. It's also hard not to hear this in Shakespeare's own voice. The true art is to depict *reality as it is*: to hold "the mirror up to nature; to show virtue her own feature, scorn her own image, and the very age and body of the time his form and pressure." It is artists who help others see, as in a mirror, what reality is truly like.

The Players, Hamlet continues, should make their outward gestures point to the inner truth of the situation. Do not tear a passion to tatters with overdoing it.

Instead, suit the action to the word. (And do *not* play to the lowest common denominator. Shakespeare—or rather, Hamlet—gets really annoyed about scene-hogging actors who go off script for cheap laughs.)

Hamlet then refers to a fine speech he heard once as "caviary to the general"—like serving caviar to palates that can't appreciate it. He complains about the limitations of the groundlings, those audience members who pay only a penny and must stand on the ground rather than sit. He says they "for the most part are capable of nothing but inexplicable dumbshows and noise"—that is, they can follow only the big gestures and flashy effects, not the sense of the words. (Considering how demanding Shakespeare's lines can be, modern readers might sympathize with these disparaged groundlings.)

But Hamlet's criticism is a bit ironic in the context. The actor playing Hamlet would declare this in front of the very groundlings he's insulting. It sounds like Shakespeare is heckling, perhaps good-naturedly, his own audience.

Moreover, the play *Hamlet* became extremely popular from the start. Somehow, Shakespeare found a way to deliver something for nearly everyone while not dumbing things down. There is caviar for those who can appreciate it in Hamlet's deep musings and exquisite wordplay. There is also a ghost, swordplay, murder, madness—and, yes, even a dumbshow—for the groundlings and the audience at large. The play works on many levels, and this was by design. Shakespeare knew his audience and how to reach them where they were.

So, even if Shakespeare preferred writing for a refined audience, he made peace with, or even welcomed, the audiences he had. He combined a popular touch with a sophisticated taste. His works played well on the London public stages as well as for the private, aristocratic audiences. This was by design, not luck.

He Continued to Evolve as a Writer

By the end of his career, he got closer to his apparent wish for a more refined clientele. In 1606, the company took possession of an indoor theater, Blackfriars, which charged about double the rate of the public Globe Theatre.

In the final five or so years of Shakespeare's career, the King's Men split their time between the outdoor Globe Theatre and, in winter, this new indoor theater. At Blackfriars, the closed and smaller theater space could allow for more elaborate stage machinery and special effects, which Shakespeare began to incorporate. In *Cymbeline*, for example, he has the god Jupiter descend "in thunder and lightning, sitting upon an eagle: he throws a thunderbolt." And in *The Tempest*, Prospero conjures up a masque, with goddesses and nymphs. The stage direction notes that

"Juno descends," followed by "a graceful dance, towards the end whereof Prospero starts suddenly and speaks," after which, "to a strange, hollow, and confused noise, [the spirits] heavily vanish" (4.1).

Prosper conjures up this entertainment, out of thin air, to entertain his daughter Miranda and her suitor. It is a masque, the genre he seemingly rejected writing several years earlier. He could create one if he *wanted* to. And here, it makes sense within his greater dramatic context.

Over his twenty-year career, Shakespeare never ceased to evolve as a writer. He continued to seek out new inspiration for his plots, as he did for *The Tempest*, in incorporating accounts of the New World. Although he never wrote a masque play, he used some of the masque's innovations in his final works.

But this was the glowing-embers phase of Shakespeare's career. His talents had developed in an oral and literary stage tradition. Words and actors were his primary tools. Music, dance, and visual arts played supporting roles only.

His talents had developed along the contours of the medium he used. His words, which on the page may seem dense and verbose, are what drew pictures for an audience on an otherwise mostly bare stage. Had he arrived 50 or 400 years later, it's anyone's guess how he would have channeled his literary gifts. But he was born at a time and place where words and performance were approaching a zenith, and he had the talent, instincts, and audiences to make the most of them.

Summary

Ben Jonson, who thought his friend should have "blotted a thousand" faulty lines, also gives Shakespeare credit as someone who worked hard at his writing:

> Who casts to write a living line, must sweat
> (Such as thine are), and strike the second heat
> Upon the Muses' anvil, turn the same
> (And himself with it), that he thinks to frame;
> Or for the laurel he may gain a scorn!
> For a good Poet's made as well as born;
> And such wert thou! (*Riverside* 65)

Jonson is affirming that Shakespeare's talent was born, but was also made—by Shakespeare himself—and that it takes both "to write a living line."

What we know about Shakespeare backs up what Jonson says here (even if Shakespeare didn't revise as much as Jonson thought he should). Shakespeare must have been gifted from birth with great intelligence and an ear for the rhythms and music of language. And he was lucky in being born at the time and place he was, where linguistic arts were a matter of national pride. But he also made himself as a writer.

Shakespeare used an array of literary models. He often echoed them, but he was not just a crow filching others' feathers to adorn himself. What Shakespeare found in others was just the starting point of his artistic process. He was discerning about what he borrowed, and he made judicious changes to suit his vision.

He took risks and innovated in nearly every aspect of his writing, becoming by far the most successful playwright in his era. And from the start of his career to the end, he never stopped evolving in his use of new techniques, new themes, new sources.

In his daily milieu, he got plenty of feedback, and from this he learned to write in a manner that his diverse audiences could follow and appreciate. In another era, he would have composed differently. There's no point in trying to mimic how Shakespeare wrote. Even he would have moved on.

This opening chapter has outlined some ways Shakespeare learned how to write. The following chapters will focus on his techniques, illustrated by examples from his work. These techniques focus in particular on creating protagonists, plots, and antagonists. His example may inspire us to make ourselves as writers, for as Jonson says, "a good poet's made as well as born."

Takeaway for Writers

From Shakespeare's works, and from what we know of his biography, we can infer some ideas about his how he developed and practiced as a writer. Shakespeare:

- Learned early how to write by imitating good models
- Observed life around him
- Broadened his horizons
- Got his foot in the door and took his knocks
- Collaborated and learned his trade thoroughly
- Adapted to circumstances
- Exploited his opportunities
- Knew his own strengths and followed his instincts
- Read widely and borrowed judiciously

- Wrote quickly and revised little
- Withdrew for deep study
- Respected his profession and his power
- Continued to evolve as a writer

Extras

Many chapters end with a selection of relevant passages from Shakespeare or other sources, for more uninterrupted reading. All Shakespeare passages are taken from *The Riverside Shakespeare*.

Sonnet 73 evokes a profound human experience by making connections between a person's end of life and natural phenomena:
That time of year thou mayst in me behold
When yellow leaves, or none, or few, do hang
Upon those boughs which shake against the cold,
Bare ruin'd choirs, where late the sweet birds sang.
In me thou seest the twilight of such day
As after sunset fadeth in the west,
Which by and by black night doth take away,
Death's second self, that seals up all in rest.
In me thou seest the glowing of such fire
That on the ashes of his youth doth lie,
As the death-bed whereon it must expire,
Consum'd with that which it was nourish'd by.
This thou perceiv'st, which makes thy love more strong,
To love that well, which thou must leave ere long.

In **Hamlet, Act 3, scene 2,** Hamlet addresses the traveling players, and provides his views of art and the role of the artist in showing reality.
HAMLET Speak the speech, I pray you, as I pronounc'd it to you, trippingly on the tongue, but if you mouth it, as many of our players do, I had as live the town-crier spoke my lines. Nor do not saw the air too much with your hand, thus, but use all gently, for in the very torrent, tempest, and, as I may say, whirlwind of your passion, you must acquire and beget a temperance that may give it smoothness. O, it offends me to the soul to hear a robustious periwig-pated fellow tear a passion to totters, to very rags, to spleet the ears of the

groundlings, who for the most part are capable of nothing but inexplicable dumb shows and noise. I would have such a fellow whipt for o'erdoing Termagant, it out-Herods Herod, pray you avoid it.

PLAYER 1: I warrant your honor.

HAMLET: Be not too tame neither, but let your own discretion be your tutor. Suit the action to the word, the word to the action, with this special observance, that you o'erstep not the modesty of nature: for any thing so o'erdone is from the purpose of playing, whose end, both at the first and now, was and is, to hold as 'twere the mirror up to nature: to show virtue her feature, scorn her own image, and the very age and body of the time his form and pressure. Now this overdone, or come tardy off, though it makes the unskillful laugh, cannot but make the judicious grieve; the censure of which one must in your allowance o'erweigh a whole theatre of others. O, there be players that I have seen play— and heard others praise, and that highly—not to speak it profanely, that, neither having th' accent of Christians nor the gait of Christian, pagan, nor man, have so strutted and bellow'd that I have thought some of Nature's journeymen had made men, and not made them well, they imitated humanity so abominably.

PLAYER 1: I hope we have reform'd that indifferently with us, sir.

HAMLET: O, reform it altogether. And let those that play your clowns speak no more than is set down for them, for there be of them that will themselves laugh to set on some quantity of barren spectators to laugh too, though in the mean time some necessary question of the play be then to be consider'd. That's villainous, and shows a most pitiful ambition in the fool that uses it. Go make you ready.

Ben Jonson knew Shakespeare well. His censure of Shakespeare's too-free facility with words more makes his appreciation of his friend's other qualities stand out all the more:

I remember the players have often mentioned it as an honour to Shakspeare, that in his writing (whatsoever he penned) he never blotted out a line. My answer hath been, "Would he had blotted a thousand," which they thought a malevolent speech. I had not told posterity this but for their ignorance who chose that circumstance to commend their friend by wherein he most faulted; and to justify mine own candour, for I loved the man, and do honour his memory on this side idolatry as much as any. He was, indeed, honest, and of an open and free nature, had an excellent phantasy, brave notions, and gentle expressions, wherein he flowed with that facility that sometimes it was necessary he should be stopped. "*Sufflaminandus erat,*" as Augustus said of Haterius. His wit was in his own power; would the rule of it had been so, too. Many times he fell into those things, could not escape laughter, as when he said in the person of Cæsar, one speaking to him, "Cæsar, thou dost me wrong." He replied, "Cæsar did never wrong but with just cause;" and such like, which were ridiculous. But he redeemed his vices with his virtues. There was ever more in him to be praised than to be pardoned. (*Timber,* De Shakspeare nostrat.—Augustus in Hat. section)

CHAPTER 2: PROTAGONIST TRAITS

I t's 1592, and a 28-year-old Shakespeare is watching rehearsals for *Edward II*, a new tragedy by Christopher Marlowe. Shakespeare is the less experienced writer, but he has sold a couple of plays to this acting troupe and is at work on a new piece about the reign of Richard III.

On this day, he's come to get a sense of Richard Burbage's range as a leading actor. But most of all, he wants to get an advance look at Marlowe's latest.

Marlowe and Shakespeare were born just two months apart, but Marlowe got a head start and his rise was meteoric: *Tamburlaine, Dr. Faustus, The Jew of Malta*— stunning innovations in themes and characters. Marlowe gives his protagonists outsized powers, hubris, gorgeous language, and spectacular downfalls. The newcomer from Stratford soaks it all in.

Edward II is another revelation. Who would think to make a hero of this miserable English king? Edward II is a weak and self-centered leader. He heaps titles and wealth on his male favorite, Gaveston, and defies his courtiers and queen, who want to separate them: "I will have Gaveston, and you shall know, / What danger 'tis to stand against your king" (1.1). But Edward finds himself overmatched and is gruesomely murdered by his wife's lover.

London audiences will be once again enthralled by Marlowe's audacity. In his writing, he pushes everything to the edge. He did the same in his personal life. Within a year of writing *Edward II*, this meteor crashed to earth. In May 1593, under murky circumstances, Marlowe was killed. A witness claimed to authorities that Marlowe died in a squabble over a tavern bill, while others have long suspected a plot.

Marlowe had been in trouble with authorities in the past, even imprisoned. The Queen herself intervened to release him, citing his service to country. It's thought that Marlowe had spied for the crown and perhaps had highly placed enemies. But Marlowe was also indiscreet in his personal life, suspected of atheism and homosexuality, both of them capital offenses. As one contemporary opined, Marlowe had "Wit lent from heaven, but vices sent from hell."

The writer's short life was nearly as dramatic as those of his protagonists. It had the compressed tragic arc meant for the stage, not for real life. The literary world felt his loss profoundly, Shakespeare among them. In his later works, Shakespeare would evoke Marlowe and even directly quote him. In As You Like It, he is invoked as a dead shepherd (in allusion to his pastoral poetry): "Dead shepherd, now I find thy saw of might, "Who ever loved that loved not at first sight?" (AYL 3.5). He even seems to alludes to Marlowe's murder as "a great reckoning in a little room" (AYL 3.3): a reckoning meant the bill to be paid, and a great reckoning could be one's final accounting for one's life.

Shakespeare learned enormously from Marlowe, and an important lesson was to take risks—if not in his personal life, then certainly in constructing his protagonists. He learned to make them big and vivid, even shocking. Around the time of *Edward II*'s premiere, Shakespeare was creating his own astonishing protagonist in *Richard III*. Many critics think it was with this play that Shakespeare came into his own as a playwright.

Shakespeare's Early Protagonist: Richard III

What made Richard III a daring choice for a protagonist? Like Marlowe's Edward II, Richard is an anti-hero more than a hero. In fact, he's presented as repulsive. The other characters in the play don't like him, not even his own mother. Richard has a hunchback and a withered arm; he skulks at the edge of the court, like the spider to which he's often compared.

His older brother reigns as king and has two sons as heirs. But Richard has boundless ambition, he's witty, and he can adopt any persona needed to gain his ends. After the king dies, Richard sees his chance. He will arrange the murder of another brother and his nephews, and cynically woo a widow whose husband he had killed, all in pursuit of the crown.

Embodying Richard: Physical and Psychological Traits

From the history chronicles he consulted, Shakespeare would have learned many details about the real Richard, including the fact he had a somewhat stooped posture. Perhaps that's where Shakespeare started: stooping over himself, then exaggerating his posture by twisting and contracting his body. As an actor himself, Shakespeare would have found it natural to physically feel his way into his character when he came to write the part.

This physical experiment may have suggested to him the image of Richard as a spider that we hear of often in the play. And this also might have helped him imagine how it would feel to be scorned as a monster, or to suggest that Richard might become bitter and vengeful, or develop a sardonic sense of humor to deflect insults.

In any case, Richard's distinctive physical and psychological traits are emphasized from the start. Clearly, Shakespeare found these traits key to this protagonist.

In the soliloquy that opens the play, we see a misshapen Richard bitterly observe he has no function in a kingdom at peace. The King can enjoy himself by "capering nimbly in a lady's chamber, / To the lascivious pleasing of a lute," while Richard himself is "not shaped for sportive tricks."

Instead, as he tells the audience, he was born

> Deformed, unfinished, sent before my time
> Into this breathing world, scarce half made up,
> And that so lamely and unfashionable
> That dogs bark at me as I halt by them.

But he conceives of a plan:

> And therefore, since I cannot prove a lover
> To entertain these fair well-spoken days,
> I am determined to prove a villain
> And hate the idle pleasures of these days.
> Plots have I laid, inductions dangerous…. (1.1)

Shakespeare is spelling it all out for the audience in this opening speech: *Because I cannot succeed as a lover (because of my deformities) I will focus on being a villain and lay plots.* Richard's physical deficits warp him morally. These traits make him seek power no matter the cost. The outward appearance and the inward nature are connected.

This is a strategy at which Shakespeare would become increasingly adept at in his career: depicting both the outward and inward dimensions of a character. Here, with Richard, he wants to establish for the audience a plausible reason for Richard's villainy. Shakespeare is sensitive to the physical and psychological dimensions of his protagonists, and seeks ways to communicate these traits to the audience.

Making Richard Central and Extraordinary

Richard III is the culmination of Shakespeare's early four-part series of history plays that begins with the reign of Henry VI. In this final work of the series, we can see that Shakespeare has resolved a dilemma he faced with those earlier plays. Namely, he was not entirely successful in depicting a broad and bloody swath of English history without the major characters blending into each other.

In *Henry VI, Parts 1, 2,* and *3,* Shakespeare focuses on the sweep of history, with many important figures coming in and out of the story. In *Richard III,* he tries something different: although he continues the history, wrapping up the overarching story of this first tetralogy, he pulls one character out to be the sole protagonist. He makes Richard the central and most fascinating character in the play. It is through Richard's perspective that we view much of the action.

From Marlowe, Shakespeare had a great model for building a protagonist. This character must stand out from the rest, whether through greater charms, greater threats, or greater appetites, it hardly matters. To stand out, the protagonist needs to be *exceptional* and must hold our interest throughout.

One way Shakespeare makes Richard stand out and dominate his story is through his distinctive traits. Through them, Shakespeare makes the character's journey seem plausible and emotionally compelling. Richard takes extraordinary risks not in spite of his physical and emotional deficits, but because of them.

What Is a Protagonist?

The protagonist, often called the hero, is a nuts-and-bolts feature of most storytelling—one of the most important elements for a writer to master. The hero's actions, desires, fears, and problems are what the audience will most care about.

The term "protagonist" derives from ancient Greek and means "first actor," that is, the most prominent character of a story. This character must become the central figure of an unfolding plot.

There are many ways of analyzing and constructing a protagonist. We can describe this character in terms of what they do and experience during the story; this can be called the protagonist's journey or arc. The protagonist will have a problem, duty, or need that is resolved by the end of the story. It is this problem that delineates the protagonist's arc across the plot.

Although this journey normally runs in close parallel with the plot, they are not identical. No matter how fundamental the protagonist is, the plot is more comprehensive and more important still. We'll examine the kinds of journeys Shakespeare gives his protagonists as well as the plots that structure his stories in subsequent chapters.

Another, and even more basic way to see how Shakespeare designs his protagonists is in terms of their traits. This means what the character is *like*. In effect, a protagonist's traits can be hard to separate from their experiences: we get a sense of a character through their responses to situations. But traits can be established early on. As he did with Richard III, Shakespeare will establish key traits for his protagonists before much of the plot has started. The traits alert us to what we should expect from this character and suggest to us where that character might be heading.

Traits of Shakespeare's Protagonists: Basic Principles

Traits in a literary character are what we perceive as their outward nature as well as anything that reflects their inward qualities. Imagining these characters as actual people, we could say their traits are the features they already possesses or perhaps gain along the way. These traits may evolve through experiences.

In building his protagonists, Shakespeare generally follows these basic principles:
- The protagonist will be exceptional in some way.
- Their traits will be appropriate and relevant in the context of the story.
- Their traits often point to the challenge ahead.
- Their traits can be depicted through a range of techniques.

Shakespeare designs his protagonist's traits with as much care as he does in providing exposition and setting the tone.

A Protagonist Is Exceptional

Shakespeare designs his protagonists to be more interesting than the characters surrounding them. They must be exceptional to hold our interest. But there are many ways to get there.

Typically, he invests them with at least one, and often several, of these attributes:
- Highly attractive, appealing, or otherwise admirable
- Great intelligence and wit
- Powerful over others

31

- Profound emotions or desires
- Extraordinary courage or perseverance

What Shakespeare does not create is a protagonist with moderate desires and manner, of average intelligence, or of ordinary abilities. His protagonists are far from perfect, of course, and may be deficient in some vital traits, such as wisdom, poise, or capacity to rule. They will often be prone to certain frailties, but these flaws will have a dramatic purpose as well.

Sometimes the exceptional nature arises from inherited power, such as the ill-fated Henry VI, whose reign will be disastrous. He did not earn his position through personal effort, but what he does and what happens to him affects the whole country.

But most interesting of all are the characters whose traits we'd find fascinating in another person—attractiveness, wit, courage, power, resourcefulness, ambition, the wherewithal to overcome great challenges.

This still opens the range up quite a bit. An adolescent boy and girl can be exceptional, as we find in *Romeo and Juliet.* So can the postulant nun Isabella in *Measure for Measure,* who seeks only to take her final vows when life outside the convent intervenes.

Richard III is exceptional in his brashness, ambition, and extreme physical and psychological characteristics: he's more clever and more damaged than those around him, and as a result, more dangerous; to us, that makes him more interesting.

Establishing Appropriate and Relevant Traits: Romeo and Juliet

Shakespeare takes care to establish distinctive and relevant traits early on, typically in our first views of a character. He wants us to see who his hero is very early and suggest the challenges that might lie ahead because of the protagonist's nature.

Whatever the traits Shakespeare gives his protagonists, he doesn't choose them randomly. Any distinctive traits will be related in some way to their journey. Otherwise, those traits will just distract. Why give a protagonist extreme youth, a profound spiritual nature, or physical deformities if these traits do not contribute in some way to the story?

Isabella the postulant is unswervingly moral and disciplined; these traits are what cause her such difficulty when she must cope with others who are less upright. Circumstances force her to leave her purer existence in the convent and engage with the more faulty characters in the world as it is; her traits of moral rectitude make this a dramatic challenges for her.

Romeo and Juliet are very young and passionately swept up in love; these traits are central to the choices they make that lead to their tragedy. But Shakespeare endows them with other dispositive traits.

Romeo and Juliet: "With love's light wings"

The protagonists of *Romeo and Juliet* are not exceptional in the way the kings and generals of Shakespeare's other works are. Although they come from prominent families in Verona, these young lovers are not noteworthy in their society. They are barely older than children and have few responsibilities or cares beyond their own youthful preoccupations. How does Shakespeare make them stand out? In large part, by making them so appealing. They are exceptional in their fresh innocence and idealism; and Shakespeare shows that through falling in love, they become even finer beings than they were before.

We are introduced to them separately. The first scene depicts a skirmish between the feuding households in the town square; Romeo arrives just after the fight has been broken up. He had been wandering the woods, nursing his heartbreak over Rosaline's rejection of him. Romeo comports himself like a conventionally lovesick swain straight out of romantic poetry. "The all-seeing sun," he tells Benvolio, "Ne'er saw her match since first the world begun," and he vows he would die before he would declare another more fair (1.2). His friends tease him and seek to distract him by luring him to a party hosted by their rivals.

Next, we meet Juliet, who appears demure and compliant to her parents' wishes to consider the well-born suitor Paris for marriage:

LADY CAPULET   Can you like of Paris' love?
JULIET I'll look to like, if looking liking move.
 But no more deep will I endart mine eye
Than your consent gives strength to make it fly. (1.3)

Juliet is agreeing to her mother's request that she when she meets Paris, she will see if she could love him; the girl obediently adds she will not look even further than what her mother consents her to do.

Individually, the protagonists are charming in the way lovely youth always are, but otherwise are unexceptional. Romeo's friend Mercutio stands out as more brilliant and volatile, although Romeo holds his own during their battle of wits.

But then comes their fateful first meeting at the Capulet party at the end of act 1. Shakespeare shows that when Romeo and Juliet first meet, they transform into something exceptional in front of our eyes. We are in the midst of the festivities, with servants bustling around, the host heartily urging on the dancers, and Tybalt, a young Capulet, spoiling to fight the Montague intruder.

Romeo spies Juliet from across the room and goes straight to her, takes her by the hand, and we are brought suddenly into a more rarefied world. Their first lines to each other are stylized and refined, taking the form of a sonnet plus a quatrain:

ROMEO If I profane with my unworthiest hand
This holy shrine, the gentle sin is this,
My lips, two blushing pilgrims, ready stand
To smooth that rough touch with a tender kiss.
JULIET Good pilgrim, you do wrong your hand too much,
Which mannerly devotion shows in this:
For saints have hands that pilgrims' hands do touch,
And palm to palm is holy palmers' [pilgrims'] kiss.
ROMEO Have not saints lips, and holy palmers too?
JULIET Ay, pilgrim, lips that they must use in prayer.
ROMEO O then, dear saint, let lips do what hands do.
They pray—grant thou, lest faith turn to despair.
JULIET Saints do not move, though grant for prayers' sake.
ROMEO Then move not while my prayer's effect I take.
He kisses her. Thus from my lips, by thine, my sin is purged. *[Kissing her.]*
JULIET Then have my lips the sin that they have took.
ROMEO Sin from my lips? O trespass sweetly urged!
Give me my sin again. *[Kissing her again.]*
JULIET   You kiss by th' book. (1.5)

For them, love is playful *and* instinctively holy. Romeo likens Juliet's hand to a holy shrine, saying his lips are two blushing pilgrims ready to make amends for any roughness he has committed in taking it up. Juliet picks up his metaphor and absolves him by noting that pilgrims are allowed to touch saints with their palms' "kiss." The two continue to play wittily off of each other's replies. Romeo justifies why it is a holy act for them to kiss, while Juliet remains modestly responsive.

Shakespeare accomplishes a lot in this first meeting between his protagonists. The formal structure of the exchange sets it apart from what has preceded: the young protagonists speak differently now. They are so delicately attuned to each other they complete each other's rhymed couplets and build on the other's imagery. They show they are physically drawn to each other and affirm this attraction is not shameful, but holy.

Shakespeare depicts here what love at its sweetest can do to a person: it makes them united in thought and feeling with another; it harmonizes and elevates them. The conventionally lovelorn Romeo is gone. Now that he has met someone who fully reciprocates his emotions he speaks in more genuinely novel turns of phrase. And Juliet responds in kind as his equal.

It's hard to imagine a more romantic meeting than this, and their behavior establishes the fineness of their spirit. There are many, many ways to depict lovers. This is how Shakespeare sets his famous pair apart. And there are other ways he adds to this.

Embodying the Characters

Shakespeare wrote *Romeo and Juliet* fairly early in his career, when was about 30 years old and a long-since married father of three. How did he find his way into the mind of a 13- or 14-year-old falling in love at first sight? How did he make their language and behavior seem suited to such innocent youth?

Perhaps he recalled his own earliest passions. Or, with a daughter approaching Juliet's age, maybe he was inspired by questioning her. But certainly, as he did with Richard III, Shakespeare pays careful attention to their physicality. He builds his protagonists with a particular corporeal nature that suits them. Their nature is composed of lightness and quickness.

As Juliet rushes to Friar Laurence's cell to be married, the Friar observes:

Here comes the lady. O, so light a foot
Will ne'er wear out the everlasting flint;
A lover may bestride the gossamers
That idles in the wanton summer air,
And yet not fall... (2.6)

That's what youth and love are like: they seem to float and skip along, and never wear out the pavement.

It is similar for Romeo, who easily scales the garden walls enclosing Juliet's chamber. When she wonders how he reached her—for "The orchard walls are high and hard to climb"—he declares: "With love's light wings did I o'erperch these walls, / For stony limits cannot hold love out" (2.2). Romeo later evokes how it feels to approach her by comparing it to how schoolboys dash out the door from school.

Imagery of Brightness and Sublimity

Aside from their physical lightness, Shakespeare establishes the nature of his young protagonists through what they focus on and the imagery they use. The lovers compare each other to things brilliant and/or high above the ground. Romeo says of Juliet that she is a jewel hanging "upon the cheek of night," and that "she doth teach the torches to burn bright." In the balcony scene he stares up at her window as he would toward the heavens, exclaiming: "What light through yonder window breaks? It is the East, and Juliet is the sun!" Juliet's imagination also turns to the upper realms; she says her beloved should become a constellation when he dies so that all the world can admire his beauty forever.

The protagonists express their love in the extreme and unguarded language of youths discovering love for the first time. But the phrases don't sound like they come from books; they are not conventional. She tells Romeo she declared her love for him "before thou didst request it, / And yet I would it were to give again." When Romeo asks why she would withdraw her love, she explains it is only so that she can give it again, since "My bounty is as boundless as the sea, / My love as deep; the more I give to thee, / The more I have, for both are infinite" (2.2).

So much does she love giving him her love, she wants to take it back in order to give it again. This turn of phrase is both child-like in its simplicity and extreme. She, like Romeo, speaks in novel, yet expansive absolutes: Love is as endless as the sea. Not even stone walls can keep love out.

Romeo and Juliet's Traits Seen in Themselves and in Contrast with Others

The traits of Shakespeare's two protagonists are established not only through what they say and do, but by reflection from others. A range of other characters provide contrast, including the earthy and pragmatic nurse who counsels Juliet, finally, to forget Romeo and marry someone else; Juliet's restrained, almost chilly mother, who also married very young; the sardonic, short-tempered Mercutio whose life is also cut short by the feud. These contrasts make the young lovers' nature stand out more clearly in relief.

The lovers share many traits in common:

- They are very young, physically light and buoyant.
- Their thoughts gravitate toward light and bright things: the sun and stars, a precious jewel in the sky, burning torches.

- They feel and speak in idealistic extremes: Juliet's love is infinite like the ocean; their love is holy like a pilgrim kissing a saint; Romeo's love is stronger than stone walls.
- Their initial meeting elicits from them literal poetry, a harmony of spirits that leads them to complete each other's verse patterns.
- They conceive of their love as being holy and at the same time carnal, physical; they feel no shame in their attraction to each other.

These traits are all relevant. Their youth and idealistic innocence make it easy to accept how impulsively they act. The story would have a very different energy if Romeo and Juliet were not around 14 years, but 24 years old. Or if their attraction for each other were devoid of a physical passion, or if that passion were framed as sinful. Their innocence and idealism—which Shakespeare is at pains to depict in their actions and language—relate integrally to their ultimate end.

Traits that Point to the Challenge Ahead: King Lear

King Lear is one of Shakespeare's late tragedies and one of his greatest works. On the face of it, Shakespeare would seem to be taking a risk in creating a protagonist like Lear. An old and irascible king, who is about to hand over his power, might not sound like a promising dramatic hero. But Shakespeare is in full command of his character-building skills here.

He establishes Lear's volatility, commanding nature, and a number of other traits early on for good dramatic reasons: the audience is not only being introduced to a vivid character; they are also being prepared for the challenges that lie ahead for him.

King Lear: "Every inch a king"

With his first entrance in the play, Lear is literally a commanding presence: he gives orders to the Duke of Gloucester and makes proclamations about the future of the state. We learn that he is dividing up his kingdom among his daughters so that he can lessen his burdens and prevent future strife:

LEAR Attend the lords of France and Burgundy,
Gloucester.
GLOUCESTER I shall, my lord. *(Exit.)*
LEAR Mean time we shall express our darker [hidden] purpose.
Give me the map there. Know that we have divided
In three our kingdom; and 'tis our fast intent

> To shake all cares and business from our age,
> Conferring them on younger strengths, while we
> Unburdened crawl toward death
> …. that future strife
> May be prevented now. (1.1)

He then turns to his daughters and demands they vie with each other in declaring who loves him most: "Which of you shall we say doth love us most, / That we our largest bounty may extend" (1.1). He wants a ceremonial display of love before he announces their portion. But this demand indicates something is amiss: Lear is conflating love with power. *Tell me you love me and I'll give you something in return.* It's not a demand a father or a king should make.

Yet his two elder daughters unctuously comply. It's the third daughter, Cordelia, who resists: "I cannot heave / My heart into my mouth." She says she loves him according to her bond, no more, no less. For Cordelia, the words he seeks can only come from the heart, not on demand.

Lear grows furious and disowns her, his feelings wounded.

When the advisor Kent begs the king to reconsider, pointing out she doesn't love him any less for not saying so, Lear threatens him, too:

> Peace, Kent!
> Come not between the dragon and his wrath;
> I loved her most, and thought to set my rest
> On her kind nursery. [*To Cordelia.*] Hence, and avoid my sight!

But Kent pushes on:

> KENT   Royal Lear,
> Whom I have ever honored as my king,
> Loved as my father, as my master followed,
> As my great patron thought on in my prayers—
> LEAR The bow is bent and drawn, make from the shaft.
> KENT Let it fall rather, though the fork invade
> The region of my heart; be Kent unmannerly
> When Lear is mad. What wouldst thou do, old man? ….
> My life I never held but as a pawn
> To wage against thine enemies, ne'er feared to lose it,
> Thy safety being motive.

Kent is saying here that he must be "unmannerly" when the king behaves madly; he would rather sacrifice his life than see Lear make this error. But for his continued pleading, this good counselor is banished as well.

After Lear and others leave the stage, the daughters Goneril and Regan confer. His behavior is a troubling sign for them. "You see how full of changes his age is," says Goneril. "He always loved our sister most, and with what poor judgment he hath now cast her off appears too grossly." "'Tis the infirmity of his age," responds Regan, "yet he hath ever but slenderly known himself" (1.1).

Although these daughters are not trustworthy witnesses, we have seen for ourselves his rash and faulty judgment. What Shakespeare leaves unclear is how long the king has shown poor judgment. Regan implies he has lacked self-knowledge—wisdom, in other words—for some time. Kent appears surprised by Lear's actions, and calls him mad as if it's out of character.

Yet however rashly the king behaves, Shakespeare still shows him as lucid. Lear will lose his wits in due course, but in this scene, Lear still sounds sane. Shakespeare shows him as rash, but responsible for his decisions.

But clearly, Lear's behavior and decisions foreshadow ominous developments for his court and himself.

What Are Lear's Traits?

With efficient brushstrokes, Shakespeare establishes in this first scene a number of key traits of the protagonist. We see that Lear is:

- Elderly
- Imperious—used to giving orders and being obeyed without question
- Demanding of love, and angry when it isn't returned as he wishes
- Impulsive enough to make hasty decisions on matters of great importance
- Unwise, lacking in "self-knowledge"; he does not see through the hypocrisy of others, and he cannot perceive Cordelia's superior response
- Stubborn, arrogant; he refuses to listen to the good counsel he's given

As a king, he wields great power, which he demonstrates from his opening lines. His whole realm depends on his choices, sound or not. This alone makes him exceptional. But he is also exceptional in his extreme temperament: his demanding nature, his sense of entitlement not simply to obedience but to love, his deeply wounded feelings when his favorite daughter won't comply with his wish. He may not be likeable, but there is no one in this first scene who is more exceptional or compelling than Lear.

Shakespeare depicts these traits primarily through what Lear says and does. But almost as telling is how others react to him. All eyes are on him. All attempt to placate him in one way or another. Only when he makes his unwise demands do some of them resist. He elicits hypocrisy from his elder daughters, but also selfless loyalty from Kent, and we will later see others equally devoted to Lear, including the Fool and Cordelia.

Why These Traits?

All of the traits we find in Lear in this opening scene are relevant to the tragic path on which Shakespeare will lead him. If he were not responsible for his initial actions, nor as arrogant and rash as we see him here, the rest of the play could not be as tragic.

When he writes this scene, Shakespeare clearly knows where he plans to take Lear. He will bring Lear from the heights of power to the depths of powerlessness: from supreme ruler to homeless outcast; from one whom others serve submissively, to one who is hunted and whose own body and mind begin to fail him.

In the opening scene, Kent warns Lear to "see better," and Regan claims he has always lacked self-knowledge. These details, too, are pointing to Lear's journey ahead. Shakespeare establishes early on this lack of wisdom as a key trait, and he does it because that is what Lear's painful journey will end up being about: to see the truth about love, justice, and his own past faults.

Lear *will* learn to see better. Through suffering, he will "feel how others feel," as he says during the storm scene, and will recognize that he neglected the unfortunate when he was still in power. By the end of the play, he will humble himself to kneel to Cordelia and ask her forgiveness: "Pray you now, forget, and forgive. I am old and foolish" (4.7).

But it is not only through passive suffering that he learns. He evolves because he *demands* to find justice and truth. This fierceness is signaled in the first scene as well with his disowning of Cordelia and banishment of Kent.

This unbending nature we see in the first scene is what drives him to remain outside in the storm, after his companions seek shelter, because his sense of outrage cannot let him rest: "This tempest in my mind / Doth from my senses take all feeling else / Save what beats there" (3.4).

He will attempt to put his elder daughters on trial for their ingratitude. And he will rail against the heavens for not taking his side and for refusing to show themselves. Even as Lear grows more vulnerable in body and mind, we will see that imperious, demanding nature that Shakespeare established in Act 1, scene 1.

Lear starts out a king who wielded power by virtue of his crown. Later, as he grapples with existential questions, a more authentic nobility emerges. The homeless and still delusional Lear will call himself "every inch a king." The irony is painful, but Shakespeare wants us to see in it a paradoxical truth. Only now, after his suffering, is Lear becoming a wise, and no circumstances can rob him of his essential greatness.

Strategies to Establish a Character: Hamlet

We often discuss protagonists as if they are real people, with intentions, desires, and inherent traits. This is just a shortcut, of course. They are invented, and their inner nature as well as their outward behavior must be communicated to an audience.

Shakespeare uses a variety of strategies to establish the nature of his protagonists. We've seen these already in the examples so far:

1. Traits **emerge from what the character says, does, and focuses on.** This is basic. When we see a character speaking and acting with passionate devotion, fixating on a grievance, or plotting to take power, we add that to our growing picture of that character. Lear demands a display of love in exchange for power; Romeo and Juliet fall in love on first sight and declare their love readily. We form a sense of their nature because of what we see them do and hear them say. This impression can be modulated later, of course. But with Shakespeare, what you see is usually what you get. A *character* may be deceived about the nature of another, as Othello is when he mistakes Iago's true intentions, but we in the audience have been let in along the way through Iago's own words and actions.

2. Some traits **are conveyed stylistically.** Romeo and Juliet express themselves with fine, poetic phrases and fresh and bright imagery. Lear speaks in harsh commands to his daughter: "Nothing will come of nothing! Speak again," and he angrily dismisses Kent for his interference; Kent, in his reply, begins in a flattering manner, then becomes impatient and switches to bluntness: "See better, Lear."

3. Traits can be **established through the protagonist's physical appearance and even through the surroundings** in which they are placed. Richard III draws attention to his own twisted and frustrated nature, which is mirrored in his deformed posture. By seeing Romeo and Juliet within their tight-knit social groups of peers and family, we can get a sense of the strong bonds they must extricate themselves from in order to be with each other.

4. We **learn about the protagonist from others and in how they reflect back on the protagonist.** We are shown Lear as the center of attention, one

whom others try to solicit and appease. From Lear's elder daughters, we are alerted that this king has lacked self-knowledge. From Romeo's friends who tease him, we are prepared for his romantic nature—he has already fallen in love and claims there is no one who can surpass Rosaline's beauty. Juliet shows a fiery nature in her dealings with the Nurse; but because her mother, Lady Capulet, appears far more distant and unsympathetic, we can see why the girl might turn, unwisely, to the Nurse for support for her plan.

Shakespeare uses all of these strategies when he introduces us to his most famous protagonist, Hamlet. What are the traits Shakespeare wants us to notice about him? And how does Shakespeare make him known to us?

Hamlet: "But I have that within which passeth show"

In *Hamlet*, as elsewhere, Shakespeare uses our initial view of the protagonist to signal that this character is exceptional and to lay the groundwork for where their journey is heading. And the writer does it with remarkable efficiency.

Our First View of Hamlet (1.2.1-132)

When we first meet Hamlet, in the midst of a crowd at court, he is clad in black mourning attire, but is silent for a good while. The scene is dominated initially by his uncle Claudius, who has recently ascended the throne and has married his brother's widow Gertrude. Claudius makes grandiloquent speeches and grants favors to his petitioners. The realm of Denmark appears to be in good hands, ruled by this confident and gracious king. An audience at this point might even think Claudius is going to be our protagonist.

And then, at line 66, the King finally turns his attention to Hamlet:

KING But now, my cousin Hamlet and my son—
HAMLET *[Aside.]* A little more than kin, and less than kind.
KING How is it that the clouds still hang on you?
HAMLET Not so, my lord, I am too much in the sun.

Hamlet's first line in the play is an aside, which is a rather muted way to make a first impression. What Hamlet is saying is that his uncle is too much his *kin* now that he has married Hamlet's mother, and that this union is unnatural (*less than kind*). He's using wordplay to express his disgust.

When Claudius then suggests that Hamlet is moping about, Hamlet retorts: "I am too much in the sun." This is more wordplay, a pun on *sun/son*. What Hamlet says can be interpreted as "I am only too much in the 'son' role now that my uncle has married my mother." He is also too much in the "sun" of the King's presence. And a third, more obvious and benign meaning would be, "I'm not withdrawn (under any clouds); I'm too much in the open (out in public)."

A single phrase with three possible interpretations. Does Hamlet expect Claudius to get any of this? Perhaps he's trying to taunt him while having deniability. This is the tactic Hamlet uses with Polonius and Ophelia later. He pushes the limits of how insolent he can be and then feigns innocence if they catch on.

But Hamlet can go only so far in giving offense to a king. He shows here that if he wants to deflect Claudius, he must be clever. He has to outwit him. That is why Hamlet's opening lines, which might seem throwaway, are actually purposeful. They show us Hamlet's quickness and also his guardedness toward Claudius. His clever language alerts us that it's worth listening carefully to him.

Next, his mother tries to engage him. She, too, implies that Hamlet should be less gloomy, remarking that everyone loses their father at some point, and inquires, "Why seems it so particular with thee?"

It might sound like motherly concern, but her choice of the word *seems* sets him off. "Seems, madam? Nay, it is, I know not 'seems,'" he insists. His downcast manner and black clothes might indeed be an act that others put on to simulate grief, "But I have that within which passeth show, / These but the trappings and the suits of woe" (1.2). In other words, don't you dare think I'm just acting. There's more grief inside than what my outward appearance can show.

His outburst hints at a wellspring of frustration. This is followed by Claudius denying Hamlet's request to return to his studies abroad. There is nothing Hamlet can say to this; the king's word is law.

Soon after, the rest of the court exits, while the protagonist remains alone with the audience.

The scene so far has efficiently introduced the protagonist; we see that he is set apart from others, and that he deeply distrusts the King. He is grieving and downcast. Yet he is mentally agile, verbally aggressive, and highly sensitive to and adept with words. We see his prickly relationships with his mother and uncle, and a hint of his sense of alienation.

But Shakespeare has not finished yet. He takes us even more deeply into the character's inner world.

Showing What's Within: First Soliloquy (1.2.133-164)

Once he is alone on the stage, Hamlet launches into a lengthy soliloquy, the first of several in the play. And now we do indeed see that there is more within than could be conveyed by his "suits of woe" or other standard expressions of grief.

This anguished soliloquy doesn't provide much new backstory, but we learn more about his fixations. Hamlet begins by expressing a longing to disappear and a distaste for all aspects of life:

> O, that this too, too [sullied] flesh would melt,
> Thaw, and resolve itself into a dew!
> Or that the Everlasting had not fixed
> His canon 'gainst self-slaughter! O God, God,
> How weary, stale, flat, and unprofitable
> Seem to me all the uses of this world!

In the next two-dozen lines he reveals his distress over his mother's hasty remarriage. How could his mother sink so low to move from his father, a man he revered, to someone so inferior to him? To descend from "Hyperion to a satyr"? Hamlet finds her behavior worse than bestial, for "a beast that wants discourse of reason / Would have mourned longer."

It bodes ill, Hamlet concludes, yet he can say nothing: "But break, my heart, for I must hold my tongue."

From this speech we learn he is so disillusioned with life that he contemplates suicide. It also depicts a reflective nature, an inclination to make moral and ethical distinctions, as when he discusses what is proper for humans versus beasts, and identifies the reason why suicide is not an option.

Shakespeare also reinforces what he showed earlier in the scene, that Hamlet feels isolated from the world around him. A great man has died, and yet the court seems to have moved on already, even his widow. This is a disillusioned young man recognizing how compromised life can be and how weak his mother is—a frailty he extends to women in general.

Hamlet is not simply mourning his father's loss or disgusted by his mother's remarriage. Life itself is tainted. Women are frail. The world yields only weary, stale, flat and unprofitable experiences.

Which Traits Are Established First?

In Hamlet's first appearance, Shakespeare provides us with abundant information about the character. Our sense of him will be expanded throughout the play, but these are the traits Shakespeare wants us to notice first. In Hamlet we find:

- Mental dexterity and precision
- A reflective and melancholic nature
- Deep frustration, a sense of constraint in his current situation
- Somber dress and a downcast manner
- Loyalty and appreciation for his late father, whom he saw as a great man
- A prickly response to his mother, revulsion at her hasty remarriage, and a distrust that he extends to women generally
- Disillusionment with life, melancholy, even suicidal thoughts

These are largely interior qualities. Except for his attempts to rebut the King and his mother, Hamlet shows little in terms of his outward prowess. We hear nothing of his particular aims besides wanting to disappear. The only physical features highlighted are his mourning clothes, which Hamlet draws attention to, and a downcast manner, which Claudius and Gertrude note. Otherwise, we have no sense of an outward-directed character; on the contrary, he is frustrated and turned inwards.

This focus on the character's inner reality is noteworthy for a protagonist, and differs from how Shakespeare introduces his other great tragic protagonists. Each of those protagonists is associated with active duties or pursuits:

- Othello first appears onstage because he has been called upon by the Venetian senate to save them from the Turkish naval threat and because he has eloped with Desdemona, whose father has lodged a complaint. The fact that Othello is black, and therefore an outsider in Venice, is also focused on.
- Lear is elderly, but in command and making consequential decisions that affect many lives: dividing up his crown between his two elder daughters, banishing a counselor, and disowning his youngest daughter.
- Macbeth is returning from a battle where he performed heroically, and we soon hear (from the witches) that he will be king. Almost immediately he contemplates seizing the crown by murdering Duncan.

Whereas these three protagonists are associated early on with power and decisive actions, Hamlet, is hemmed in, frustrated, at an impasse; he cannot even speak openly. Shakespeare clearly is seeking to highlight the inward nature of this protagonist from the start and to suggest a frustration in his outward interactions.

How does Shakespeare communicate these traits effectively to the audience? And why does he establish these particular traits as primary ones?

Shakespeare paints this picture through the strategies we noted outlined above, namely, through what Hamlet says and does; through style; through his relationship with others and how they view him; and through his physical appearance and surroundings.

Conveying Traits Through What He Says and Does

Shakespeare gives Hamlet an aside as his first line—a private comment—and ends the scene with a self-reflective soliloquy. In between, Hamlet refers to his inner reality—to "that within," which surpasses any mere show. These all direct our attention toward this character's interior world.

And Hamlet's speeches show a quick and aggressive mind and emotional volatility. He cleverly parries Claudius' questions to him and slyly insults the king to his face. He turns on his mother for her ill-chosen word choice and forcefully defends his display of grief. He conveys his deep frustration in finding the path of suicide closed to him and declaring he must let his heart break rather than speak his mind openly.

Conveying Traits Through Style

In Hamlet's soliloquy in particular, Shakespeare uses a linguistic style that reflects a tormented, frustrated mind, in which Hamlet moves from topic to topic without finding resolution and fixates on certain ideas. We will analyze the style of this speech in more depth in Chapter 4.

Conveying Traits Through Relationship with Others

In this introductory scene, Shakespeare sets up a contest for our interest: the confident king vs. the melancholic prince. As the scene progresses, it becomes apparent that Hamlet, with his tormented, inwardly focused nature, is the more compelling of the two, despite the King's outward suavity and seeming magnanimity. This contrast with Claudius helps to depict Hamlet. Whereas Claudius is acting with outward competence, Hamlet shows himself to be stuck. Claudius is restricting his movement (refusing to let him return to his studies) and Hamlet himself must keep silent about his true feelings.

Hamlet's nature is further reflected in his relationship with his mother. We see a sharpness towards her that he didn't dare show to the King. In his soliloquy we will learn even more how disgusted he is by how quickly she remarried and how this has tainted his view of all women.

And in this scene, we see that Claudius and Gertrude take keen notice of Hamlet's mourning, and want him to move on. Hamlet apparently makes them uneasy. We don't know *why* yet, but we soon will.

Conveying Traits Through Physical Appearance and Surroundings

Shakespeare establishes Hamlet's exceptional and difficult circumstances, in part, by setting him in isolation from others. He shows this physically through Hamlet's mourning clothes and by the fact he is silent onstage for a length of time at the beginning, and at the end of the scene, when, he is alone onstage during his soliloquy. This sense of Hamlet being at odds with others is conveyed through Hamlet's tense exchanges with Claudius and his mother.

In the soliloquy, Shakespeare takes Hamlet's alienation further: this is a person at odds with own existence, contemplating suicide. He wants to disappear like the dew.

Why These Traits?

Shakespeare's approach in introducing the character this way is somewhat unconventional, but he has at least a few good reasons for doing so:

1. *Builds tension and prepares us for future conflict*

The situation in which we first see Hamlet has tension already built in. Hamlet seems like a powder keg ready to explode. He is constrained from speaking his mind; is resentful toward the King; and is deeply dismayed by his mother's behavior, which he finds worse than a beast's. He is even considering suicide.

Hamlet finds no allies in this scene, not even his own mother, to whom he reacts in a prickly way. But we can see who will likely be his main adversary: his uncle, whom he detests. By showing Hamlet in this combative and frustrated state, Shakespeare has wasted no time in generating a tense dynamic, and preparing us for future clashes—with the King and possibly his mother, as well as with his own self.

By showing him as set apart and alienated from others, Shakespeare hints at Hamlet's future struggles, and this already piques our interest.

2. *Marks Hamlet out as exceptional, interesting, and accessible*

A protagonist must be exceptional is some way to hold our attention, and Hamlet indeed appears exceptional from the start. This is not in the way that Othello, Lear, and Macbeth are exceptional, but rather, through the depth of his anguish and the quickness of his mind.

We will listen more carefully to him, be more attentive to his shifts of mood, because we have witnessed his clever turn of mind and seen him turn volatile and combative.

And Shakespeare suggests that we will have access to the "real" character within. Hamlet insists there is more to him than can be shown through outward signs such as mourning clothes or other signs of grief, and soon afterward takes us into his confidence on what is tormenting him.

3. *Sets expectations of what the story is about*

This introduction to the character of Hamlet is particularly focused on setting the audience's expectations about what this story will be about.

Shortly after this scene, Hamlet will encounter the Ghost and be called upon to avenge his father's murder. It will become very much an action-packed revenge tragedy.

The revenge tragedy is a genre Shakespeare's audiences knew well. They would expect to see a lot of violence, probably a specter along the way, and ultimately, the deaths of the avenged and probably the avenger. Shakespeare will provide all this. But he did not want the story to be *only* about this.

So, in our introduction to the protagonist we see someone not particularly suited to the standard role of a doer. This protagonist is not a coward (though he will question later whether he is), but he is perceptive and sensitive. He wrestles with moral and ethical questions even before he discovers his father was murdered.

Through this scene, Shakespeare is alerting us that this story will not simply be a struggle between two adversaries, the powerful king and the aggrieved nephew/stepson. It will *also* delve in Hamlet's inner dilemmas; it will not *only* be about revenge for a father's murder but a confrontation with life's imperfections and mysteries.

This makes the story more universal, of course. Few of us are called on to revenge a murder, but many of us face the disappointment with our parents' frailties, become disillusioned with life, and wish we could end our sorrows. Shakespeare wants to frame Hamlet in this broader light: he is more than just an avenger; he is one who faces existential questions we all face.

Hamlet's traits of inward reflection and psychological turmoil are central to how Shakespeare conceives of this protagonist, and these are firmly established in Hamlet's first scene.

In subsequent scenes, Shakespeare will reinforce these traits, and expand our impression of him. We will see many more facets to him, but all the traits established here are central to the story ahead. This early view of Hamlet prepares us for a plot that will explore not only his duty to take revenge but also his turmoil inside.

Summary

Traits are fundamental elements of Shakespeare's characters, and are usually established very early in a story. Shakespeare uses the traits of his protagonists to make them interesting to the audience, but they contribute in important ways to how the story unfolds.

A protagonist will be exceptional in some way—this is to hold our interest, but there are numerous ways to single a character out. Unlike Lear and Hamlet, Romeo and Juliet are not that important socially, but they are exceptional in their own way. It is their extreme youth, their impulsive idealism, and their fine romanticism that compel our interest. For Hamlet it is his lightning quick wit and emotional volatility. For Lear, it is his powerful, imperious nature—he is every inch a king, even after he forfeits his power. One might think an elderly king bereft of power would not be interesting. But he is.

There are many tools Shakespeare uses to depict a character's traits. In our first view of Hamlet, Shakespeare uses a range of them—his appearance; his interactions with others; his words that depict a keen intellectual and emotional inner world. We see his behavior through the eyes of other key characters. He is presented both in a public setting and in a private, inward-turning soliloquy, which allows him to show still more breadth of his nature.

As important as a character's traits are, these are not enough to tell a story. The character has to be engaged in actions of some kind and seen at critical moments. Later chapters will describe the kinds of journeys on which Shakespeare takes his protagonists. But in the next chapter, we will examine how Shakespeare fleshes out his protagonists to make them seem realistic and complex.

Takeaway for Writers

In building his protagonists, Shakespeare follows these general principles:
- They are exceptional in some way. This typically means they display at least one, and often more, of these traits:
  - Highly attractive, appealing, or otherwise admirable
  - Great intelligence and wit
  - Powerful over others
  - Profound emotions or desires
  - Extraordinary courage or perseverance
- Their traits will be appropriate and relevant in the context of the story. The traits are not superfluous. Every prominent trait we perceive in the protagonist early on will prepare us for how they behave later.
- Key traits are established almost immediately, although some of these traits may transform as the story continues and the character is forced to reckon with new circumstances. For example, a lack of self-knowledge turns to wisdom.
- Their traits often point to the nature of the challenge ahead; these traits are selected with the rest of the plot in mind.
- Their traits can be depicted through a range of techniques: through what the protagonist says and does and through stylistic choices, but also in what others say about the protagonist or how they react to them.

Extras

In the **long opening speech in *Richard III*,** given by the hunchbacked future king, Shakespeare tells us a lot about the nature of his protagonist, who will dissemble and murder his way to the throne.

> RICHARD Now is the winter of our discontent
> Made glorious summer by this son of York;
> And all the clouds that low'r'd upon our house
> In the deep bosom of the ocean buried.
> Now are our brows bound with victorious wreaths,
> Our bruised arms hung up for monuments,
> Our stern alarums chang'd to merry meetings,
> Our dreadful marches to delightful measures.

Grim-visag'd War hath smooth'd his wrinkled front;
And now, in stead of mounting barbed steeds
To fright the souls of fearful adversaries,
He capers nimbly in a lady's chamber
To the lascivious pleasing of a lute.
But I, that am not shap'd for sportive tricks,
Nor made to court an amorous looking-glass;
I, that am rudely stamp'd, and want love's majesty
To strut before a wanton ambling nymph;
I, that am curtail'd of this fair proportion,
Cheated of feature by dissembling nature,
Deform'd, unfinish'd, sent before my time
Into this breathing world, scarce half made up,
And that so lamely and unfashionable
That dogs bark at me as I halt by them —
Why, I, in this weak piping time of peace,
Have no delight to pass away the time,
Unless to see my shadow in the sun
And descant on mine own deformity.
And therefore, since I cannot prove a lover
To entertain these fair well-spoken days,
I am determined to prove a villain
And hate the idle pleasures of these days.
Plots have I laid, inductions dangerous,
By drunken prophecies, libels, and dreams,
To set my brother Clarence and the King
In deadly hate the one against the other;
And if King Edward be as true and just
As I am subtle, false, and treacherous,
This day should Clarence closely be mew'd up
About a prophecy, which says that G
Of Edward's heirs the murtherer shall be.
Dive, thoughts, down to my soul, here Clarence comes! (1.1.1-41)

CHAPTER 3: COMPLEX AND "REAL" PROTAGONISTS

Why, look you now, how unworthy a thing you make of me! You would play upon me, you would seem to know my stops, you would pluck out the heart of my mystery, you would sound me from my lowest note to the top of my compass; and there is much music, excellent voice, in this little organ, yet cannot you make it speak. 'Sblood, do you think I am easier to be played on than a pipe? Call me what instrument you will, though you fret me, yet you cannot play upon me.
  —Hamlet, to Rosencrantz and Guildenstern (3.2)

Shakespeare is admired for his mastery of many aspects of writing, but perhaps most of all for his ability to create complex and believable characters. They are fictional, yet readers have the impression of knowing them more intimately than people in their own lives. When Hamlet rebukes his old friends for trying to manipulate him as if he were a mere pipe to play on, he points to "the heart of my mystery," his inner depths, which he says they cannot touch. Hamlet's reference to his own mystery and his anger at their attempts to manipulate him are just one subtle touch among countless others by which Shakespeare render this fictional character believable.

It can be an uncanny experience to encounter Shakespeare's characters for the first time from across the centuries. If we leave aside their literary and at times archaic speech patterns, they can seem utterly modern and real. Shakespeare's characters have even been studied as proxies for actual human behavior. Sigmund Freud, when formulating his theories of psychoanalysis, turned often to Shakespeare as a guide in searching the dark corners of human motivation.

First, we should concede we cannot pluck out the heart of Shakespeare's mystery. He must have observed people with an extraordinary perception; he must have been gifted with, or developed, preternatural insights into human complexity and motivation that have rarely been matched.

But even if we take it as a given that Shakespeare's understanding of human nature is truly exceptional, we can still analyze *how* he built characters. We can see the mechanics behind his realistic and complex protagonists.

In this chapter we will touch on some of those techniques. The techniques can be applied to character drawing in general, and Shakespeare often imbues even minor characters with uniqueness and complexity. But it is in his protagonists, and particularly in his great tragic protagonists from his middle to late period, that Shakespeare explores human nature to its depths.

Before we get to specific strategies he used, let's begin with what he *avoided:* conventionality.

Avoiding Conventionality

A protagonist's traits might mark this character out as exceptional—they are depicted as powerful, intelligent, beautiful, passionate—yet are still uninteresting. This could be because the character is too conventionally depicted—a stereotype.

It requires discipline in a writer to resist what is easy and predictable, and to find instead what is more authentic or "real." With a stereotypical hero, we can predict too easily what they'll do, how they'll react, what motivates them. They don't surprise or challenge us enough, and this makes us lose interest.

Complex characters require us to work a little harder: we have to keep expanding our picture of them, making sense of apparent contradictions. Their nuances and complexity go a long way toward interesting us and making them seem believable.

There are no particular traits that signal complexity. Rather, this emerges from a breadth of traits and behaviors that seem plausible in a single individual.

Shakespeare recognizes stereotypes and avoids them. He even gives a tongue-in-cheek warning about cliches. His Sonnet 130 pokes fun at them, depicting his beloved in terms of what she is *not* (namely, *not* these cliches):

> My mistress' eyes are nothing like the sun;
> Coral is far more red than her lips' red;
> If snow be white, why then her breasts are dun [dull colored];
> If hairs be wires, black wires grow on her head.
> I have seen roses damasked, red and white,
> But no such roses see I in her cheeks,
> And in some perfumes is there more delight
> Than in the breath that from my mistress reeks [is exhaled].
> I love to hear her speak, yet well I know
> That music hath a far more pleasing sound;
> I grant I never saw a goddess go;

My mistress when she walks treads on the ground.
　And yet, by heaven, I think my love as rare
　As any she belied with false compare.

Far from insulting his mistress, he is simply acknowledging the difference between what poets claim and what the reality is. He uses that discrepancy to make his claims of love ring truer. My beloved mistress walks on the ground, has eyes that are less bright than the sun, lips that are less red than coral, and so on. But for all that, I know my love is more real because I see the real person, not some fantasy.

So, Shakespeare's implicit warning to writers is that if you claim your beloved has breath sweeter than perfume or floats like a goddess, you are not seeing the *real* woman; you are thinking, seeing, and expressing yourself in others' ideas.

Raising and Rejecting Cliches

This sonnet is not the only time Shakespeare invokes cliches in order to reject them. He employs the strategy on a few other occasions, such as in the following examples, one from a comedy, another from a tragedy.

As You Like It: Rejecting Romantic Excess

In the comedy *As You Like It*, the main protagonist is Rosalind, who spends much of the story disguised as a boy called Ganymede. The lovelorn Orlando takes advice from Ganymede (not knowing this is actually Rosalind) in hopes of learning how to win the woman he loves (Rosalind herself). Orlando claims he will die if Rosalind rejects him. "No, faith," replies Ganymede/Rosalind. She lists famous lovers who are said to have died for love. "But these are all lies: men have died from time to time and worms have eaten them, but not for love."

Orlando objects: "for I protest her frown might kill me," but Rosalind again corrects him: "By this hand, it will not kill a fly." (4.1)

Orlando is suffering from romantic excess. Rosalind wants to squelch that in him so he can love the real person, *her*, not his conventional idea of a beloved, whose frowns can kill. It's a subtle detail, but with it, Shakespeare makes Rosalind a bit more real to us because she (like us) sees through romantic fantasies.

Hamlet: Beyond Mourning Conventions

Hamlet's first appearance in his play, discussed in the previous chapter, shows a similar strategy. Shakespeare wants to make Hamlet to stand out right away as real to us, and to show him as truly in deep grief over the loss of his father. So, he has Hamlet wearing the standard clothes of mourning—the "customary suits of solemn black." But he also has Hamlet react defensively when his mother asks why, when everyone must lose their father, he seems so particularly sad.

Seems?! Hamlet asks his mother. *How dare you think I am just pretending!*

Hamlet's response immediately makes a claim to our attention by the way he sees through trappings of mourning. He lists the signs a person might display, but which might indeed be simply for show:

> Seems, madam? Nay, it is, I know not "seems."
> 'Tis not alone my inky cloak, good mother,
> Nor customary suits of solemn black,
> Nor windy suspiration of forced breath,
> No, nor the fruitful river in the eye,
> Nor the dejected havior of the visage,
> Together with all forms, moods, shapes of grief,
> That can denote me truly. These indeed seem,
> For they are actions that a man might play,
> But I have that within which passes show,
> These but the trappings and the suits of woe. (1.2)

He acknowledges that people might make themselves sigh (suspiration of forced breadth) or have a dejected expression, even shed tears, without actually feeling grief. *But this is not what I'm doing.* The conventional signs of mourning are acknowledged, but only to say that his are not put on for show, but come from true grief.

This is a typically bold Shakespearean move. He has his stage actor (Richard Burbage) playing a fictional character (Hamlet) who objects to being seen as just acting a part, instead of having genuine sorrow. Shakespeare makes his characters just that much more real to us by daring us to even consider them as fictitious. How dare we not believe that Hamlet is *real?*

Obviously, this strategy of invoking and then rejecting cliches to make a character seem more authentic can be used only so often. We find Shakespeare using other approaches, though, that are far more pervasive throughout his works.

Naturalistic Touches: Juliet

If Shakespeare avoids conventions, what does he do instead? How does he make a character seem to have depth and reality?

One approach may seem deceptively simple: he paints his characters through an abundance of subtle, naturalistic details. These details make the character individualized, yet recognizably human; unique, but relatable. None of the details may be particularly striking in themselves, but they accumulate to draw a multifaceted portrait of a person.

They add up to a seemingly three-dimensional, rather than the stylized or formulaic, character, and at the same time, will seem coherent within one personality. It's the nature of real people to be sometimes contradictory, and as we will see, Shakespeare does incorporate what might seem to be contradictory traits, but in a way that still makes them seem plausible within that character.

Naturalistic Touches in Creating Juliet

Building a character through naturalistic touches is a skill that can be hard to emulate, but a sign of mastery. It will be easier to see through examples than through explanation. Let's start with a fairly simple protagonist. Juliet is not complex in terms of her psychology or intellect, but she is vivid, believable, and her unique nature suits the role she plays in the story.

Novel Expressiveness

In *Romeo and Juliet,* Juliet is encountering romantic love for the first time, and she, like Romeo, expresses herself in extremes. This tendency to superlatives is a believable reflection of how young people often behave in a similar situation.

But what keeps her from seeming conventional? Why doesn't she sound like a generic teenager in love? Largely, it is the language she uses—how she observes, describes, and reacts to situations. These sound fresh and novel. One example is when she declares that Romeo should become a constellation after his death so that the whole world can fall in love with him as she does now. She does not use the sort of cliched language Shakespeare pokes fun of in Sonnet 130. Instead, her imagery seems to emerge from her own felt perceptions instead of from books. She sees the world in an original way, which helps us to believe this character is "real" and is feeling this powerful love for the first time.

Naturalistic Behaviors

Beyond her speech patterns, Shakespeare has her behave in ways we wouldn't expect from a cliched young maiden in love. Although she usually views Romeo in ideal terms, this young girl is not all sweetness and unvarying light. She is obstinate with her father when he tries to force her to marry Paris. She is testy with her Nurse on several occasions. When she learns Romeo has just killed her cousin Tybalt in a street fight, she turns furious and repudiates him at length before reproaching herself for her lack of loyalty:

Shall I speak ill of him that is my husband?

Ah, poor my lord, what tongue shall smooth thy name

When I, thy three-hours wife, have mangled it?

But wherefore, villain, didst thou kill my cousin?

That villain cousin would have killed my husband. (3.2)

In many such details, Shakespeare is expanding on the hints he found his source story, *Romeus and Juliet*, Arthur Brooke's lengthy translation of an Italian poem. He takes it farther than Brooke by foregrounding what we might call naturalistic behaviors. (No one in real life speaks in verse, so Shakespeare is not writing "naturalism" in the strict literary sense; but we adopt this term to indicate a comparatively more realistic way of behaving.)

Consider the scene in which Juliet eagerly awaits Romeo's message about when and where they will marry. The Nurse has gone to find out the information.

Brooke simply mentions that once the Nurse learns it, she returns home "with speedy pace," and has the Nurse praising Romeo before Juliet pushes her to get to the point of when their wedding will be (*Romeus and Juliet* 673–88).

Shakespeare expands greatly on this moment. He begins the scene with Juliet alone, impatiently counting the minutes till the Nurse's return, and imagining all kinds of reasons for her delay:

The clock struck nine when I did send the Nurse.

In half an hour she promised to return.

Perchance she cannot meet him—that's not so.

O, she is lame! ....

Had she affections and warm youthful blood,

She would be as swift in motion as a ball.... (2.5)

When the Nurse finally arrives, Juliet accosts her, demanding Romeo's message and searching her expression for any hint of good or bad news. But the Nurse ignores this to complain about her aching bones, which leads Juliet to retort, "I would thou hadst my bones, and I thy news."

JULIET Now, good sweet nurse—O Lord, why lookest thou sad?

Though news be sad, yet tell them merrily;

If good, thou shamest the music of sweet news

By playing it to me with so sour a face.

> NURSE I am a-weary, give me leave awhile.
> Fie, how my bones ache! What a jaunt have I!
> JULIET I would thou hadst my bones, and I thy news.
> Nay, come, I pray thee, speak, good, good nurse, speak.
> NURSE Jesu, what haste! Can you not stay awhile?
> Do you not see that I am out of breath?
> JULIET How art thou out of breath, when thou hast breath
> To say to me that thou art out of breath? (2.5)

Shakespeare accomplishes a couple of things in the way he alters Brooke's original version. He portrays, in these subtle details, a naturalistic behavior of someone very young and in love. But he also sharpens the contrast of the Nurse's mundane, middle-aged ailments with Juliet's youthful passion.

Another example comes near the end, when Juliet is about to drink the potion that will make her appear dead. Shakespeare takes us through a series of reactions she has.

At first, she panics. Like the near-child she is, she wants to call her nurse to comfort her, but stops herself. She then worries the potion might not work and she'll be forced to marry Paris, which makes her consider stabbing herself. Next, she fears the Friar may have given her poison in order to cover up his role in her marriage to Romeo:

> I have a faint cold fear thrills through my veins,
> That almost freezes up the heat of life.
> I'll call them back again to comfort me.
> Nurse! — What should she do here?
> My dismal scene I needs must act alone.
> Come, vial
> What if this mixture do not work at all?
> Shall I be married then tomorrow morning?
> *[Laying down her dagger.]*
> No, no, this shall forbid it. Lie thou there.
> What if it be a poison which the Friar
> Subtly hath ministered to have me dead,
> Lest in this marriage he should be dishonored
> Because he married me before to Romeo?

And finally, she imagines in macabre detail the scene she will face when she wakes up in the crypt next to her dead kinsmen:

Where for this many hundred years the bones
Of all my buried ancestors are packed,
Where bloody Tybalt, yet but green in earth,
Lies fest'ring in his shroud… (4.2)

Comparing this with Brooke reveals just how many subtle, naturalistic details Shakespeare adds. Brooke gave him only the idea of Juliet imagining, at great length, a grisly scene upon waking up (*Romeus and Juliet* 2341–2402). Shakespeare surpasses his source in broadening the range of fears she has, and in reflecting the kind of rapid-fire progression of thoughts that someone in her situation might experience as they try to anticipate all possible threats she is facing.

Consider, by contrast, if Juliet had acted with perfect faith and simply quaffed the potion and fallen unconscious. She would seem less believable. Instead, with this sequence of highly charged reactions, we see her face up to her fears and mature in front of our eyes. This confrontation with the possibilities makes her heroic as well, because in spite of her trepidation and awareness of the dangers that might await her, she takes the potion anyway; her love is greater than her fears.

These details do not impact the plot, but they add a few more brushstrokes to the portrait. They help us find this protagonist more fleshed out than a conventional girl in love. Juliet shows flashes of temper; she doesn't trust blindly; she shows a natural fear of death and instinct for self-preservation. She acts, in other words, as we can easily imagine ourselves acting in a similar situation.

Juliet is not even among Shakespeare's most complex and realistic protagonists. But we can see the steps he takes, even early in his career, to keep her from becoming two-dimensional. He avoids cliched expressions of young and passionate love, instead finding novel ways for her to express herself. And he provides an abundance of small, naturalistic touches, such as her impatience at the Nurse's slowness, or the many fears that haunt her when she is about to swallow the potion.

Multiple Contexts for a Protagonist: Hamlet

Shakespeare does not conceive of characters as a static and unitary thing. They are more like a mosaic, composed of traits as well as circumstances and relationships. No character is an island.

One of Shakespeare's most effective techniques of character-drawing is rather simple: he places them in a multiplicity of contexts. That is, we view the character in various situations and relationships, each instance of which adds nuance to the character. We behave differently depending on who we are interacting with and what is happening in our lives, yet we are still ourselves. So it is with Shakespeare's protagonists.

The Many Sides of Hamlet

Once, when teaching a Shakespeare seminar, I asked students to write down what they thought was Hamlet's most prominent trait; then we went around the room giving our answers. Halfway through, some students were looking perplexed. We had all read the same play, but we weren't seeing the same character, at least, not the same leading trait.

One student noted great intellect. Depressed, said another. Then came competitive. Obsessed with his mother. Skeptical. Noble. Sarcastic. Loyal. Indecisive. Ambitious. Verbally gifted and witty. Mistreats his girlfriend. Arrogant. Erratic mood swings. Romantic. Likes to pull the strings. Insightful. Good-natured. Sensitive. Impulsive. A decent guy trapped in impossible circumstances. Philosophical.

Of 24 students in the class, there were 21 distinct answers—positive traits, negative traits, traits that might seem incompatible with each other. For these students—as for nearly anyone who gets to know this character—Hamlet is so fleshed out and real that he can be seen in any or all of these perspectives. A full, life-like character will be interpreted variously by a range of people, and even their views can change over time. If I polled that same group decades later, they'd likely identify a different leading trait. We are alert to what most interests us, and to what we can most relate to, at that moment in time.

Making Hamlet Multifaceted

So, how does Shakespeare construct this character in such a way that readers perceive a different dominant trait?

Soliloquies, as we have noted, give the audience the sense that they have access to Hamlet's innermost thoughts. But beyond that, we see him also see him in a wide range of situations. We see him in public displays and in private moments. He interacts with friends and enemies. He comments on how others view Denmark, and reflects on philosophical questions about human capacity and frailty, and about what happens after death. He even gives a lengthy discourse to the actors on how to act and on the value of their art.

He announces to Horatio that he intends to play-act as mad to throw Claudius off his scent ("I am but mad north-north-west"), but his overwrought nature still gets the best of him. He veers from melancholic to manic, from romantic to sarcastic, as he responds to the changing cast around him. And this is Shakespeare's technique: to show Hamlet in the round by giving him such a varied breadth of situations and social encounters.

Interaction with a Wide Range of Other Characters

Hamlet engages with individuals across the entire social spectrum, from the King and Queen to his friends and love interest to the gravedigger. He even talks to the Ghost. And of course, to a skull. And to each individual he naturally shows a different side of himself. It's how we all are. By having Hamlet interact with a wide range of other characters, Shakespeare can reveal more about him.

These interactions place him in the roles of son, prince, disillusioned lover, peer (of Fortinbras), competitor (with Laertes), and intimate friend (of Horatio). Hamlet acts as an impresario and critic with the traveling players; he taunts a meddling counselor (Polonius) from a position of intellectual superiority; and spars with the gravedigger as if they are on equal footing. In speaking to Rosencrantz and Guildenstern, he harkens back to his earlier days as a student; and earlier yet, as a young boy, to the skull of Yorick. In remarks from Ophelia and Fortinbras, we get a glimpse of what his future might have been. There's virtually no aspect of this character's existence—past, present, or projected future—that Shakespeare doesn't invoke in some way. He can do this because of the breadth of relationships he gives to Hamlet.

Let's consider each of these different relationships, in turn, to see how they help to display a different facet of Hamlet's nature:

1. With **his uncle, the King,** no matter how much he loathes him, Hamlet follows social protocol and contrives to appear to obey his commands, or at least not push the boundaries too far. Hamlet is a prince and must publicly act the part. But his frustration and antagonism toward his hated uncle are palpable from the start. He cannot act openly against the King, so Hamlet will plot against him behind the scenes; he will even act mad in order to disguise his intentions. Claudius' superior power and malevolence force Hamlet to be clever in self-defense.

2. With **his mother, Gertrude,** Hamlet is emotionally attached, sometimes respectful, sometimes confrontational and angry. He is revolted at how she could move on so quickly to marry the brother of her husband. Her physical

relationship with Claudius disturbs him, and he urges her to stop going to their shared bed. The Ghost warns him to "leave her to heaven," and not to punish her, which makes Hamlet steel himself to "speak daggers, not use them" on her. Her example prompts him to reflect that humans, though they can have the gifts of angels, may instead behave worse than beasts. Gertrude's seeming weakness so disturbs him that he accuses all women of frailty—an accusation he later hurls at Ophelia.

3. His encounter with **the Ghost of his dead father** unleashes a torrent of emotions. After this meeting, Hamlet turns giddy, almost manic. Plausible enough: How would *you* behave if you saw the ghost of your dead father and learned he had been murdered, just as you already vaguely suspected? When the Ghost instructs him to revenge his murder, Hamlet acts as someone suddenly released from his shackles and who thinks he has the key to his problems. His manic, whirling speech after this is understandable. But later he veers back to a more skeptical view. Is this Ghost really my father? Could this be a false spirit sent to lure me into mortal danger? It opens up a realm of questions he must grapple with. The encounter with the Ghost has made him realize, as he tells Horatio: "There are more things in heaven and earth, Horatio, / Than are dreamt of in your philosophy" (1.5). By having Hamlet encounter this Ghost, Shakespeare can depict the protagonist's intuitive nature, his loyalty and courage, his mania, and later, his caution. All these traits plausibly coexist, particularly in a context such as this.

4. With **Ophelia**, Hamlet displays a romantic as well as a cruel side. We even hear one of his love letters he sent to her read aloud. It is not good poetry, but it is ardent. His previous love for her turns to distrust,when he thinks she is conspiring with others to expose him. He becomes almost abusive to her. He confesses, "I did love you once," but when Ophelia replies she did believe it, he then declares, "You should not have believed me.... I loved you not" (3.1). We have not seen Hamlet and Ophelia together during happier times, but it is suggested they might have married one day. As Gertrude says in the cemetery: "I hoped thou shouldst have been my Hamlet's wife; / I thought thy bride-bed to have decked, sweet maid, / And not have strewed thy grave" (5.1). The Ophelia subplot shows how much Hamlet has lost because fate requires him to avenge his father.

5. We see a more relaxed, even normal young man when his friends **Rosencrantz and Guildenstern** arrive. Hamlet falls into easy banter with them, even venturing into off-color jokes. And yet Hamlet is quick to put up

his guard, as he does with Ophelia, when he senses they are there to spy on him, declaring them: "my two schoolfellows, / Whom I will trust as I will adders fanged" (3.3). As with Ophelia, the relationships with his friends show how relatively carefree Hamlet's life used to be, and how tainted things have become since his father's murder.

6. With the traveling troupe of **Players** arrive, Hamlet shows yet another side— as theatrical impresario and director. He even says he will pen some new lines for the Players to insert in their performance before the King. (It's hard not to see Hamlet here as an alter ego for Shakespeare.) Hamlet shows himself a natural leader, seizing on their opportune arrival to serve his ends; he displays his artistic acumen in his advising the actors how to act well and in declaring an exalted role for art. The Players are not just used as a means for Hamlet to confirm Claudius' guilt. They become an opportunity for Hamlet to display, as it were, a Shakespearean side of himself.

7. A satirical side emerges in Hamlet's encounters with **Polonius**. Polonius is a loquacious fount of received wisdom ("neither a borrower nor a lender be"), but when Hamlet engages with him, the young man talks circles around him. Hamlet taunts him, in part, because the older man believes that he can elicit the true cause of Hamlet's melancholy, but Hamlet sees through his stratagems. Polonius is himself a pawn being used by Claudius. But there are tragic consequences to Polonius' interference. In the Closet scene, Hamlet impulsively stabs through a curtain when he hears a noise, killing Polonius. This pushes Ophelia into insanity and provokes Laertes to seek revenge against him. Polonius plays a key role in the plot, but he also is used to show Hamlet's unwillingness to suffer fools, and to draw attention to the high-stakes battle Hamlet and Claudius are waging, which leads Polonius and his children to their deaths.

8. In his exchanges with **First Gravedigger**, the prince shows an ease with even the lowliest of subjects. Hamlet spars with him about the nature of the Gravedigger's job. As with Polonius, this interaction allows Hamlet to show his witty side while exploring questions about death and damnation—topics that arise naturally because of where they are (a cemetery) and what the other character is doing (digging what we later learn is Ophelia's grave).

9. This exchange transitions directly to Hamlet's next "encounter"—with the skull of his old playmate, the court jester. In addressing **Yorick's skull,** Hamlet conjures up his youth as a carefree boy who would ride on Yorick's shoulders and laugh at his japes. Yorick's skull also leads Hamlet to extend

his reflections about the visceral reality of death: "Here hung those lips that I have kissed I know not how oft," and "Now get you to my lady's chamber, and tell her, let her paint an inch thick, to this favor [visage] she must come; make her laugh at that" (5.1).

Shakespeare often has his protagonists encounter foil characters. A foil resembles the protagonist in key respects, but has differences that highlight and reflect back on the unique nature of the protagonist. Fortinbras, Laertes, and Horatio are all about the same age as Hamlet, and each has strengths that Hamlet comments on and admires. Shakespeare uses these foils to put Hamlet's own nature in a clearer light—his gaps and his strengths.

10. Ophelia's brother **Laertes** is a foil for Hamlet on several levels. Both men are devastated by Ophelia's death, but her burial leads them to a highly tense confrontation. At the cemetery, not knowing Hamlet is present, Laertes addresses Ophelia and reproaches "that cursèd head / Whose wicked deed thy most ingenious sense / Deprived thee of!"—that is, he condemns Hamlet, who killed her father, thereby driving Ophelia into madness. Out of grief, Laertes leaps into the grave after her. This enrages Hamlet, who steps out of hiding, and the men begin to scuffle. Hamlet insists on competing with him over who loved her more:

> I loved Ophelia. Forty thousand brothers
> Could not with all their quantity of love
> Make up my sum. What wilt thou do for her? ….
> Dost thou come here to whine?
> To outface me with leaping in her grave?
> Be buried quick with her, and so will I. (5.1)

What causes this sudden ire and makes him boast of how much he loved her? He told Ophelia earlier he did not love her, but here he is declaring he loved her forty-thousand times more than any brother could. It's a highly volatile response, presumably arising from guilt and shock at her loss. By showing Hamlet side by side with Laertes, Shakespeare can bring out the peculiar, guilt-ridden reaction of Hamlet's.

Later, Hamlet expresses his regrets over how he behaved:

> But I am very sorry, good Horatio,
> That to Laertes I forgot myself,
> For by the image of my cause I see

The portraiture of his. (5.2)

He is telling Horatio that Laertes has a similar "cause" for anger: Laertes's father was killed—by Hamlet himself—just as Hamlet's father was killed. Both sons want to avenge their father's murder. Hamlet sees this. At the fencing match, he shows himself far more respectful. He apologizes to Laertes for his outburst at Ophelia's grave, and asks his forgiveness over his "mad" action that led to Polonius' death.

This foil character helps to show Hamlet as reasonable and fair-minded, at least when he is not in the throes of emotion. He can see the situation from Laertes' perspective; he is respectful toward him. But the match provides an incisive moment of contrast between these two characters. Laertes, unlike Hamlet, is so eager to get revenge against Hamlet for his father's death that he is willing to conspire with Claudius in using a poisoned rapier in the fencing match, while Hamlet shows himself as gentleman.

11. **Fortinbras** has very few lines in the play, but is often invoked by others. He is, like Hamlet, the son of a dead king; he, too, loses the throne to his uncle. But Fortinbras turns his energy outward and fights for meaningless plots of land in faraway Poland. He and Hamlet do not meet, but Hamlet speaks admiringly of the Norwegian prince's readiness to wage battle, even if the prize is worth no more than a straw. To him, Fortinbras is the image of decisiveness.

   For his part, Fortinbras speaks gracious words about Hamlet, providing a final appraisal of the dead prince: "For he was likely, had he been put on, / To have proved most royal" (5.2). Through this foil relationship, we conclude that Hamlet, too, might have become a worthy leader. But we also see key differences. What is heroic about leading soldiers to their death over an unimportant plot of land in a distant country? Hamlet might admire this decisiveness, but this is also coming from someone who fears he lacks it himself. Hamlet, with his far more reflective nature, would be less likely to commit to such a quixotic cause. Through this contrast with Fortinbras, Hamlet's gift of moral reflection appears more obvious. He might well "have proved most royal," but in a different way than Fortinbras shows himself.

12. The foil-relationship with **Horatio** vitally rounds out Hamlet's character. Hamlet careens from melancholic to high-strung to calmer phases, this volatile state is not what Hamlet prefers. His friend Horatio represents for him the ideal: "For thou hast been / As one

in suffering all that suffers nothing" (3.2). He praises his friend Horatio for his stoical equanimity:

Give me that man
That is not passion's slave, and I will wear him
In my heart's core, ay, in my heart of heart,
As I do thee. (3.2)

But Hamlet, unlike Horatio, has been placed in extraordinary situations. While seeking to resolve his problems, he often does seem enslaved to passion. His bond with Horatio is his only one in the play that is not strained or adversarial in some way. In their interactions, we can see who Hamlet is at his best and most calm: a loyal and appreciative friend, and one who aspires to be poised and more stoical.

Shakespeare has the protagonist himself make explicit connections between each of these foils and himself. Hamlet wishes himself more decisive like Fortinbras and admires his willingness to fight for a straw when honor is at the stake. With Laertes, he perceives the same plight as his own—a father murdered. With Horatio, he sees a model to aspire to.

The effect of these foil-relationships is to bring Hamlet's nature into sharper perspective. Although Hamlet admires the warrior Fortinbras, it does not seem in Hamlet's nature to wage battles that will cost the lives of countless soldiers over a relatively worthless plot of land.

In contrast to Laertes, Hamlet cannot act swiftly and single-mindedly to enact his revenge. For Laertes, it's a simple decision: he will use even underhanded means to get revenge. For Hamlet, it has been a painfully circuitous one, punctuated with frequent self-examination and self-reproach.

Shakespeare gives Hamlet a broad range of encounters: with loved and hated family members who also happen to be the king and queen; with meddling courtiers; with friends and an erstwhile sweetheart; with traveling players and a gravedigger; with a distant peer, who is Prince of Norway; with the spirit of his father and the memory of his old court jester, represented by a skull. Each encounter shows Hamlet engaging in a different social register.

Consider if Shakespeare instead restricted the cast to members of the Danish court. Or what if Hamlet behaved toward members of the lower classes, including the actors, as if they were inferiors unworthy of his attention, rather than engaging frankly with them?

The situations in which Hamlet is placed allow Shakespeare to bring out a range of nuances in Hamlet's psychological and emotional character. He can show his relaxed wit and friendly nature; his satirical wit; his romantic side; his philosophical acuity; his resourcefulness and fine artistic sensibility, and so on.

Take a few of the supporting characters away, and Hamlet would still be a multifaceted protagonist. But remove four or five of them? Or pare down the character lists to just Hamlet, Claudius, Gertrude, and the Ghost? Think of how much of Hamlet we wouldn't know.

Depicting Complexity in Unity: Cleopatra's "Fire and Air"

Juliet and Cleopatra make two useful bookends. They are Shakespeare's most passionate female protagonists. Each strives to be with her beloved; each goes to extremes in pursuit of her desires; each is enchantingly drawn.

But in other respects, what a world of difference. Juliet is young and guileless; Cleopatra is worldly and full of wiles, the "serpent of old Nile," as Antony calls her. Juliet emerges early in Shakespeare's career. Cleopatra arrives after Shakespeare had another 10 or 15 years of experience under his belt, and Shakespeare was at the zenith of his interest in complex and realistic character-drawing. (His style of character-drawing, in fact, would soon change as he moved into his final period.)

Shakespeare's Daunting Challenge

So, Shakespeare was bringing the full force of his character-building arsenal to Cleopatra. By this stage of his career, he had explored virtually every technique imaginable for realistically depicting protagonists, and he uses many of them to good effect here.

But still, Shakespeare had a unique challenge here. Bringing Cleopatra convincingly to life is a much steeper task than drawing a teenager in the first flush of love.

Few figures in history have captured the imagination as Cleopatra has. From the historian Plutarch and his other sources, Shakespeare would have learned that she was beautiful, yet it was her intelligence and charisma that set her on another level.

She became ruler of Egypt at the age of 19, soon wresting full control from her co-ruler and brother Ptolemy. For the next two decades she leveraged her political and other gifts to consolidate her power. She entered an alliance—and had children—with not one but two of Rome's greatest leaders: Julius Caesar in her youth and Mark Antony in her maturity.

How did the real Cleopatra manage to stay in power in a man's world? That question is something Shakespeare had to wrestle with.

He had to be able to show her as quite extraordinary in her own right, and powerfully seductive, or there would be little rationale for her fame nor for Antony to risk his power for her. Lacking this, Antony would appear unimpressive, too.

Added to this is the fact that on the London stage, female roles were enacted by men or teenaged boys, so the sensual appeal of this character would largely depend on the writing.

Shakespeare had his work cut out for him. How to make his stage version live up to her perennial fame and not be disappointingly mundane?

Shakespeare's Solution: Mutability

In reflecting on how to bring this character to life, Shakespeare very likely found his mind wandering back to his favorite classical author, Ovid, to whom he often turned for ideas. Ovid's *Metamorphosis* shows gods and other creatures in perpetual change. Change is the underlying principle of nature. Without metamorphosis—that is, changing from one form to another—life ceases.

If change is irresistible, was this perhaps Cleopatra's particular charm? It seems plausible that Shakespeare came to the conclusion that the great Julius Caesar and Mark Antony, not to mention the public ever since, could only be captivated by someone whose essence is like the mystery of life itself, perpetually in motion and never the same for long.

Shakespeare's solution, in any case, sounds very much like the principle he found in Ovid. The playwright makes Cleopatra as close to mutable as humanly possible. He shows her moods as almost constantly in flux. Her behaviors are often unpredictable and provocative to others. In this, she resembles the constantly moving elements of fire and air, to which she compares herself.

Typically, she shifts her mood or demands within each scene in which she appears, sometimes multiple times. She is lustful and demanding; then shrewd; then exuberantly fun. Exasperating and unreasonable; stately; reckless; petty and vain; brilliantly imaginative; and, particularly at the end, majestic. Shakespeare's Cleopatra is the opposite of monotonous, or one-toned. He makes her more like a prism of light, each color flashing in turn, while emerging from a single source.

Yet for all this multiplicity, Cleopatra seems a believable unity. Shakespeare never lets us doubt that, despite her shifting moods, she always seeks to be in control, and that no matter how much she loves Antony, she looks out for her own interests. This indomitable sense of self is the anchor of her character. At the end, when she makes her glorious departure with the aid of an asp, vowing to follow Antony to the next world, it is only after she fails to strike an acceptable deal with Caesar. If we are hoping for a self-sacrificing lover in this Cleopatra, let alone a proper and conventional lady, Shakespeare will disappoint; but he does make her believably complex as a character.

Strategies to Portray Her Mutability

Shakespeare emphasizes her mutability not only in what she says and does, but in how others perceive her.

Numerous characters remark on her behavior, and each—even among the Romans—interprets her a little differently. To Philo, she's a strumpet; Caesar calls her one as well, but later finds her shrewd and regal. Dolabella so commiserates with her loss at the end that he reveals to her Caesar's secret plan to parade her in Rome. To Antony's friend Enobarbus, "Age cannot wither her, nor custom stale / Her infinity variety" (2.2). And to Antony she is, alternately, heaven and hell. But he cannot live without her: "Let Rome in Tiber melt and the wide arch / Of the ranged empire fall. Here is my space" (1.1).

No one, not even Antony, can contain her because when they expect her to be one way, she will have moved on to something else. She cannot be pinned down.

Notably, Cleopatra is one of the rare protagonists for whom Shakespeare saw no need to give a soliloquy. We never see her alone. She is always engaging or tangling with others, always keeping things around her in motion. Who is Cleopatra by herself? It seems her essential nature is inseparable from her effect on, and movement around, others.

First View of Cleopatra

Shakespeare frames her first entrance by having the Roman Philo grumbling about the shocking self-indulgence of this pair of lovers. Then we see them ourselves, and they do indeed seem self-indulgent considering how much of the world depends on them.

CLEOPATRA If it be love indeed, tell me how much.
ANTONY There's beggary in the love that can be reckoned.
CLEOPATRA I'll set a bourn how far to be beloved.
ANTONY Then must thou needs find out new heaven, new Earth. (1.1)

Cleopatra's first words are prodding Antony to tell her how much he loves her. Antony is more reasonable, replying that love that can be tallied up is a poor imitation. But Cleopatra insists, and she gets what she wants. He tells her his love is beyond earthly limits. This is how the leader of Egypt and the co-ruler of the Roman Empire are spending their time.

But then a Messenger arrives from Caesar. Antony is irritated at the interruption, but Cleopatra makes her first shift. She now taunts him that his wife Fulvia or fellow triumvir Caesar might have orders for him.

> MESSENGER News, my good lord, from Rome.
> ANTONY Grates me, the sum.
> CLEOPATRA Nay, hear them, Antony.
> Fulvia perchance is angry; or who knows
> If the scarce-bearded Caesar have not sent
> His powerful mandate to you: "Do this, or this;
> Take in that kingdom, and enfranchise that;
> Perform 't, or else we damn thee."

When he objects, she continues to taunt him, accusing him of lying about his love for her, until Antony pleads for peace: "Let's not confound the time with conference harsh." Antony again complies with her wishes, ignoring the Messenger to focus on their mutual enjoyment:

> ANTONY   Fie, wrangling queen!
> Whom everything becomes—to chide, to laugh,
> To weep; whose every passion fully strives
> To make itself (in thee) fair and admired!
> No messenger but thine, and all alone,
> Tonight we'll wander through the streets and note
> The qualities of people. Come, my queen,
> Last night you did desire it. [To the Messenger.]
> Speak not to us.

What do we learn about Cleopatra from this opening scene? Shakespeare introduces Cleopatra with concise strokes, establishing some key traits right away. She is demanding, sensual, and playful. She makes her own rules about how much love is enough. And when something arises that can distract her hold over Antony, she can shift gears quickly to manage the situation.

Shakespeare suggests in this opening salvo much of what we will see in Cleopatra throughout the play, including how rapidly she changes her approach.

Cleopatra's Attempts to Control Others

Shakespeare builds on this initial impression soon after, showing how she expertly molds others to her desires. Her ploys to keep Antony enthralled seem to be second nature to her. When she sees that Antony is meeting with Caesar's messenger after all, she avoids Antony and instead sends her servant Alexas with these instructions:

> See where he is, who's with him, what he does.
> I did not send you. If you find him sad,
> Say I am dancing; if in mirth, report
> That I am sudden sick. Quick, and return. (1.3)

This is her plan: she *intends* to be contrary. Alexas must act as if she didn't send him and provoke Antony's interest by reporting her as the opposite of whatever state he is in at the moment.

Cleopatra's waiting woman Charmian disapproves of this and warns her she should be more submissive to Antony in order to keep his love:

> CHARMIAN Madam, methinks if you did love him dearly,
> You do not hold the method to enforce
> The like from him.
> CLEOPATRA   What should I do, I do not?
> CHARMIAN In each thing give him way, cross him in nothing.
> CLEOPATRA Thou teachest like a fool: the way to lose him. (1.3)

Cleopatra is doing everything she can think of ("What should I do [that] I do not [already]?"), and she knows what she's doing. As Antony admits, he is in thrall to her and fears losing himself: "These strong Egyptian fetters I must break, / Or lose myself in dotage" (1.2).

Antony periodically stretches, but never breaks, his fetters, as when he chooses to marry Caesar's sister to cement his political ties. But he will return to Cleopatra.

As we see later in the play, her powers to seduce others have limits. It's not for lack of trying. After she and Antony lose the Battle of Actium, Caesar sends Thidias to negotiate with her. She lets him speak and even offers him the honor of kissing her royal hand. In the end, Cleopatra fails to win what she wants, but it is the great and famously self-controlled Caesar she is unable to manipulate.

Cleopatra Through the Eyes of Others

Shakespeare builds our sense of this protagonist not only in what she says and does, but most effectively, in her encounters with many other characters. Antony, of course, offers the fullest perspective on her, both her good traits and the bad.

She is his universe—he would let the empire fall and Rome melt in the Tiber for her. But nearly every other character reflects back on her a portion of her nature.

Her attendants, with whom she has an easy familiarity, find her admirable, with Charmian praising her as "A lass unparalleled," and some will readily die with her at the end. Other Egyptians find her arbitrary or unreasonable: she punishes the Messenger who dares to reports bad news to her and is beaten for it; and goes into a rage when her treasurer Seleucus refuses to back up her lies about her accounts to Caesar.

But it is especially through the Romans' eyes that we see how she can be different things to different people. They judge, deplore, and/or appreciate her.

Caesar, who had earlier called her a whore, says of her after her suicide: "Bravest at the last, / She leveled at our purposes and, being royal, / Took her own way" (5.2).

Through Enobarbus' Eyes

Other than Antony, the character who offers the most capacious view of Cleopatra is Enobarbus, Antony's great friend and advisor. Shakespeare establishes Enobarbus as a tolerant and fair-minded observer; indeed, he functions throughout the play as a kind of chorus, framing how we view each of the protagonists and their relationship. Shakespeare uses him to amplify what he wants us to see in Cleopatra's charms, and he speaks some of the most famous lines in the play.

For example, Enobarbus describes to his fellow Romans the sublime effect of Cleopatra floating on her barge in the Nile, surpassing what even Venus could show. But she is not just beautiful. Enobarbus points to an uncanny charm in everything she does:

I saw her once
Hop forty paces through the public street;
And having lost her breath, she spoke, and panted,
That she did make defect perfection,
And breathless, power breathe forth. (2.2)

Whatever she does, even something unqueen-like as hopping through the street and getting out of breath, she elevates to something sublime.

In his view, she is beyond compare, and this is due largely to her mutability— her infinite variety. When one of his fellow Romans notes that Antony must leave Cleopatra now that he has taken Caesar's sister as his new wife, Enobarbus dismisses the possibility. Why?

Age cannot wither her, nor custom stale
Her infinite variety. Other women cloy
The appetites they feed, but she makes hungry
Where most she satisfies. (2.2)

To Enobarbus's description of her charms, his listener Maecenas feebly responds, "If beauty, wisdom, modesty, can settle / The heart of Antony, Octavia is / A blessed lottery to him" (2.2).

If Antony would be content with beauty, wisdom, and modesty, Octavia might be enough. But course, this won't satisfy Antony's appetite when he could have infinite variety. By evoking this paragon Octavia as the perfect wife for Antony, this only serves to reflect back on Cleopatra's far greater, if unorthodox appeal.

Metamorphosis is a principle of life itself. Life is change. In Cleopatra, Shakespeare is showing this Ovidian principle in action and how captivating it can be to witness someone change from one form to another.

At the end, after Antony has died and she seeks to join him, she declares she is fire and air, the elements that rise to the heavens and are in constant motion.

Methinks I hear
Antony call; I see him rouse himself
To praise my noble act. .... Husband, I come!
Now to that name my courage prove my title!
I am fire and air; my other elements
I give to baser life. (5.2)

Earth and water are the dross she leaves behind. In life, and even more so in the hereafter, her essence is mutable.

Summary of Techniques Shakespeare Uses for Cleopatra

To recap, Shakespeare brings this concept of a character—Cleopatra as mutable, in a state of constant transformation—to practical form through a range of techniques. Primarily he does this by:

- Showing her mood and aims changing swiftly, at least once within each scene, while maintaining a certain core sense of her character (she seeks control and is indomitable).
- Making explicit that she changes her self-presentation at will in order to control others, as when her servant is told to report her as the opposite of whatever mood Antony is in.

- Portraying the multiple perspectives that others have of her; many characters observe and comment on her, but none see the same person.
- Foregoing any attempt to portray her "inner life"; there are no soliloquies, no scenes of Cleopatra by herself. She is always placed in relation with others, always reactive, like the elements of air and fire.

Complexity is not the same as pulling together parts that are incompatible or randomly connected. To make a character that is believably complex requires a capacious-enough perspective on that character. Seemingly contradictory traits can be integrated and appear plausible in one character, as Shakespeare shows in Cleopatra. He establishes a core nature for her: we see she is powerful and will never willingly let go of control. From this core, she can plausibly express a nearly endless stream of variety. She is an actor who can adopt a new persona at will and knows nearly infinite ways to enchant her audiences.

Should All Protagonists Be Complex and Realistic?

There is no protagonist more complex and realistic in Shakespeare than Hamlet (although Cleopatra comes close). But that protagonist is suited for his specific purpose. *Hamlet* is a revenge tragedy, a particular subgenre popular in Shakespeare's day. In this tradition, the hero takes revenge for a great wrong done to a loved one, usually at the cost of their own life.

Shakespeare's innovation was to explore the psychic costs to a revenger. He probes the spiritual and emotional underpinnings of a situation in which an otherwise good character is setting out to kill another person. In what conditions is it morally and ethically right to take revenge? What effect might this duty have upon an avenger who is by nature intelligent and sensitive?

It's a weighty subject, and it makes sense for Shakespeare to create a protagonist with a complex psyche into which he could delve deeply. This requires that the play spend a *lot* of time on Hamlet, to flesh him out fully and to depict his inner world.

But are complexity and "realness" always needed or desirable in a protagonist? The answer is no. Although we can say that Shakespeare was fascinated by human variety and delighted in it for its own sake, there are occasions when he dispenses with character complexity if it doesn't contribute to the overall work.

Protagonists to Suit the Style and Genre

The nature of his protagonists depends largely on the genre in which he's writing. The more serious the work—such as the tragedies and history plays—the more deeply he tends to explore their psychology. He may examine to some degree the inner dimensions of his comic protagonists, but rarely to the same extent.

This might account for why the main comic protagonists, especially in the cheerful romantic comedies, can appear less distinct from each other. Viola (*Twelfth Night*) and Rosalind (*As You Like It*) are rather similar: both are resilient, witty, loving, and resourceful; they speak in a similar style. For *Much Ado About Nothing*, with its two female leads, Shakespeare has a reason to differentiate them, and so he does, making Hero more a bit more passive and conventional, and Beatrice wittier and more assertive. In *A Midsummer Night's Dream*, Shakespeare creates numerous lovers, intentionally making many of them mirror each other; this underscores the concept that love makes us project onto others what we want to see, not what is objectively there. In these comedies, the highly differentiated nature we find in Hamlet would be overkill in a romantic heroine.

Different Protagonist Style in the Romances

Near the end of his career, we find a new development in Shakespeare's approach to character. With his final plays, termed the romances, he moves into a more mythic, less highly realistic style overall. The romances have elements of both comedy and tragedy. Their *stories* take greater precedence, while their protagonists tend to be drawn in broader strokes.

They are still not conventional, and Shakespeare does gives them individualizing touches, but they veer closer to archetypes: the jealous husband, the long-suffering wanderer, the transformative virgin, the magus, the lost daughter, and so on. Shakespeare obviously *could* have depicted more of their inner lives, but evidently it was not what he deemed the stories needed.

We can see this difference in how he portrays a destructively jealous protagonist in his middle period and again near the end of his career.

Othello depicts in detail how an otherwise good and loving husband can be ensnared by jealousy, culminating with his murdering his wife. Shakespeare uses the entire play to show *how* it is possible. This is psychological exploration at its deepest and finest.

In *The Winter's Tale*, one of Shakespeare's late works, a jealous fit overcomes King Leontes early in the play with fatal consequences. We don't get a backstory on why Leontes irrationally suspects his wife with his best friend. For this story, it doesn't matter. We aren't led to dwell on what caused it, but instead on the consequences. The focus is on his and others' subsequent suffering and the working out of unexpected grace that brings back much of what he destroyed.

It is, as its title suggests, a "winter's tale" —the kind of story told around the hearth during the cold, dark months. Shakespeare veers closer to folk tale than to realistic tragedy in this play, and creates a more archetypal figure to take the place of a highly differentiated individual whose psychology we explore.

We likewise see some of the archetypal nature in the heroines of the romances. The female protagonists are young and resourceful daughters—Marina *(Pericles)*, Imogen *(Cymbeline)*, Perdita *(The Winter's Tale)*, and Miranda *(The Tempest)*. Each is placed in highly unusual circumstances as a result of their father's decisions or his fate. In *Cymbeline*, Imogen secretly marries against the king her father's wishes, and both her father and her husband put in her dangerous circumstances.

These daughters share many of the same traits. They all are instinctively virtuous, resilient, resourceful, and loving. There are fewer individualizing details such as we find even in Juliet. Rather, they are a type of ideal daughter (or ideal wife), one who surmounts challenges and helps restore the faith of the older generation when all seems lost. As Prospero tells Miranda about the days just after they were banished from Milan and set adrift:

PROSPERO   O, a cherubin
Thou wast that did preserve me. Thou didst smile,
Infusèd with a fortitude from heaven,
When I have decked the sea with drops full salt,
Under my burden groaned, which raised in me
An undergoing stomach to bear up
Against what should ensue. (1.2)

While the daughters' traits are similar, it is their adventures that distinguish them. Even the names of three of them indicate a key feature of their story: Marina is born at sea; Perdita means the lost one. Miranda means admirable, to be wondered at; she herself is full of admiration: when she sees a group of humans on her uncharted island for the first time, she declares, "O brave new world / That has such people in't!" (5.1). ("Tis new to thee," responds her more jaded father.)

To tell these fantastical tales—which call to mind myths and romance narratives—a focus on finely nuanced differences among characters is not needed or even desirable.

And so, the answer is no: Shakespeare does not make all of his protagonists complex or fleshed out to the same degree. It depends on the needs of the work.

But there is no question that Shakespeare's instincts from the start led him to explore what makes us individual. When we speak of a Shakespearean protagonist, it is those from his early through his late-middle periods that we are typically thinking.

Summary

Shakespeare clearly had a profound gift for understanding human nature; his characters, especially his protagonists, can seem remarkably fleshed out, even knowable the way we know people in real life. While this gift may not be teachable, we can analyze techniques he uses to render his characters complex and seemingly real.

But Shakespeare also does not choose to invest all of his protagonists with the same degree of specificity. For some of them—particularly his tragic protagonists—he depicts their psychological motivations and differentiating qualities in exquisite detail. But for others, he may focus less on their individuality and more on their function within the plot. He varies, in other words, how complex and real he tries to make his characters depending on the needs of the story.

Among the ways Shakespeare brings his characters to life is by reflecting their states of mind or their circumstances in the style in which they speak, a topic we explore in the next chapter.

Takeaway for Writers

Shakespeare renders his protagonists complex and realistic through a variety of strategies. These include:

- Avoiding conventionality or cliches
- Providing abundant "naturalistic" touches
- Placing the protagonist in multiple contexts and in relationship with many different kinds of other characters; this brings out more nuances in a character.

For Cleopatra, who presented Shakespeare with a steep dramatic challenge and who is one of his most complex and engrossing protagonists, he uses fundamental techniques as well as at least one very specific approach. He constructs Cleopatra through these standard methods:

- What she says and does
- In relationship with others
- Through the eyes of others—what others say about her; how they react to her (Enobarbus' lavish descriptions of her indelibly shape how we think about this character)
- By contrast or comparison with other characters (she is contrasted, for example, with Antony's new wife, Octavia, a paragon of Roman female virtue)

But more unusually:

- Cleopatra has no soliloquies, asides, and other private moments. Shakespeare deems her private musings would not be useful, and focuses instead on her interactions with, and effect on, others.
- Most specifically, Shakespeare shows her, in virtually every one of her scenes, changing her mood, her decisions, her strategies. The character is constructed to appear like mutability itself; she is likened to the elements of fire and air. For the audience, this makes her fascinating and maddening to watch, just as other characters in the play find her.

The nature of the protagonist depends on the particular work; Shakespeare did not choose to invest his characters with the same degree of complexity or individuality.

Terms

Archetype: The term archetype, from Greek word *archetypos*, or "original pattern," is, "in literary criticism, a primordial image, character, or pattern of circumstances that recurs throughout literature and thought consistently enough to be considered a universal concept or situation." (Britannica https://www.britannica.com/art/character-writer)

Foil: A foil is "a character whose qualities or actions serve to emphasize those of the protagonist (or of some other character) by providing a strong contrast with them." (Baldrick)

Extras

In act 1, scene 3, lines 15–127, Shakespeare provides a stretch of dialogue between Cleopatra and Antony that displays her extreme mutability, lofty imagination, and relentless manipulation of him — all key elements in depicting her complexity and her hold on Antony.

After accusing him at length of deserting her for his wife Fulvia, Cleopatra is momentarily chastened when Antony tells her that Fulvia is dead; but within four lines, she begins to fault him for not feeling remorse for Fulvia's death, and claims he will show no genuine remorse at leaving her, either.

Link to *Antony and Cleopatra* (1.3.15–127) from The Folger Shakespeare:
https://www.folger.edu/explore/shakespeares-works/antony-and-cleopatra/read/1/3/

CHAPTER 4: SPOTLIGHT: ADAPTING LANGUAGE STYLE TO THE SITUATION

The Spotlight chapters focus on a special topic in some depth. In this first Spotlight, we'll examine how Shakespeare adapts the language style of two of his protagonists to suit their particular situations. This permits him to convey more nuance about the nature of the character and to express a certain tonal quality in the moment. A parallel example might be the manner in which different orchestral instruments bring alternate shades of expression to a melody.

The language styles we will focus on come from passages of Prince Hal from early in *Henry IV, Part 1,* and from the prince Shakespeare created a few years later, Hamlet.

Adapting the Language Style to the Situation

Among his many other attributes, Hamlet displays well developed notions about art. He advises the Players that in their acting they should "Suit the action to the word, the word to the action, with this special observance, that you o'erstep not the modesty of nature" (3.2). That is, the actor's speech, gestures, and behaviors should be in sync; they should harmonize, with none of them appearing unnatural.

The writer's role in this would be to make the language of a character in sync with the action. This would entail finding an appropriate linguistic style for a character and adjusting as circumstances demand.

Not surprisingly, Shakespeare does just this for his protagonists. He suits the speech to the action, and both to the context. Granted, Shakespeare is working within a highly structured format. He usually composes in unrhymed iambic pentameter verse form, sometimes switching to a less formal prose style, and occasionally to even more patterned verse forms with special rhyme and meter schemes.

But within the constraints of these formats, he shows a careful attention to suit the diction and tone of a character, and adjusts it during the course of the story depending on the situation. One style doesn't not fit all. And he particularly diverges from the norm when he wants to make a point. Their linguistic styles add another layer of meaning to the protagonist and the situation.

Hal the Lad vs Hal the Future King

Prince Hal makes his first appearance in *Henry IV, Part 1*. He will be the main protagonist in this and the two remaining works of the Henriad tetralogy, so Shakespeare wants to make the right first impression with him. He uses language style to help signal to us Hal's engaging, versatile, and ambivalent nature.

We first meet the Prince of Wales in Act 1, scene 2, in a tavern in Eastcheap, London—a world away from the court of his father Henry IV. Hal's companion Falstaff asks him what time it is, and Hal retorts that Falstaff couldn't care less what time it is, since he's only interested in food, drink, and bawdy women:

FALSTAFF Now, Hal, what time of day is it, lad?

PRINCE Thou art so fat-witted with drinking of old sack, and unbuttoning thee after supper, and sleeping upon benches after noon, that thou hast forgotten to demand that truly which thou wouldst truly know. What a devil hast thou to do with the time of the day? Unless hours were cups of sack [wine], and minutes capons, and clocks the tongues of bawds [pimps], and dials the signs of leaping-houses [brothels], and the blessed sun himself a fair hot wench in flame-colored taffeta, I see no reason why thou shouldst be so superfluous to demand the time of the day. (1.2)

The speech is in prose, not verse, and filled with informal terms, many referring to Falstaff's world of carnal indulgence: sack, capons, bawds, leaping houses, a hot wench. Hal piles on examples of Falstaff's self-indulgence with the linguistic exuberance that Falstaff himself will excel at. Hal can match Falstaff's tone to a T. He's one of the lads.

After this, we are introduced to many of Falstaff's cronies, and we hear of their plans to rob travelers. Hal refuses to participate in this plot, but privately agrees to another companion's plan to rob the robbers, just for the fun of hearing how Falstaff will lie about it.

Finally, at the end of this tavern scene, the other characters leave the stage. When Hal is alone he delivers a soliloquy that sharply contrasts with what we've just seen of him.

He announces that he is acting a part for his own purposes, and reveals just how discriminating, even calculating he is. The speech's linguistic style emphasizes this sudden shift of tone.

Hal's Oratorical Soliloquy

The style of this soliloquy, no less than the content, is remarkable. It is oratorical, with strong, balanced, almost lawyer-like sentences. Each sentence is end-stopped (it finishes out the full verse line), and this lends a sturdiness to the rhythm. To sum things up with a flourish, Hal even concludes with a neat rhymed couplet: "I'll so offend to make offense a skill, / Redeeming time when men think least I will." It's a soliloquy, yes, but this protagonist is not searching his soul; he is justifying his position to the audience and displaying his mastery of his situation.

This table breaks up the soliloquy sentence by sentence and summarizes the idea that Hal is expressing in each.

PRINCE (1H4 1.2.195–217) Soliloquy, sentence by sentence	Idea expressed
I know you all, and will a while uphold The unyoked humor of your idleness.	*What I am doing* (I am putting up with your unyoked idleness).
Yet herein will I imitate the sun, Who doth permit the base contagious clouds To smother up his beauty from the world, That when he please again to be himself, Being wanted, he may be more wondered at By breaking through the foul and ugly mists Of vapors that did seem to strangle him.	*Why I'm pretending* (I imitate the sun, who allows the clouds to smother his beauty, in order to be more impressive when the clouds disperse.)
If all the year were playing holidays, To sport would be as tedious as to work; But when they seldom come, they wished for come, And nothing pleaseth but rare accidents.	*Illustration justifying what I'm doing* (People appreciate what is rare.)
So when this loose behavior I throw off And pay the debt I never promised,	*What the outcome will be*

By how much better than my word I am, By so much shall I falsify men's hopes, And like bright metal on a sullen ground, My reformation, glitt'ring o'er my fault, Shall show more goodly and attract more eyes Than that which hath no foil to set it off.	(I will be more impressive when I exceed expectations, since the contrast with my past will make me appear all the more dazzling.)
I'll so offend to make offense a skill, Redeeming time when men think least I will. *He exits.*	*Recap of what I intend* (I will so skillfully offend that people will be surprised at my redemption.)

This is commanding and confident language, fit for a monarch. Shakespeare uses it as a tonal contrast to Hal's behavior with the tavern denizens earlier in the scene. He is showing us—not only in its content, but in its style—the broad range Hal is capable of. Although he can be chummy with the lowest rung of society, underneath is a pitilessly shrewd prince, who will throw these friends off when he judges the time is right. He acts as a supreme leader must, and as ordinary mortals would not readily do.

Hamlet, the Anguished Prince

Finally, let's compare that soliloquy of Hal's with Hamlet's first soliloquy, which we've already discussed. Not by coincidence, Hal's and Hamlet's soliloquies occur in the same location in both plays, namely, at the end of act 1, scene 2. Shakespeare has had time to introduce to the protagonist and give adequate exposition, and now brings us in for a close-up. We are ready for a peek at the "real" character; we will learn their motivations or concerns, which those around him are not privy to.

While both soliloquies serve this similar purpose, stylistically, they could hardly be more different.

Hamlet's Naturalistic, Anguished Soliloquy

One obvious difference between Hal's and Hamlet's soliloquies is in how the sentences and ideas flow in the speeches. Hamlet's soliloquy is not like a rational argument, in which a speaker is trying to describe a problem or persuade someone

83

of something. Far less is he confiding information to the audience about his motives for what he does, such as Hal is doing.

Rather, Hamlet conveys a sense of being stuck and distressed. He shifts from idea to idea without making overt logical connections. Yet, what Hamlet says is not random or disordered. There is a perceptible connection between these thoughts, but Shakespeare leaves it to us to infer that connection.

When we break up what he says into separate units of thoughts, we find this sequence:

1. I want to disappear.
2. Life is meaningless.
3. How can it be my mother could have forgotten my father after such a short a time and married his less worthy brother?
4. I must not speak of this, even though it breaks my heart.

Re-read the speech now to notice how Shakespeare's stylistic choices reflect this disjunctive flow of ideas, and how it contrasts with the more orderly speech by Hal.

This table breaks up the soliloquy into its idea-units and summarizes what is being expressed in each section. I've added parallel slash lines // to indicate where the sentence and other section breaks are.

HAMLET (1.2.129–59) **Soliloquy divided into idea-units** (mid-line sentence breaks indicated by parallel slash lines: //)	**Idea expressed**
O, that this too too [sullied] flesh would melt, Thaw, and resolve itself into a dew! Or that the Everlasting had not fixed His canon 'gainst self-slaughter! //	*I want to disappear*
O God, God, How weary, stale, flat, and unprofitable Seem to me all the uses of this world! Fie on't, ah fie! // 'Tis an unweeded garden That grows to seed. // Things rank and gross in nature Possess it merely. //	*Life is meaningless*
That it should come to this: But two months dead//—nay, not so much, not two. So excellent a king, that was to this	*How could my mother forget my father so soon after his death and*

Hyperion to a satyr, so loving to my mother That he might not beteem the winds of heaven Visit her face too roughly. // Heaven and earth, Must I remember? // Why, she would hang on him As if increase of appetite had grown By what it fed on. // And yet, within a month— Let me not think on't! // Frailty, thy name is woman!—// A little month, or ere those shoes were old With which she followed my poor father's body, Like Niobe, all tears//—why she, even she—// O God, a beast that wants discourse of reason Would have mourned longer—//married with my uncle, My father's brother, but no more like my father Than I to Hercules. // Within a month, Ere yet the salt of most unrighteous tears Had left the flushing in her galled eyes, She married— // O most wicked speed: to post With such dexterity to incestuous sheets, It is not, nor it cannot come to good.	*marry his far less worthy* *brother?*
But break, my heart, for I must hold my tongue. [*Stage direction*] *Enter Horatio, Marcellus, and Barnardo.*	*I must not speak of this, though* *it breaks my heart.*

Speech Content and Progression of Thought

What exactly is he saying here? Let's first review the basic content and progression of thought through the soliloquy.

Hamlet begins with his despair. His first thought is of disappearing, of wishing suicide were not against God's law.

Then, he generalizes his despair by finding the world itself has nothing worthwhile to offer. ("'Tis an unweeded garden / That grows to seed.") Why does he wish to be gone? Why does he think the world has no meaning?

Although he makes no explicit connection, we can infer the cause from what he says next. He fixates on his father's death and on the anguish and revulsion he feels that his mother could move on so quickly from a worthy man like his father to marry his far inferior brother.

The final line is that he has no recourse. He must let his heart break because he can say nothing. ("But break, my heart, for I must hold my tongue.")

The progression of thought is nothing like an argument, nor is he directly informing the audience what is going on (even though we pick up some backstory from it). Rather, the oblique flow of ideas only reinforces the sense of someone who is flailing. The ideas go nowhere, because he sees no way forward—he must hold his tongue. It reflects the kind of inertia one feels when wrestling unsuccessfully with an emotional dilemma.

Style of Diction

Hamlet's sentence structure and word choice similarly reflect turmoil. Unlike Hal's end-stopped sentences, Hamlet's sentences are ragged, with breaks in the middle of the line. As befits a speaker in an anguished state of mind, his lines are punctuated with clauses and exclamatory short phrases, such as "O God, God…" and "Fie on 't, ah fie!" "Heaven and Earth!" The sentences stop and restart.

There are other naturalistic speech patterns that Shakespeare includes. Consider this single, very long sentence. Shakespeare constructs it so that it breaks up, shifts direction, embeds two other short sentences (marked here by the dashes), and then resumes its course:

> And yet, within a month—
> Let me not think on't! Frailty, thy name is woman!—
> A little month, or ere those shoes were old
> With which she followed my poor father's body,
> Like Niobe, all tears —why she, even she—
> O God, a beast that wants discourse of reason
> Would have mourned longer— married with my uncle,
> My father's brother, but no more like my father
> Than I to Hercules.

That is a tortuous sentence to diagram, but it is designed to reflect a tormented cast of mind. It has repetitions and interjections, along with multiple clauses, as if he starts to express one idea and new thoughts intervene.

That sentence appears within this longer extract, below, which reveals further patterns. Hamlet makes a statement, then corrects himself: "But two months dead—nay, not so much, not two." He returns three more times to this idea, showing how fixated he is on the speed with which his mother moved on. Below, the bolded phrases indicate repetitions regarding how long ago the king died (**two months dead**… **within a month**… **A little month**… **Within a month**). Italics show where the interjections appear, which again chop up the flow of the passage: *"nay, not so much, not two…. Heaven and Earth, / Must I remember?… Let me not think on 't! Frailty, thy name is woman!)…O God, a beast that wants discourse of reason / Would have mourned longer!")*

> That it should come to this:
> But two months dead—nay, not so much, not two.
> So excellent a king, that was to this
> Hyperion to a satyr, so loving to my mother
> That he might not beteem the winds of heaven
> Visit her face too roughly. *Heaven and earth,*
> *Must I remember?* Why, she would hang on him
> As if increase of appetite had grown
> By what it fed on. // And yet, **within a month**—
> Let me not think on't! Frailty, thy name is woman!—
> **A little month**, or ere those shoes were old
> With which she followed my poor father's body,
> Like Niobe, all tears—why she, even she—
> O God, a beast that wants discourse of reason
> Would have mourned longer—married with my uncle,
> My father's brother, but no more like my father
> Than I to Hercules. **Within a month,**
> Ere yet the salt of most unrighteous tears
> Had left the flushing in her galled eyes,
> She married….

We can see that Shakespeare constructs Hamlet's language in a way that we might think or speak if we were upset or struggling to understand something (leaving aside, of course, the fact that we do not speak in blank verse).

All of these stylistic features contribute to our sense of the speaker as being tossed from one emotion or thought to another, and back again, and returning to something he is fixated on.

Shakespeare's intentions can be seen more clearly by contrasting Hamlet's style here with that of Hal's oratorical "I know you all" soliloquy, above.

If Shakespeare had depicted Hamlet's distress through the same kind of balanced sentences that Hal speaks, it would not suit the context. How would we be able to feel Hamlet's anguish if his language was measured and lucidly expository? Instead, the lines sound as if they are freshly erupting from Hamlet's mind, one emotion or observation tumbling out and overlapping into another.

The distress conveyed through the content as well as style of his speech helps the audience feel they are getting access to his inner life and emotions. It prepares us, as well, for Hamlet's later volatility, in which he will swing from aggressiveness to lethargy.

By carefully adjusting the style of Hamlet's speak to suit this particular situation, Shakespeare generates a sense that we're witnessing Hamlet's true nature, his inner turmoil, gives us a glimpse of "that within which passeth show."

Takeaway for Writers

The stylistic features of a character's language can be used to reflect their situation. Shakespeare shifts gears linguistically as the context demands. In these few examples from Hal and Hamlet, we see some of Shakespeare's techniques in action:

- Shakespeare depicts Hamlet's speech in a quasi-naturalistic way (true naturalism, of course, would avoid verse). He breaks up the sentences with numerous interjections and clauses, ends most sentences in the middle of the verse line, and reverts to the same notions again and again to indicate what Hamlet is fixated on. This style conveys Hamlet's distress better than a more measured linguistic style would.
- Hal's initial speech, in which he taunts Falstaff, is ebullient, informal, and witty. He shows that, although he is the Prince of Wales, he can relate easily even to the more dubious elements of society.
- In Hal's soliloquy, Shakespeare wants to sharply contrast our initial impression of Hal with the "real" and self-controlled prince. Although Hal has been roistering with the lads in Eastcheap, he actually has things under his steely-eyed control. Hal conveys this through his soliloquy's clear and balanced sentences, which take the form of a persuasive argument, complete with a summary couplet.
- The language style of each helps Shakespeare to fine-tune how the audience perceives the protagonists and the situation in which they find themselves.

CHAPTER 5: PROTAGONIST JOURNEYS

FIRST WITCH: All hail, Macbeth, hail to thee, Thane of Glamis!
SECOND WITCH: All hail, Macbeth, hail to thee, Thane of Cawdor!
THIRD WITCH: All hail, Macbeth, that shalt be king hereafter!
BANQUO (to Macbeth): Good sir, why do you start and seem to fear
Things that do sound so fair? (Mac. 1.3)

Macbeth has been a loyal subject. He is returning from a battle on behalf the king when he and his companion Banquo are accosted by three eerie-looking women. They seem to know a lot about him. They know he is Thane, or lord, of Glamis. They hail him as Thane of Cawdor, though he doesn't yet know the king has rewarded him with that title. And they predict he will be king.

Banquo observes that Macbeth looks more horrified than pleased to hear this. Is it because the witches have exposed a secret desire? If these creatures have supernatural knowledge—as they seem to—maybe he *is* meant to be king.

With their cryptic lines, the witches plant a seed in Macbeth. His mind soon conjures up the thought of murder, although at first, he resists: "If chance will have me king, why, chance may crown me / Without my stir" (1.3). But ambition takes greater hold, and he and Lady Macbeth decide not to wait for chance.

Shakespeare shows that Macbeth will conceive of his murderous plan shortly after this temptation. The play is largely about the nature of evil—evil outside influences and the evil we choose to commit. Among the questions Shakespeare wants us to ponder is whether Macbeth would ever have taken that lethal first step if he had not been tempted by the witches or goaded by his wife, who is as ambitious as he is and prods him once she learns of their prophecy.

In this chapter, we will examine how Shakespeare constructs the protagonist's journey. This includes the ways he starts his protagonists down their path, continues them through hurdles and self-defining choices, and shows them finding a resolution of their aim or problem. The specifics of their journeys vary, but certain elements are found commonly across his works.

Central Problem

The course that a protagonist follows in Shakespeare is not random or shapeless; we can think of it as a journey, or an arc. Shakespeare's protagonists are typically propelled into action by a more or less explicit central problem. This problem may be a goal they deeply desire, a conflict they've been drawn into, a dilemma they must face, or an untenable situation from which they must extricate themselves or others.

The protagonist may not even be aware of the problem at first, but is swept up in a situation and must find a way to deal with it. But whether or not *they* know their goal, Shakespeare will establish it for the audience. We will see that the protagonist is compelled in a certain direction and must respond in some way to a problem.

Another common feature of a protagonist's journey is that, in engaging with this problem, the hero will likely undergo significant change. Almost always they change more than any other character.

From *Macbeth*, we see one way that Shakespeare initiates a protagonist's journey. Macbeth's central problem—his goal and motivating force—is how to seize and maintain power. But his encounter with the witches triggers a potential that might have remained latent. He, with the encouragement and complicity of his wife, makes a fatal choice he might not have made otherwise. The rest of the story works out the consequences.

But in other works, the protagonist will not be as active in selecting or accepting a particular aim. Othello, for example, does not realize until the end of the play that he has been practiced on, and that all along he was fighting the wrong foe. In this case, it is another character, Iago, who sets events in motion, and the protagonist is forced to respond.

But no matter how the central problem emerges, it still shapes a path the protagonist must follow.

Types of Protagonist Problems in Shakespeare

Although each of Shakespeare's protagonists is unique, the problems they face tend to fall under one or more of these themes:

1. To unite with another
2. To find one's way in a new or threatening world; to adapt to changing circumstances

3. To attain justice; to right a wrong
4. To discern the truth of a situation
5. To gain power and maintain it
6. To defend against a threat to themselves or their world
7. To withstand great loss; to patiently endure
8. To stand apart as an individual against the group

This list is just a high-level summary of the central problems Shakespeare gives his protagonists. The actual problem will often straddle more than one of these themes.

To unite with another

In his plays involving romantic love, there are protagonist pairs whose main goal is to be with each other. That is where their energy is directed. Most of Shakespeare's comedies fall in this category, including *A Midsummer Night's Dream, Two Gentlemen of Verona,* and *Much Ado About Nothing.* So do the romantic tragedies *Romeo and Juliet* and *Antony and Cleopatra.*

There will invariably be hurdles posed by disapproving parents, jealous competitors, or other blocking figures. The barriers might arise from a hostile community (*Troilus and Cressida, Romeo and Juliet*) or from conflicting political goals (*Antony and Cleopatra*). Sometimes, in their seeking to unite with another, a protagonist suffers rejection or betrayal by their loved one (*All's Well That Ends Well, Troilus and Cressida*).

In these plays, the protagonists typically know their goal early on. The challenges revolve around how to overcome the hurdles or balance conflicting desires. Helena in *All's Well* aims to win her beloved Bertram in marriage—which she does by healing the King, who has promised to fulfill whatever she requests—and then win him again after her new husband abandons her.

The protagonists' problems are typically resolved when the lovers are at last able to marry, or are reconciled, or (as in *Romeo and Juliet* and *Antony and Cleopatra*) are united forever in death. *Troilus and Cressida* ends bitterly, with the two protagonists estranged forever.

To find one's way, to adapt in a new world

Some protagonists find themselves plunged into new and difficult circumstances and must find a way to survive or adapt. Several of the comedies as well as the late romances fall in this category. The effort to adapt may entail extraordinary measures, as when the female protagonists disguise themselves as men. In *Twelfth Night,* Viola has been shipwrecked on the shores of Illyria. She must find her way in a strange land. To protect herself, she adopts a male's name (Cesario) and attire.

In the romance *Pericles, Prince of Tyre,* the young princess Marina must find a way to preserve her dignity and chastity after she has been kidnapped and sold to a brothel. Even the tempestuous Katharina in *The Taming of the Shrew* is learning to adapt to a new world: she must learn to tame herself if she wishes to enjoy a harmonious life with Petruchio.

We find this theme in tragedy as well. In *King Lear,* when the old king gives away his crown, his elder daughters turn against him and he loses the power and security he was accustomed to. He even finds his physical and mental faculties slipping from him. His journey requires him to adapt in some way to this new and terrifying world in which he is losing his bearings.

To get justice, to right a wrong

Attaining justice or righting a wrong is another common goal for Shakespeare's protagonists. It is central in *Hamlet,* in which the protagonist accepts the dread task given him by the Ghost. Yet for much of the play he finds himself unable to follow through:

> I do not know
> Why yet I live to say, "This thing's to do,"
> Sith I have cause, and will, and strength, and means
> To do't. (4.4)

Like Macbeth, he is also battling an internal hurdle. So, although this protagonist clearly knows his aim, he struggles to fulfill it.

In *Measure for Measure,* there are two, or arguably even three protagonists, each with conflicting goals. But these goals all reflect on the widespread vice in Vienna, where laws have been laxly enforced. The challenge posed by the play overall, and to each of the protagonists, is to restore respect for the law without resorting to overly harsh measures.

The Merchant of Venice overlaps, to an extent, with all three of these categories so far: This is a love story, and the protagonist Portia wishes to be united with her suitor Bassanio (Theme 1). But one hurdle is the danger into which Bassanio has inadvertently put his friend and financial benefactor: Antonio has enabled Bassanio to woo Portia by taking out a loan from Shylock on terms that now threaten his life. To rescue the situation, the protagonist impersonates a legal scholar and must make her way in the unfamiliar world of law (Theme 2). She does this in pursuit of justice (Theme 3), appealing to Shylock to not insist on the letter of the law, but to accept justice informed by goodwill and mercy.

To gain power and maintain it

One of the most prevalent goals among Shakespeare's protagonists is to seize power and/or maintain it against their adversaries. Not surprisingly, this problem emerges regularly in the history plays. It shapes the arcs of many of his kings, including Richard III, Henry IV, and Henry V. The tragic protagonist Macbeth also pursues this goal.

In *Richard II*, Henry Bolingbroke seizes the crown from the rightful, if weak, king and becomes crowned Henry IV. In the sequels, *Henry IV, Part1* and *Part 2*, we find Henry IV in a constant battle to hold onto power. He aims to rule in peace, and shows himself to be a rather capable ruler. He even tries to prepare his son, Prince Hal, to be a wise ruler after him. But across both parts of *Henry IV*, he is confronted with rebellion from his nobles and the truancy and apparent vice of his son, the Prince of Wales. Henry IV expresses the desire to lead a crusade to Jerusalem, but has no choice but to stay home to subdue his adversaries.

Macbeth wants to attain the Scottish crown and then eliminate any other claimants. Much of the play revolves around his efforts to fight these enemies. But the play also shows that his most formidable enemy is himself. Led on by the witches, he commits the crimes that plague his peace of mind, destroy his wife, and lead to his own demise.

To discern the truth of a situation, including of oneself

Protagonists may have as the central problem the need to discern the truth of a situation. This goal frequently overlaps with other protagonist problems. For example, Hamlet's main objective is to take revenge—to bring justice to his father's murderer. But as part of this, he also needs to discern the truth of whether Claudius if truly guilty or if the Ghost is an evil spirit sent to damn him by leading him to murder. King Lear's overriding problem is to "see better": to grow in self-knowledge, to perceive others' true nature and where he has been at fault.

Othello's central problem is to discern the truth, but through most of the play, he is looking in the wrong direction, where Iago is pointing him. This protagonist *thinks* his goal is to discover whether his wife is faithful or not, and then to enact what he considers justice by killing her. In fact, his actual challenge is to be wise enough to resist Iago's trap, to see through Iago's machinations—a threat he sees only when it's too late.

To defend against a threat to themselves or their world

Protagonists often wrestle with a problem bigger than themselves. Rather than aiming for personal advancement or benefit, their goal may be defensive or protective. We find this in many of the tragedies and histories. What happens to the protagonists will also dictate the fate of others. Like Hamlet, these protagonists may be enmeshed in a world that is out of balance and must try to set things right.

In *Julius Caesar*, Brutus loves Caesar as a friend, but fears he will become a tyrant, and so he takes part in his assassination. His goal is to save the Roman Republic.

When the problem involves defending themselves from a threat, these protagonists will typically be swept up in an event or circumstance and must find out what is to be done. Richard II finds himself under threat by his cousin, Bolingbroke, who seeks to regain his lands and, ultimately, to usurp Richard's throne. Most of the play shows Richard veering from moments of manic confidence—"Not all the water in the rough rude sea / Can wash the balm off from an anointed king" (3.2)—to an abyss of despair when his forces are defeated and he is imprisoned. His aim through most of the play is reactive and defensive: to hold on to his power and then, once lost, to reframe his understanding of himself and the spiritual and political worldview he believed in.

Othello's problem of discerning the truth is related to this goal: he cannot defend himself from Iago unless he discerns the reality behind Iago's lies.

In *Henry V*, the newly crowned king, whom we know from earlier plays in the cycle Prince Hal, is shown exploring legal claims that would justify an invasion of France; he also takes offense when the Dauphin of France provocatively insults him. When Henry decides to invade, he claims he simply wants what belongs to England and to defend his and the country's honor. Shakespeare, however, introduces several notes of skepticism about this rationale, raising the possibility that Henry is using a dubious legal claim as a pretext for war. His overt goal is to defend England's interests, but Shakespeare also shows there's a thin line between defense of honor and a war of conquest.

To withstand great loss, to endure patiently

In several of Shakespeare's later works, the protagonist faces a great loss early in the story: the loss of a loved one, loss of position, loss of home and identity.

Leontes in *The Winter's Tale* is told (falsely) that his wife died in childbirth, and his son actually does die shortly after; on Leontes' orders, his newborn daughter is taken away to be abandoned. In *Pericles*, the title character similarly believes he has lost his wife and, later, their daughter. These protagonists do not know that many of the losses are recoverable. The great hurdle facing them is to endure that pain with patience. In Leontes' case, it is also to come to terms with his grave mistake earlier in which he wrongly accused his wife of infidelity, which led to his many losses.

King Lear's challenge similarly consists of enduring and adapting to loss. Like Leontes, Lear has brought this calamity on himself. He gives up his power early in the play thinking he is "unburdening" himself from cares. But his cares only worsen as he faces not just the hostility of his two elder daughters, but also the progressive loss of his physical and mental strength.

While suffering can seem like a passive goal for a protagonist, withstanding great hardship can be as difficult as any more active endeavor. Pericles enunciates a fundamental crisis in life when he cries, "O you gods! / Why do you make us love your goodly gifts / And snatch them straight away?" (3.1). Shakespeare's challenge is to find a way to make this goal appear active and dramatic.

Through this type of problem, Shakespeare explores the nature of justice, the human condition, and our relationship with "the gods." It is through painful loss that Shakespeare's protagonists are set on the path to encountering some of the most profound questions.

To stand apart as an individual against the group

In at least two plays, Shakespeare sets up his protagonists in opposition to their communities. *Coriolanus* and *Timon of Athens* pose a central problem for the heroes in which they must try to reconcile their own extraordinary, flawed selves with the fickle and craven society in which they live.

Coriolanus is a great war hero for Rome, but he is also a patrician snob who despises the masses, and for this they drive him from the city. His primary aim is to regain his honor by taking revenge on them. To that end, Coriolanus unites with a former enemy, Aufidius, to invade Rome. But at the point of victory, he relents at his mother's entreaty. This act of mercy infuriates Aufidius, who kills him for it.

Timon is an extraordinarily generous bon vivant, lavishing his fortune on others, but when he becomes bankrupt, he finds all doors closed to him. Extravagant during the good times, he is equally intemperate in his poverty, lashing out against Athenians for their hypocrisy. Like Coriolanus, he becomes an enemy to his city. Although he chances upon buried gold later in the story, he uses it not to return to his former lifestyle, but to fund an attack on Athens out of spite.

Rejecting their communities for the sake of their personal aims comes at a catastrophic cost. There are some individuals, Shakespeare shows, whose natures will not permit them to compromise with or accept society as it is. The protagonist acts out of anger. Their goal is tragic in nature—to punish or reject the community that does not live up to their standards. It's a goal in which to succeed (and destroy their city) is to fail as well.

Each protagonist in Shakespeare is unique, but from a higher vantage point we can see the central problems that initiate and shape their journey tend to fall into a finite number of categories.

Protagonist's Arc

With their central problem, Shakespeare starts them off in a particular direction and gives them a particular impetus. Where does the protagonist go from there?

Let's review the broader picture now, the journey that the protagonist will trace from beginning to end during a story.

This path from the establishment of the problem to its resolution is often referred to as the character or protagonist arc.

The following graphic represents the protagonist arc. The protagonist's problem will be established (A). Challenges or hurdles will occur as the protagonist addresses the central problem (B). These challenges may occur at any point in the arc, but the most intense ones will typically occur around the midpoint of the plot, and again near the end. The arc concludes when their central problem is resolved (C).

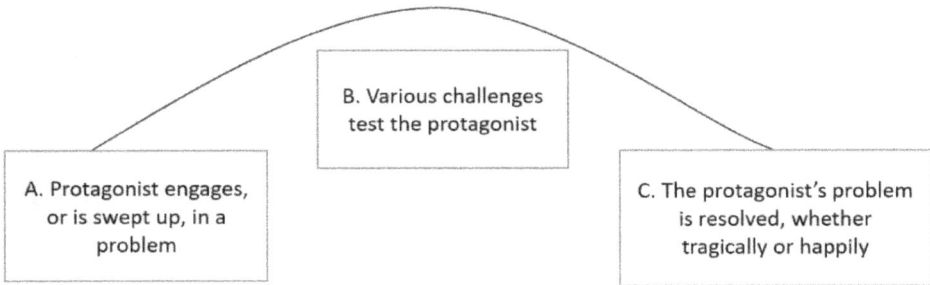

| | B. Various challenges test the protagonist | |
| A. Protagonist engages, or is swept up, in a problem | | C. The protagonist's problem is resolved, whether tragically or happily |

Protagonist Arc as Similar to Essay Structure

It can be useful to conceive of the protagonist's arc as similar to a standard essay structure. This is highly simplified, of course, and fictional narratives are certainly not essays. Yet both types of writing will typically set up an expectation that a specific issue will be addressed, spend the bulk of the content addressing it, and conclude once the issue is resolved. This is essentially what Shakespeare does with his protagonists. Although *Hamlet* is a highly complex play, the arc of its protagonist develops in way that resembles how an essay is structured:

A. Protagonist's Central Problem (similar to thesis, which is a statement to be proven)

A ghost resembling the old king is haunting the battlements of Elsinore. Something is rotten in the state of Denmark. Hamlet encounters the Ghost, who entreats him to avenge his murder. Hamlet agrees to do it. This is his central problem. How can he accomplish this task? He declares the time is out of joint and curses his fate that he must set it right.

B. Confronting the Problem (similar to exploration or testing of thesis)

In the following four acts, Hamlet must overcome many hurdles as he attempts to achieve his aim of revenging his father's murder and setting things right. These hurdles include:

- Protecting himself from Claudius and others who try to thwart him or betray him
- Confirming whether Claudius really killed his father
- Seeking the proper conditions in which to take revenge (when Claudius is in a state of sin)

- Grappling with his own troubled spirit on many levels: his disgust at his mother's behavior; his worry that the Ghost might be a damned spirit sent to ensnare his soul; his alienation from Ophelia; his procrastination in killing Claudius; and his psychospiritual distress over many of life's mysteries

C. Resolution (similar to an essay conclusion, which shows the thesis has been addressed)

Hamlet makes peace within himself before the plot's resolution ("if it be not now, yet it will come—the readiness is all," he concludes to Horatio in act 5, scene 2).

In the final moments of the play, he at last fulfills his duty to revenge his father's murder. The bloodshed in this scene purges the Danish court of all who were corrupt or tainted, including Hamlet himself. This makes way for the Norwegian prince Fortinbras to ascend to the throne. Although it is at the cost of his own life, Hamlet has set the time right again.

By keeping in mind that protagonists have a central problem, must confront the problem, and then resolve it, the shape of their arc becomes easier to visualize.

Challenges/Tests

The smooth curve of an arc is perhaps too tidy an image to represent the protagonist's journey. Although it proceeds from A (establishment of central problem) to C (resolution), the part in the middle, the B section, won't be a smooth glide path. Rather, it will be filled with surprises and setbacks, with risks and suspense, and partial resolutions along the way.

In a story, as in life, a character's strengths as well as their frailties may not become apparent until they are tested. This middle section will present challenges or development of some sort. If the path to C is too smooth and straightforward, it will feel preordained and predictable. But if the various hurdles seem random or digressive, we lose a sense of the direction in which the protagonist is heading.

Romeo and Juliet each have as their goal to unite with the other. Some of the hurdles that arise include challenges the two protagonists experience together—for instance, how to manage to get married by the Friar and spend their wedding night together. Other challenges they encounter individually. For example:

- Romeo kills Juliet's cousin in a duel, which threatens to shatter the happiness they just experienced in getting secretly married.

- Juliet later is threatened by her father that she must marry the man of his choosing or be expelled from the house to fend for herself.
- When the Nurse urges the newly married Juliet to commit this bigamy and marry Paris, Juliet is alienated from her one ally at home.
- As a consequence, Juliet agrees to the Friar's plan that she drink a potion that will make her appear dead. At the moment when she is about to drink it, she panics at the many ghastly possibilities that await her, but carries through with her intention.
- Romeo later hears a report that she has died, having missed the message informing him of the Friar's plan. So, he acquires poison to kill himself.
- After he poisons himself at her side in the crypt, Juliet awakens and sees he is dead. Rather than live without him, she stabs herself.
- Their resolution comes in the fact that they are united at last, albeit in death.

Audiences want to see problems solved, in the same way that we feel satisfied when a journey is completed. Even tragic resolutions are gratifying. The most compelling protagonist journeys are those in which this character develops or learns something significant along the way, and we along with them.

Typical Protagonist Challenges or Developments

As with the central problems, Shakespeare provides his protagonists with a wide range of challenges that tend to fall in certain categories. Some prominent ones are shown below, but there are too many variants to include all.

1. **An unforeseen setback** shows the severity of the challenge and the protagonist's depth of commitment. Examples:
   - Hamlet struggles to understand why he delays taking revenge although he knows he has ample cause and opportunity.
   - When Romeo kills her cousin Tybalt, the newly married Juliet initially repudiates Romeo, but then reaffirms that she owes her loyalty to him.
2. **A painful loss or humiliation** along the way shows how much the goal is costing the protagonist: Examples:
   - Many of Shakespeare's female protagonists endure cruel treatment from the men with whom they hoped to be united, such as Helena in *All's Well* and Hero in *Much Ado*; others suffer actual physical threats and privations, such as Katharina in *Taming of the Shrew*.
   - A distraught and distrustful Hamlet rebuffs Ophelia, although at other times he says he loved her; eventually she dies as a consequence of his actions.

- Troilus learns that his Cressida, who pledged to be true to him, has been seduced by the Greek Diomedes.
3. **A difficult sacrifice** or **challenging dilemma** confronts the protagonist, and this must be addressed to resolve the problem.
    - Isabella, the novice of *Measure for Measure,* is told she must submit to the judge Angelo's lust or her brother will be executed.
    - At the end of *Two Gentlemen of Verona,* Valentine is torn between his love for Sylvia and loyalty to his friend Proteus, who also desires Sylvia; Valentine offers to cede his claims to her out of friendship to Proteus.
4. **False or misleading information** leads the protagonist to make errors, often with dire consequences. Examples:
    - Othello is entrapped by Iago's lies about Desdemona's fidelity.
    - Macbeth believes the distorted proclamations of the witches, which lead him to think he is invincible.
    - Romeo gets false information that Juliet is dead, which leads him to commit suicide.
    - Claudio in *Much Ado* is led to believe his betrothed, Hero, has been unfaithful, so he spurns her at the altar.
5. **Physical threats, imprisonment, or other obstacles** the protagonist must work through or around. Examples:
    - Lear faces dire conditions as he wanders the heath in a storm, which in turn further degrades his mental state.
    - Richard II is defeated by Bolingbroke and held captive.
    - In turn, Bolingbroke, who becomes Henry IV, faces ongoing civil rebellion as he tries to rule.
    - Marina in *Pericles* must use her wits to avoid being forced into prostitution.
6. **A surprising encounter or discovery** that puts the problem in a new light. Examples:
    - Lear meets with the mad beggar Poor Tom, who provides Lear with an opportunity to "see better"—to reflect on humanity's nature; Lear has a parallel encounter with the storm. He projects his anger and despair onto "the heavens," perceiving in this natural phenomenon insights into how the gods do or don't involve themselves in human affairs.

- Hamlet learns that traveling players are visiting the castle; this prompts him to devise the Mousetrap performance to try to catch the conscience of the king.
- In *A Midsummer Night's Dream*, Titania, who has been put under a spell to fall in love with the next creature she sees, does indeed fall in love with one of the "rude mechanicals," Nick Bottom, who has also been bewitched and given an ass's head.
- In *Much Ado*, friends of Beatrice and Benedick contrive to have them eavesdrop, each in their turn, on them declaring how much Benedick or Beatrice is in love with the other. This leads the sworn bachelor and maid to release their seeming antipathies and realize they are, in fact, in love with the other.

There are many other ways that a protagonist is challenged in their pursuit of a goal; these may be internal (a psychological or spiritual dilemma), and not only external.

How the Challenges Lead to Resolution of Central Problem

Shakespeare is selective in the challenges he sets for his protagonists. He chooses challenges that not only deepen our sense of the character, but that also advance the character in some way toward the resolution of their aim.

Here are two examples of the challenges Shakespeare gives his protagonists—one comic, one tragic—as he takes them along the arc from their central problem to resolution. In each, the challenges help reveal more of the character and bring them closer to their endpoint.

Twelfth Night: *Viola's Challenges*

In the romantic comedy *Twelfth Night*, the main protagonist is Viola, a young woman we first meet after she has been shipwrecked on a foreign shore. She exclaims to the ship's Captain: "And what shall I do in Illyria? / My brother he is in Elysium" (1.2). She believes her brother has drowned in the wreck, and she doesn't know what to do now. She knows only that she must take care of herself. Viola must find her way in a strange land.

And that she does. But she acknowledges along the way that there are limits to what she can control: "What else may hap, to time I will commit" (1.2). By the end she has found a new home, a husband-to-be, and even her brother again.

How does Shakespeare shape her arc to get here there? This is a romantic comedy. The hurdles she faces are almost all comic and light-hearted. Luck is clearly on her side. But her challenges still are crafted to show her as meriting her ultimate good fortune.

Her first hurdle is how to find her way in a foreign land as an unprotected female. She starts by adopting a male name, Cesario, and male attire. Then, in this guise, Viola finds employment in the household of Count Orsino.

A complication arises when she falls in love with her master. But she is now stuck in her role as a boy.

Her next challenge comes when Orsino instructs her to transmit messages of love to the Lady Olivia on his behalf. She vows to perform her task faithfully, and she does so, even while preferring her mission not succeed. "I'll do my best / To woo your lady," she promises, but this comes at a cost, as she admits in an aside: "Yet a barful strife! / Whoe'er I woo, myself would be his wife" (1.4).

She executes her duty with persistence and good wit, refusing to take no for an answer when Olivia tries to avoid her. As Cesario, Viola counters every argument Olivia makes for why she cannot return Orsino's love. In her wooing-by-proxy, we get a sense of the protagonist's deep capacity for love:

VIOLA [as CESARIO] With such a suff'ring, such a deadly life,
In your denial I would find no sense.
I would not understand it.
OLIVIA   Why, what would you?
VIOLA Make me a willow cabin at your gate
And call upon my soul within the house,
Write loyal cantons of contemnèd love
And sing them loud even in the dead of night,
Hallow your name to the reverberate hills
And make the babbling gossip of the air
Cry out "Olivia!" O, you should not rest
Between the elements of air and earth
But you should pity me! (1.5)

This points to how deeply Viola is capable of loving. If she were a man who loved someone, she would set herself up in a simple cabin outside their gate and sing love songs to her beloved without cease.

But as comic chance would have it, Viola argues Orsino's suit so persuasively that she causes Olivia falls in love with *her*. When Viola realizes what has happened, she again concedes her limitations: "O time! thou must untangle this, not I; / It is too hard a knot for me to untie!"

Viola's main hurdle is her inability to show herself as a woman. She must stand by as Orsino declares his love for another and boasts of how much greater a man's love is than any woman's:

> ORSINO: There is no woman's sides
> Can bide the beating of so strong a passion
> As love doth give my heart; no woman's heart
> So big, to hold so much; they lack retention. (2.4)

We, who know just how ardently she loves him, will think otherwise. And then we hear Viola/Cesario counter this by telling Orsino the story of her father's daughter—herself, in other words:

> she never told her love,
> But let concealment, like a worm i'th'bud,
> Feed on her damask cheek; she pined in thought,
> And with a green and yellow melancholy
> She sat like Patience on a monument,
> Smiling at grief. Was not this love indeed?
> We men may say more, swear more, but indeed
> Our shows are more than will; for still we prove
> Much in our vows, but little in our love. (2.4)

In this scene, we see Viola's fine qualities come out: she stands up for the dignity and capacity of women in love; she endures the hardship of not being able to express this love to Orsino; and she practices the patience she speaks of — allowing Time to untie the hard knot that is constraining her.

In the spirit of comedy, it is not just the active doing, but also having faith and going with the flow that gets the protagonist to their desired goal. The hard knot that Viola couldn't untie herself is untied for her at the end when her twin brother arrives on the scene, causing a peak of identity-confusion, and obliging Viola finally to reveal herself. This paves the way for Orsino to shift his affections to her once he puts two-and-two together about Cesario's past proclamations about love and devotion to him.

How does Shakespeare use these challenges to get her closer to her goal of making her way in a strange land? Her first challenge, being shipwrecked, leads her to find employment with Orsino, and with each subsequent challenge, she proves her fine character and wit; ultimately, these all lead her to the union she desires with Orsino.

The challenges (middle section) that lead from problem to resolution in Viola's arc can be shown like this.

Viola's Arc:

| Viola is alone in a strange land and must find safety and new conditions for happiness. | • Adopts male disguise to protect herself and is taken on by Orsino as a page.
• Fulfills her duty to woo Olivia for Orsino, in spite of pain this causes her.
• Faces (comic) challenges that arise because of her cross-dressing.
• Remains stoical, but speaks up for women, when Orsino tells her no woman can love as deeply as a man. | Viola is united with her beloved Orsino, recovers her brother, and her brother marries Oliva, whom Orsino had courted. |

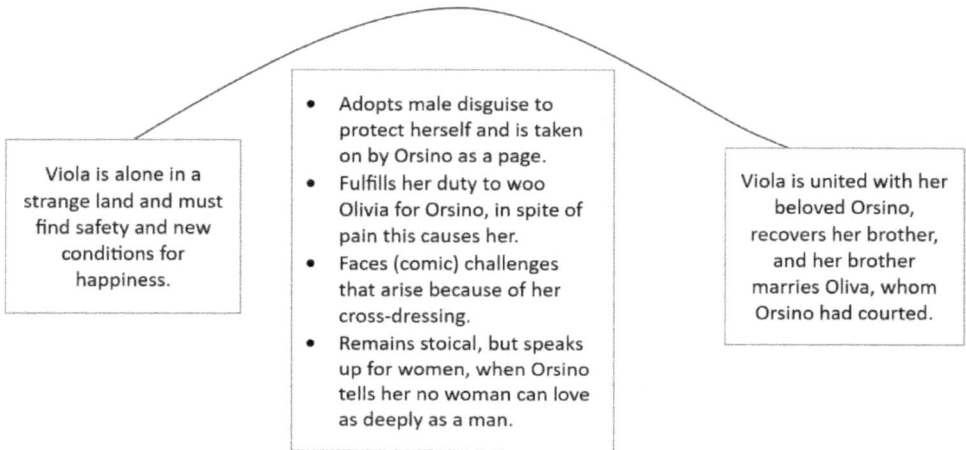

In each instance she shows herself:
- clever and resourceful in making the most of her opportunities,
- open and ready for love, and
- patient in waiting for the right circumstances in which to act.

While she is limited in what she can make to happen, she is doing everything right to be ready for love when the fates will allow.

And so, Viola accomplishes her goal: she finds her way in a strange land by a combination of resourcefulness, wit, integrity, faith, and stoical patience. She falls in love. She makes new allies. She performs her duties faithfully. And she even finds that her brother is alive after all.

She does not, and cannot, actively pursue Orsino in the situation in which she finds herself, but her responses to her challenges propel her forward to the happy resolution of her goal.

Macbeth's Challenges

Macbeth wants to attain the crown and hang on to power, and for that he is willing to commit horrific crimes, including murdering his king, his friend Banquo, and many other innocents. Macbeth pursues this goal, but as he confronts each challenge, he discovers this goal is destroying him.

The thesis Shakespeare is exploring in this tragedy is: What are the consequences of pursuing power at any costs? Macbeth quickly attains his deep desire: he becomes king. Yet in doing so, he triggers the violent opposition of other nobles and the murdered king's sons. An even more insidious enemy arises for Macbeth and his wife-accomplice: their own guilty consciences.

The particular challenges that Shakespeare gives him are selected to show how Macbeth loses his humanity step by step as a natural consequence of his choices. Each new act of violence engenders more resistance from the people he wants to rule, which prompts him to still more dehumanizing violence to suppress it. Not only his moral soundness but also his psychological health degrades in the process.

This degradation begins with his first decisive challenge: whether or not to kill King Duncan as he stays with them at their castle. Although Macbeth initially says "If chance will have me king, why, chance may crown me / Without my stir," his wife goads him and they decide to take matters in their own hands.

Killing Duncan is bloody business and fills Macbeth with horror. It also does not achieve his goal once and for all as they hoped. "A little water clears us of this deed," claims Lady Macbeth hopefully, but they have only started a chain of reactions.

Macbeth's subsequent challenges include the following. In each, his attempts to achieve a particular goal result only in making things worse.

1. **The goal**: Hold on to power for his heirs.
    Macbeth fears the witches' predictions about Banquo's line inheriting the crown, so Macbeth sends assassins to kill Banquo and his young son.
    The result: Murder of his rival, which will trigger more resistance and guilt, although the son escapes.

2. **The goal:** Consolidate his power with the nobles.
    To consolidate his power, Macbeth tries to win over the nobles by hosting a banquet, but his guilty behavior when seeing Banquo's ghost gives him away. Many of the nobles flee the country, some of them to England to unite behind Duncan's son Malcolm.
    The result: His guilty behavior makes them more suspicious of him.

3. **The goal:** Gain and maintain control through murder.
    In spite of Macbeth's efforts to maintain control so he can reign with his wife, Lady Macbeth's psyche crumbles under their sense of guilt. We see her preoccupation with the murder of Macduff's wife when she tries to cleanse her

hands while sleepwalking and mutters: "The Thane of Fife had a wife; where is she now? What, will these hands ne'er be clean?" (5.1).

The result: Psyche-destroying guilt.

4. **The goal:** Take revenge on Macduff for his resistance.

In time, Macbeth gives way to indiscriminate slaughter of any who resist him. There is no turning back, as Macbeth admits: "I am in blood / Stepped in so far that, should I wade no more, / Returning were as tedious as go o'er" (3.4). He orders the murder of Macduff's whole family.

The result: Provokes Macduff to vow to revenge; Macduff will slay Macbeth at the end.

5. **The goal:** Gain reassurance.

Macbeth seeks reassurance from the witches about their prophecy, so he visits them again. They lead him to believe he is invincible, telling him no man of woman born can defeat him and that he will not lose until Birnam Wood comes to Dunsinane—both of them apparent impossibilities which do, in fact, occur.

The result: Further entrapment in the witches' misleading encouragement.

With each step he takes to achieve his aim, Macbeth engenders resistance and a weakening of his situation. His failure becomes apparent when his symbiotic relationship with his wife falters. He pleads with the Doctor to cure his wife's psychic collapse: "Canst thou not minister to a mind diseased, / Pluck from the memory a rooted sorrow, / Raze out the written troubles of the brain" (5.3). The answer, of course, is no. The Doctor tells him: "Therein the patient / Must minister to himself." Macbeth rejects this advice: "Throw physic to the dogs, I'll none of it."

Neither Macbeth nor his wife succeed in ministering to their true threat, their guilt. Even before his wife dies, Macbeth sees how his ambitions have sapped him of all that is good in life:

> I have lived long enough; my way of life
> Is fall'n into the sere, the yellow leaf,
> And that which should accompany old age,
> As honor, love, obedience, troops of friends,
> I must not look to have; but in their stead,
> Curses, not loud but deep, mouth-honor, breath
> Which the poor heart would fain deny and dare not. (5.3)

As he arms himself for battle, he learns of his wife's death. He is now past caring. "She should have died hereafter; / There would have been a time for such a word." Instead, life has become no more than "a tale / Told by an idiot, full of sound and fury, / Signifying nothing."

Macbeth's journey takes the following shape.

Macbeth's Arc

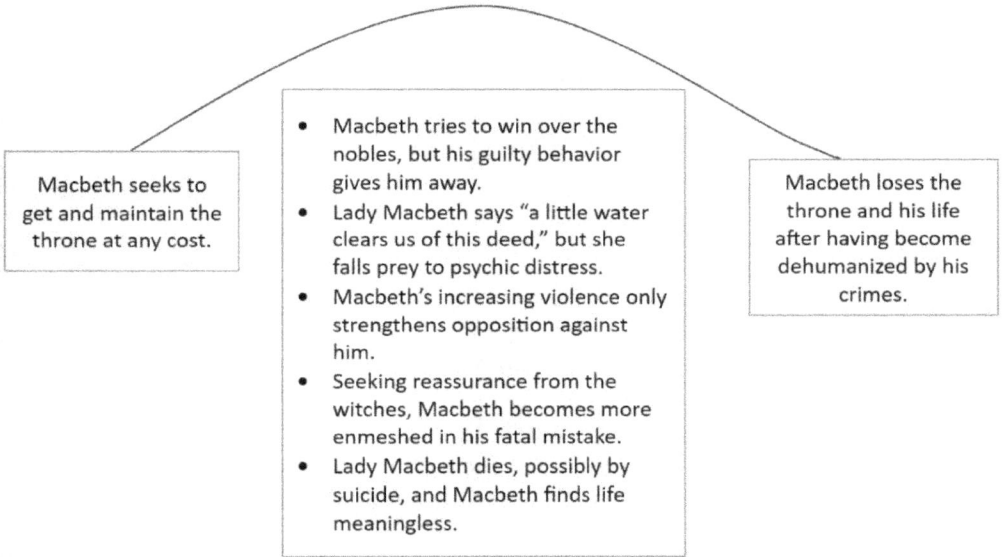

Macbeth seeks to get and maintain the throne at any cost.

- Macbeth tries to win over the nobles, but his guilty behavior gives him away.
- Lady Macbeth says "a little water clears us of this deed," but she falls prey to psychic distress.
- Macbeth's increasing violence only strengthens opposition against him.
- Seeking reassurance from the witches, Macbeth becomes more enmeshed in his fatal mistake.
- Lady Macbeth dies, possibly by suicide, and Macbeth finds life meaningless.

Macbeth loses the throne and his life after having become dehumanized by his crimes.

Notice the particular challenge that Shakespeare does *not* give him during the middle section: a military one. Macbeth's prowess as a warrior is already established. We do not see him in combat until the final scene, when he meets his doom at Macduff's hands. Shakespeare saw no need to give Macbeth the kind of challenge at which he was already so proficient. It would add nothing to his journey.

Rather, he shows Macbeth facing threats that can't be found on the battlefield and that he cannot openly confront: the witches' cryptic malevolence, and his own guilty conscience and progressive paranoia, which lead him to more violence.

Indeed, at the end, when Macbeth engages with the attacking forces, the battle comes as a relief to him. He finds himself

a-weary of the sun,

And wish the estate o' the world were now undone.

Ring the alarum-bell! Blow wind, come wrack,

At least we'll die with harness on our back. (5.5)

This, at last, is the kind of fighting he can excel at. Even though he knows it will spell his death, it will bring him a conclusion on his own terms—with harness on his back. Shakespeare is reminding us at the end that he was, in fact, a brave warrior. But it was the unseen enemies—the evil represented by the witches, and the psychological compulsions both he and his wife gave in to—that led to his downfall.

These various challenges link together as a kind of arc. The arc begins with Macbeth's goal, to get and maintain power at any cost, and concludes by showing us what the ultimate cost is: the loss of his humanity and ability to value life.

Resolution

The final phase of a protagonist's journey will be a culmination of what was initiated early in the story. The problem or goal is at last resolved. As we have just seen with the example from Macbeth, it may not be resolved in the way the protagonist has expected.

To an extent, the protagonist's resolution depends on the genre. Comedies and romances often culminate in marriage for the lovers, or in reunions of parents and children. Particularly in comedy, the complications tend to sort themselves out as if a benevolent force were taking a hand. But even so, Shakespeare's comic protagonists have almost always "earned" their happy outcomes by their resourcefulness and admirable behavior in the face of challenges.

This is true of Viola, who proved her love and strong character by acting like Patience on a monument—she behaved with grace in spite of her disappointments. Viola is rewarded with the love of Orsino, with whom she finds a new home; she has even been reunited with the brother she thought drowned.

The romances—particularly, *Pericles, Cymbeline,* and *The Winter's Tale*—portray a journey that seems to be more of a test of endurance. The challenges have been more serious, verging on tragic. Benevolent forces also seem to be at work, but these individuals suffer more and it is only after deep remorse or perseverance that they find the losses they have experienced restored to them.

In Shakespeare's final romance, *The Tempest,* the protagonist gets justice from his old enemies and is finally going home to prepare for the end of his eventful life.

The resolution of tragic protagonists, of course, often involves death. But these heroes will gain something of significance even if they lose their life. It might be they acquire a great insight or recognition—an *anagnorisis,* as Aristotle calls it in *The Poetics.* The arc might end in the attainment of justice, as Hamlet's does.

The tragic protagonist's end will almost always have a significant impact on others, not just themselves. The society or state is often left somewhat better as a result, as in *Romeo and Juliet,* as the feuding families vow to end their hostilities, and as in *Hamlet,* with the purgation of the murderous court. But not necessarily. The end of *Julius Caesar* shows the defeat of Brutus' hopes to protect the republic; instead, a bloody new period will begin, although that, too, will lead ultimately to reign of Augustus Caesar and the golden years of his Pax Romana.

What matters technically in the resolution of a protagonist's arc is that the central problem has been explored and brought to fruition or completion in a satisfying way.

Protagonist Transformation

A satisfying resolution may include transformation of some kind by this character. Shakespeare often shows his protagonists, particularly in the more serious works, learning or developing in some way, and vicariously, we do along with them. Whether they are "better" for the experience or not, few of his protagonists reach the endpoint unchanged or unscathed. They have become different because of the tests they have faced along the way.

Macbeth's Transformation

The transformation in the tragedies almost always comes too late for the protagonist: they learn something, but only after seeing the tragic consequences of their errors. Macbeth *thought* he and his wife would be content once they gained power. But his actual challenge was to resist the temptation to do evil in the first place. Shakespeare shows Macbeth's friend and peer Banquo going through a similar temptation in the play and choosing not to trust in the witches. But because Macbeth does not resist, the witches' prophecy can kindle in him an ambition he and his wife have seemingly already entertained.

Shakespeare shows the scales falling progressively from Macbeth's eyes. He finds he is now trapped by his crimes: "It will have blood, they say; blood will have blood" (3.4), yet he continues killing to maintain his hold on power. He recognizes he has driven away the sorts of joys that others can look forward to: "that which should accompany old age, / As honor, love, obedience, troops of friends, / I must not look to have" (5.3).

He loses his wife to her psychological distress and is too depleted when she dies to be able to mourn her. And at the end, he realizes the witches' have misled him, feeding his false hopes. From a bloody lust for power at any costs, his life, he admits, has become a dusty path, completely meaningless.

This is one reason Macbeth's journey is so compelling. While the supernatural eeriness and violence form the framework for the story, it is Macbeth's and Lady Macbeth's psychological battles and the progressive loss of their own humanity that make this play so harrowing. We witness what happens when a person is willing to do any amount of evil to achieve one's goal. The evil itself destroys the person. That is his resolution, and Macbeth himself recognizes it by the end. His transformation is tragic.

Viola's Transformation

Comic protagonists transform as well, but their lessons are not as hard-fought and their resolutions are happy, and the change they undergo is usually less extreme than in the serious works.

Viola, alone and mourning her protector-brother, accepts the challenge to fend for herself. In adopting a male persona, she gains her more leeway to show her mettle beyond what society would allow a woman to show. As Cesario she is able to speak her mind as freely as a man, and she shows herself no less witty and clever than those around her. She shows how persuasively she would woo the one she loves (to the point that she causes Olivia to fall in love with her). Viola will display her love and devotion well beyond what Count Orsino had claimed a woman was capable of. And she patiently endures to wait until the time that fate will bring her conundrums to a resolution.

She transforms in an outward, literal sense when she resumes her female identity, and when she unites with her beloved Orsino. But she has also transformed in showing how resourceful she could be, as a defenseless woman in a strange land, to find her way home. Her brave and cheerful engagement with her challenges shows her as deserving of the good fortune that happens at the end.

What Does a Protagonist's "Resolution" Really Mean?

This is not to say all questions are tidied up unambiguously for a protagonist. For instance, Shakespeare's problem plays—*All's Well That Ends Well, Measure for Measure,* and *Troilus and Cressida*—have famously attracted differing interpretations of what the endings mean, and consequently, how the protagonist's journey ends. It is hard to see their journeys as having as purely happy conclusions, nor as tragic ones, but something more mixed. For some readers, the resolutions can seem unsettling. Shakespeare raises profound questions in all of his plays and not all can be easily put to rest. He rarely airbrushes away thorny problems, but he does tie up in some way the questions posed by the protagonist's central problem.

Resolution of Isabella's Journey in Measure for Measure

In *Measure for Measure,* we can see how carefully Shakespeare structures his protagonist's journey. He gives Isabella a series of challenges that evolve from an issue raised at the beginning, and resolves it in such a way that he avoids making the outcome seem overly simplistic.

At the beginning of *Measure for Measure,* the protagonist Isabella prepares to take her final vows as a nun. Her view of right and wrong is unequivocal. By entering the convent, she wishes to sequester herself from the sinfulness of the world around her. Shakespeare frames this, implicitly, as the protagonist's problem: in turning away from the world, she will never be tested further and she will waste her gifts by not lighting the way for others. The Duke spells out this idea explicitly when he tells Angelo, another reclusive figure, that

> Thyself and thy belongings
> Are not thine own so proper as to waste
> Thyself upon thy virtues, they on thee.
> Heaven doth with us as we with torches do,
> Not light them for themselves; for if our virtues
> Did not go forth of us, 'twere all alike
> As if we had them not. (1.1)

Those who are virtuous, he is saying, are like torches: heaven uses them to light the way for others. What good are those gifts if they are not used?

The city of Vienna, in fact, is overrun with licentiousness and could use more of Isabella's moral strictness. Isabella's central problem will involve managing in this world she'd rather avoid.

When her brother Claudio is arrested for having slept with his betrothed before marriage, Isabella is called to speak to the judge Angelo on his behalf. But Angelo, who is reckoned to be cold and incorruptible, becomes inflamed by her purity and demands that she submit to him or her brother will be executed promptly. She refuses because to do otherwise is to lose her immortal soul; she is then led to believe her brother has been executed.

111

The Duke of Vienna, meanwhile, knows he has been an overly permissive ruler and wants to right things by having the strict Angelo take power temporarily. But he first tests him, pretending to be out of the city, while actually spying on how he handles cases.

When the Duke sees the dilemma Angelo has placed Isabella, he proposes a bed-trick: Isabella will appear to comply with Angelo's desires, but in fact, another woman will take her place in bed. This woman was previously affianced to Angelo, but he spurned her when she lost her dowry.

The resolution of the play is largely what perplexes critics. When Angelo's misdeeds are exposed, the Duke announces he will execute him, just as Angelo ordered Claudio's execution: measure for measure. But Isabella intervenes, pleading for mercy. The Duke grants it, and "punishes" Angelo instead by making him marry his former fiancée with whom he just slept. The Duke further proposes to wed Isabella. It is not clear from the text if she is happy about this turn of events or not, but her plans for a quiet convent life seem to be over.

So, is this a satisfying resolution to her journey? It's certainly been disputed. But at least from a structural perspective, we can say that it returns to and resolves the protagonist's central problem. Isabella progresses from her initially strict, almost harsh view of justice and learns to ask for merciful justice, even for the man who wronged her.

Thanks to her experiences with the messy, unjust world that she is forced to deal with, Isabella has transformed. There are other elements of the ending that may not sit right with audiences, but Isabella's transformation is unquestionably satisfying. We have witnessed her growth toward greater knowledge of the world and greater compassion, without sacrificing her principles. She asks for adherence to the law, while tempering it with mercy. She and her influence—the light she shines for others—are just what Vienna and the Duke need.

Summary

As we have seen, Shakespeare's heroes will confront a problem of some kind, and this demarcates the beginning and end of a journey. The protagonist might not even choose the journey they are following, but circumstances compel them in a certain direction and toward a particular goal. Nor do they always attain what they *think* they have been aiming at.

The protagonist's journey is not the whole story, certainly not in Shakespeare. The problem, challenges, and resolution for the protagonist will never entirely encompass all that the work conveys. (Hamlet's journey—which takes up the vast bulk of the play, comes very close, however.) There is always a larger perspective offered. From this broader view, we can see how the protagonist's desires and fears relate to the world around them.

The protagonist's arc is not identical to plot, even though they will run in parallel. No matter how important the protagonist, the plot will provide additional perspective, as we will explore in later chapters.

Takeaway for Writers

For his protagonists, Shakespeare constructs a journey that usually falls into a clear pattern:

- It begins with a central problem that sends them toward a goal, whether they are aware of that goal or not.
- The protagonist must deal with challenges along the way that test their resolve and make them clarify the situation around their goal.
- The journey ends in a resolution of the central problem.

Although each of Shakespeare's protagonists is unique, there are typical protagonist problems they tend to face, involving one or more of these themes:

- To unite with another
- To find one's way in a new or threatening world; to adapt to changing circumstances
- To attain justice; to right a wrong
- To gain power and maintain it
- To discern the truth about a situation
- To defend against a threat to themselves or their world
- To withstand great loss; to patiently endure
- To stand apart as an individual against the group

Shakespeare provides his protagonists with a wide range of challenges that tend to fall in certain categories. The main ones are shown below, but there are too many variants to include all.

- An unforeseen setback shows the severity of challenge and the protagonist's depth of commitment.
- A painful loss or humiliation along the way shows how much the goal is costing the protagonist.

- A difficult sacrifice or challenging dilemma confronts the protagonist
- False or misleading information leads the protagonist to make grave errors.
- Physical threats, imprisonment, or other obstacles the protagonist must work through or around.
- A surprising encounter puts the problem in a new light.

Some main principles Shakespeare follows in constructing journey:
- **A journey needs a destination.** Whether or not the protagonist is aware of any goal at first, the journey should be leading to a particular end point, a destination.
- **Challenges should propel the protagonist toward that goal,** often in the form of hurdles that the protagonist then overcomes. Challenges should not seem random and distracting but relate in some way to that goal.
- **Challenges need to be of sufficient difficulty,** depending on the nature of the story. For most protagonists, the goal will be hard to achieve, and therefore the challenges they face are formidable. By facing and overcoming the hurdles, the protagonist becomes a greater person than at first appeared.
- **The journey concludes when the protagonist's problem is resolved.** The entire plot may continue on, at least a short while, but the protagonist's arc is not identical to the plot, even if they run in parallel.

CHAPTER 6: SPOTLIGHT: PRINCE HAL'S JOURNEY

To see Shakespeare's mastery of structuring a protagonist journey, we can do no better than to consider Prince Hal's arc. This arc stretches across three plays and shows Shakespeare focusing very much on what Hal's central problem is, what his challenges are, and especially, the end point toward which he is heading. This protagonist provides a great example of a complex yet clearly structured journey.

One reason Hal's journey is illuminating as a model is because Shakespeare foregrounds Hal's pursuit of his goal so clearly and pays comparatively little attention to his inner nature, his psychology. Shakespeare only rarely shows the prince as grappling with serious emotional or ethical conflicts, in contrast to Hamlet, who is frequently engaged with them. Hal is focused on his ultimate aim; for this protagonist, achieving that goal is what matters above all.

In this chapter, we will trace how Shakespeare shapes Hal's journey across a multi-part work, providing satisfying resolutions in each part along with a comprehensive resolution at the end.

Hal, the Heroic Protagonist

All of Shakespeare's protagonists are heroic in one way or other, but Prince Hal (later Henry V), is probably Shakespeare's most traditionally heroic. He has a quest toward which he aims, and through personal sacrifice, he succeeds brilliantly at it, bringing himself and his country great renown.

The real Henry V was a revered figure to the English people. It is no surprise Shakespeare wanted to bring him to the stage. Shakespeare frames this monarch's story in a most effective way by contrasting him with his two predecessors, Richard II and Henry IV.

Hal's own journey spans the last three plays of Shakespeare's four-play cycle known as the Henriad. This cycle covers the English civil wars around the turn of the fifteenth century, and in it, Shakespeare explores the varieties of kingship. He begins with the weak, poetic, but rightful king Richard II. He is overthrown by the pragmatic rebel, Bolingbroke, who is crowned as Henry IV. Once we reach the usurper's son Henry V (Hal), we at last find a model of a great and successful monarch.

Journey Greater than Traits

From the start, Shakespeare associates Prince Hal with his destiny. He is the Prince of Wales, which means he is the heir apparent and will become king at his father's death. But he has other traits. He is adept at everything to do with human relations—from sparring wittily with friends, to perceiving the motivations of others, to reassuring other nobles of his fitness to lead, to rousing his troops for battle, and to wooing and winning his French princess at the end.

And yet, Shakespeare does not have Hal/Henry V bare his soul to his audience the way Hamlet does. Shakespeare portrays little of his "inner world," and focuses on how he operates in the world of men and women of every echelon. Shakespeare shows how this protagonist deliberately sets about to fulfill the task he has been given—to become a great king—and completes that task by the end of the third play. His friendship with Falstaff, however jovial and emotional at times, is sacrificed without hesitation when he ascends the throne.

One might say that Hal's leading trait—his position as future king—is identical to his goal. Even during his carousing days, he never loses sight of the fact, or forgets the burden, that he will be king. As he vows, "I'll so offend, to make offense a skill, / Redeeming time when men least think I will" (1.2).

His single-mindedness toward this goal is what explains an otherwise disconcerting coldness, verging on cruelty, that we see at key moments in the plays. It's hard to find any soft spot in Hal's heart, any vulnerability that we'd expect to find in an ordinary person. For Shakespeare, evidently, the role of ideal king and leader leaves little room for it.

Elements and Structure of the Protagonist Arc

Shakespeare spreads the full arc of his protagonist across three plays: *Henry IV, Part 1* and *Part 2* and *Henry V*. These were composed from about 1596 to 1600.

To portray this journey, Shakespeare's main challenge is to keep a sense of Hal's forward momentum from play to play, rather like a mini-series, while also shaping each individual play with a satisfying conclusion. The works were performed individually and each was premiered probably a year or more apart, so they needed to stand alone as well.

To lend this protagonist a sense of continuity, Shakespeare provides for Hal a single compelling goal, which he pursues throughout the three plays. This goal doesn't resolve until the end of *Henry V*, but there are milestones the Hal achieves along the way at the end of *Part 1* and *Part 2* that provide a sense of resolution, too.

Partial and Final Resolutions in Prince Hal's Journey

Prince Hal's overall goal is to pay the debt he never promised—that is, to become a great king. He achieves a portion of the goal in each of the plays, but reaches his complete fulfillment of the promise in the final play.

This diagram shows the overall arc to the series and the resolutions that fall at the end of each work. The journey resolves partially in the first two plays and is completed in the final one.

Hal/HenryV's Complete Journey Arc Across Three Plays:

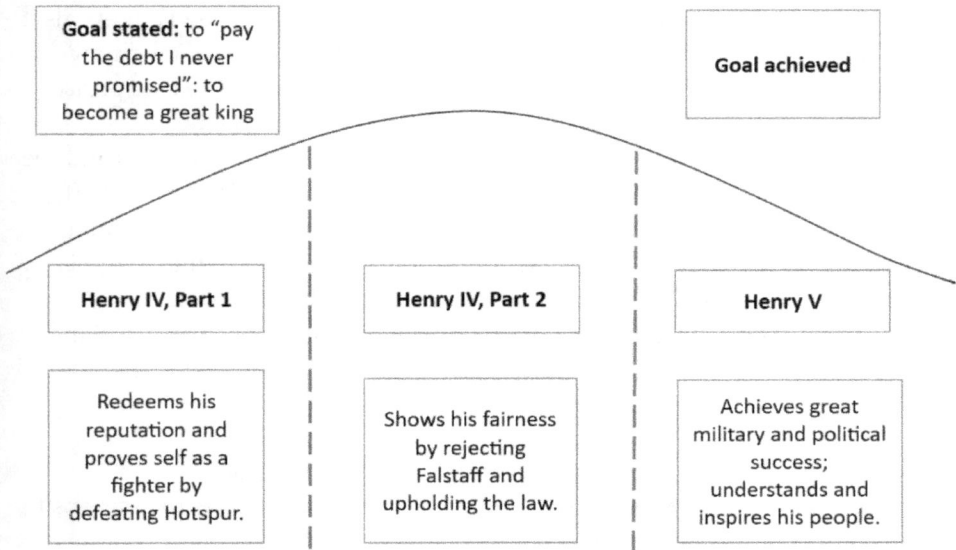

Goal stated: to "pay the debt I never promised": to become a great king		Goal achieved
Henry IV, Part 1	**Henry IV, Part 2**	**Henry V**
Redeems his reputation and proves self as a fighter by defeating Hotspur.	Shows his fairness by rejecting Falstaff and upholding the law.	Achieves great military and political success; understands and inspires his people.

Recap of Hal's Arc

Each of the plays has the standard elements of a protagonist's journey:

1. Central problem (same in each play)
2. Challenges

3. Resolution (milestones met and final resolution)

Let's start by identifying key elements of the journey within the action of each play.

Henry IV, Part 1

Hal's journey begins early in *Henry IV, Part 1*. We first meet him in a tavern in Eastcheap, London, as he carouses with his acquaintances. Most are of dubious character, such as the ebullient Sir John Falstaff, who lives by sponging off of others or through outright thievery. Falstaff and his cronies are plotting their next robbery. They invite Hal to join them, but he declines. In private, Hal's friend Poins proposes that the two of them should rob the gang after they have committed the robbery just for the fun of hearing the extravagant lies Falstaff will tell.

Hal agrees, and it all falls out as predicted. Falstaff and his accomplices drop their loot and flee, and Falstaff later claims he fought valiantly against attackers, with the numbers of his attackers increasing with each telling. When Hal reveals it was only himself and Poins who robbed them, Falstaff is undeterred, and now prides himself on his excellent intuition. "The lion will not touch the true prince. Instinct is a great matter. I was now a coward on instinct" (2.4), he boasts.

Word then comes about an impending battle between the King's forces and the rebels; the King has also summoned Hal to court the next day. Hal and Falstaff rehearse a scene to prepare him for this uncomfortable meeting. Impersonating Henry IV, Falstaff attacks Hal for his vices and praises the fat knight among his companions. He advises him to banish all the others, but keep Falstaff close, because to lose him is to lose everything: "banish plump Jack, and banish all the world." To this, Hal coolly replies, "I do, I will." (2.4)

Central Problem in Henry IV, Part 1

In act 1, scene 2, we get the clearest expression of the protagonist's central problem. It comes in a long soliloquy in which the prince articulates the reasons for his unprincely behavior and his objectives.

He knows that one day he must "pay the debt I never promised" — that is, he will become king, a role he never sought, but must accept as the heir apparent. His louche behavior now makes others fear the worst of him, but that is part of his plan. He will "imitate the sun" and disperse these clouds later, which will win him more favor than if he had never seemed to stray:

So when this loose behavior I throw off
And pay the debt I never promised,
By how much better than my word I am,
By so much shall I falsify men's hopes [expectations],
And, like bright metal on a sullen ground,
My reformation, glitt'ring o'er my fault,
Shall show more goodly and attract more eyes
Than that which hath no foil to set it off.
I'll so offend, to make offense a skill,
Redeeming time when men think least I will. (1.2)

He is managing his public relations. He is biding his time, letting his reputation seem low, in order to redeem himself "when men think least I will" for greater effect.

Challenges in *Henry IV, Part 1*

In the meantime, however, he has to deal with his father, Henry IV, who is extremely disappointed in him. His father decries that "The hope and expectation of thy time / Is ruined, and the soul of every man / Prophetically do forethink thy fall" (3.2).

The King chides Hal for his low behavior, noting "Not an eye / But is a-weary of thy common sight, / Save mine, which hath desired to see thee more." He declares he would rather learn the rebel Hotspur were his actual son, and that the two boys had been switched at birth.

He even fears his son is so depraved that he would turn against him: "Why, Harry, do I tell thee of my foes, / Which art my nearest and dearest enemy?" He accuses Hal that out of "vassal fear" and "base inclination," he is more likely to fight on Hotspur's side simply "To show how much thou art degenerate."

Hal patiently endures his father's rebukes, and then vows he will redeem himself by defeating Hotspur in battle. And that is what he will do.

The rebels, including Hotspur, are convinced that the Prince of Wales will never leave his carousing nor be a real threat. So, when the showdown comes at the end of the play, and Hal does triumph, Hotspur feels robbed not only of his life, but of his honors. He knows that Hal will be credited with "those proud titles thou hast won of me. / They wound my thoughts worse than thy sword my flesh" (5.4).

Hal, for his part, is gracious in victory:
Fare thee well, great heart!

....
Adieu, and take thy praise with thee to heaven.
Thy ignominy sleep with thee in the grave,
But not remembered in thy epitaph! (5.4)

He also spies Falstaff on the ground, who is pretending to be dead, and shows a
rare moment of tenderness for him:
[He spieth Falstaff on the ground.]
What, old acquaintance! could not all this flesh
Keep in a little life? Poor Jack, farewell!
I could have better spared a better man.
O, I should have a heavy miss of thee
If I were much in love with vanity! (5.4)

Notice Hal's conditional statement of affection: he would have a "heavy miss"
of Falstaff if he greatly loved vain things. But Hal is not of common affections. He
will miss the old rogue, but not inordinately.

Resolution in *Henry IV, Part 1*

Part 1 ends with Hal reaching an important milestone in his quest to become a
great king: he proves himself in battle, saving his father's life and reign; and, like a
great and just prince, he shows respect to his worthy foe.

Henry IV, Part 2

Hal's journey does not pick up right away in *Part 2*, the next play of the series.
Instead, Shakespeare opens with other business. The first scene shows the rebels
still plotting against the King, and the next scene picks up with Falstaff, who has
been cashing in on the reputation he gained by (falsely) claiming to have killed
Hotspur.

A key moment, and a reminder of what is at stake for Hal, comes in act 3, when
his father Henry IV first appears. The gravely ill King speaks of the heavy duty
that comes with rule: "Uneasy lies the head that wears a crown" (3.1). He is
plagued with insomnia, even though he's surrounded by comfort, while the
lowliest of his subjects can sleep soundly in the harshest conditions. This speech
recapitulates the topic Shakespeare is pursuing in this series of plays: what
kingship entails. Here we see its costs, at least to a king who tries to fulfill his
duties responsibly.

Central Problem in *Henry IV, Part 2*

In this play, Hal will continue his journey along the same trajectory that was established in *Part 1*: how to become an exemplary king—the debt he never promised, but is duty-bound to pay.

But intertwined in Hal's journey is the arc of another major character, Falstaff, who serves as a co-protagonist for *Part 2*. Falstaff here is as boundlessly witty and shameless as ever. He declares in the first act that he expects to have free run of the treasury once Prince Hal gets into power, and he is eager to exact vengeance on anyone who has crossed him in the past, such as the Lord Justice.

The lawlessness and excess that Falstaff threatens is a prominent topic of the play. It harkens back to the threats that Richard II posed to the kingdom when he unwisely elevated his favorites to positions of power. Now we see that Falstaff, who indulges in all manner of vices, expects to gain this same power once Hal ascends the throne.

The play establishes the arc of Falstaff first. Hal himself doesn't even appear until act 2, scene 2, when we find him in Eastcheap and, it would seem, back to his old habits.

At court, meanwhile, the King frets over what will happen to the country once he dies. But one of his nobles, Warwick, suggests that Hal is putting his waywardness to good use:

> The Prince but studies his companions
> Like a strange tongue…
> The Prince will, in the perfectness of time
> Cast off his followers, and their memory
> Shall as a pattern or a measure live,
> By which his Grace must mete the lives of others,
> Turning past evils to advantages. (4.3)

In other words, Warwick clarifies to the king (and reminds the audience) that there is value in Hal's low associations. Hal can discover firsthand what all classes of people are like. This knowledge will serve him later as a ruler. And Warwick rightly predicts an outcome that Hal has already foretold: that he will redeem himself with advantage.

Challenges in *Henry IV, Part 2*

Hal is called into action against the rebels to support his father; this is one of his challenges. But his greatest challenge in *Part 2* involves preparing himself, mentally and emotionally, to take on the role of king.

He must first counter his father's worst suspicions about him—fears shared by many in the court. This comes to a peak in act 4. Hal thinks the King has died, so he takes the crown and puts it on his own head, imagining the future he now must face. We have been primed for this moment by the earlier scene of Henry IV's insomnia: the crown that made Henry IV uneasy is what Hal now prepares himself to wear.

But Hal's father is still alive. When Henry IV awakens, he is outraged by his son's presumption and accuses him of wanting him dead. Hal insists, "I never thought to hear you speak again," but the King accuses him: "Thy wish was father, Harry, to that thought" (4.3).

Henry IV is once again tormented by fears of the havoc his son will wreak once no one can restrain him:

> O my poor kingdom, sick with civil blows!
> When that my care could not withhold thy riots,
> What wilt thou do when riot is thy care?
> O, thou wilt be a wilderness again,
> Peopled with wolves, thy old inhabitants! (4.3)

But Hal is able to convince his father of his sincere intention to rule wisely; he even piously invokes "He that wears the crown immortally," asking the Lord to let his father keep his earthly crown: "Long guard it yours!"

Assuaged, the dying king gives his son some final, *realpolitik* advice. Once Hal becomes king, he should wage a foreign war in order to unite the populace and make them forget his past failings.

> Therefore, my Harry,
> Be it thy course to busy giddy minds
> With foreign quarrels, that action, hence borne out,
> May waste the memory of the former days. (4.3)

This recalls Hal's own plans, expressed in the previous play, on how to gain the people's favor. Both father and son are frankly calculating in how they manage the public-relations side of kingship.

Resolution in *Henry IV, Part 2*

Part 2 concludes with the King's death and Hal being crowned as King Henry V. To the surprise of nearly everyone except the audience, Henry V behaves just as he promised his father and disclosed to us.

To the Lord Justice, who had punished him earlier for misbehavior and who now fears his revenge, Henry V absolves him and tells him he shall keep his office.

Most significant of all, he rejects Falstaff: "I banish thee, on pain of death, / As I have done the rest of my misleaders, / Not to come near our person by ten mile" (5.5).

He adds that if his old companions reform, they may be advanced later. But this banishment crushes Falstaff. His grandiose expectations of power and wealth, on the promise of which he extracted large loans from others, not to mention his affection for the prince, have ended in cruel disappointment.

Falstaff ends the play defeated. But the new monarch has achieved a second milestone in his quest to become a great leader: he has affirmed that the law must be applied fairly to all, and he has decisively thrown off his old "misleaders." Chief among them is Falstaff. The old knight had explicitly had served Hal as a father-figure. In this resolution, Henry V passes through a necessary transition to maturity: he copes with the loss his real father, and rejects his other father figure, in his passage to taking on the sacred role as head of his country. Henry V must rule alone now.

Henry V

In the course of his journey so far, our protagonist has shown greatness on the battlefield in single combat, rejected his old and inappropriate companions, and applied the law fairly. But as this play opens, he has not yet been tested as a king. As monarch he must make hard decisions of life and death, and unite a country that has been torn by civil strife. He must also protect his country's interests on the world stage.

Central Problem in *Henry V*

In *Henry V* we see the final phase of Hal's arc, which began in *Part 1* and continued through *Part 2*. His goal from the start was to pay the debt of becoming a great king, and in this final installment, the protagonist faces difficult decisions in matters of war, diplomacy, and domestic threats.

Challenges in *Henry V*

We first see the King, in a quasi-Machiavellian move, seek grounds for the foreign war his father advised him to pursue. His advisers provide him with arcane legal justifications for why Henry can claim France as subject to England's rule. His decision is sealed when the Dauphin of France rebuffs his claims with an insulting gift of tennis balls, saying these more befit one who "savor[s] too much of your youth" (1.2). The young King takes up the challenge:

"When we have matched our rackets to these balls, / We will in France, by God's grace, play a set / Shall strike his father's crown into the hazard."

Henry notes he won't be doing this alone: it's through God's grace he will venture and win in this cause.

But before he embarks for France, he must deal with the treachery of three of his own nobles, including one he counted as a dear friend. Henry has discovered they were bribed by the French to assassinate him.

Henry lures these noblemen into saying how they would treat someone who threatened the King. Falling into the King's trap, they urge him to inflict the most severe punishment. Henry then confronts them with their own guilt and condemns them to execution in line with their own judgment. Henry, once again, is strictly just, even against a friend. In this particular challenge, he demonstrates he is capable of discerning and uprooting home-grown treachery.

Once Henry proceeds to the war, we see even more of his ruthless side. He threatens the town of Calais—even the innocent—with unspeakable horrors unless they surrender to him. And we can guess from the way Henry has kept his other promises that he would indeed make good on them. The town surrenders.

We are far from the roistering, madcap Prince of Wales. A king is responsible for his country's security. Shakespeare often adds a touch of humor or charm to Henry V along the way. But he also evokes the horrors of war and the harsh methods that Henry uses in waging this fight.

There are further victories, but the English forces will suffer great losses. Henry is in retreat when he is faced with a seemingly insurmountable challenge. The French are forcing a showdown in which the English troops will be outnumbered ten to one. This is the peak challenge of the protagonist's entire journey. The outcome will make or mar who he is as a king, with the future of his country at stake as well.

With a depleted and discouraged army, Henry must prepare them for the Battle of Agincourt. He shows personal humility and entreats God to be with them. And he spends the eve of the battle visiting the camp in disguise so he can learn the state of mind of his soldiers. Incognito, he disputes with low-ranking soldiers about the justice of the King's cause, but he doesn't pull rank on them later for their criticisms, nor punish them for it. This king can hear unvarnished criticism of his leadership and not react out of ego.

Then, just before the battle, Henry gives a rousing speech to his troops. He vows that their courage and valor this day will make them the equal of the King, and assures them that in the future, this anniversary will never go by

But we in it shall be remembered—
We few, we happy few, we band of brothers;
For he to-day that sheds his blood with me
Shall be my brother; be he ne'er so vile,
This day shall gentle his condition;
And gentlemen in England, now a-bed
Shall think themselves accursed they were not here;
And hold their manhoods cheap whiles any speaks
That fought with us upon Saint Crispin's day. (4.3)

The prince, who learned the language of the commoners in Eastcheap, now shows how effectively he can touch their hearts and pride now.

The battle of Agincourt, in which the English are hugely outnumbered, falls to them, a victory that Henry humbly credits to the Almighty: "Praised be God, and not our strength, for it!" (4.7).

Henry's final deft act is to cement the peace by negotiating for the hand of the French princess, and then winning her with his humorously blunt, plain-spoken wooing. The great King need not adopt pretentious French manners to be a King of England and France.

Resolution in *Henry V*

With Henry V's stunning achievement in battle, and his skillful and romantic act of marital diplomacy, Shakespeare brings the protagonist's journey to an end. The promise Hal gave early in *Part 1* is fulfilled. He shows the humility and strict adherence to justice that Richard II failed to show. He is even more adept than Henry IV at the popular touch for managing the people. And he is free from the taint that infected his father, which was the crime of stealing the crown. The ending of *Henry V* represents not only the resolution of Prince Hal's three-play arc, but a resolution to the entire four-play sequence, in which we have seen two extreme and troubled versions of monarchy give way to a near-perfect middle ground: the ideal monarch.

Analysis of Hal's Arc

How Shakespeare Planned the Journey

In his Henriad series, Shakespeare aims to show how, after civil strife during the reigns of Richard II and Henry IV, a leader might emerge and embody a king's full promise. This journey to fulfilling that promise is the arc that Shakespeare takes Hal/Henry V on.

To become a great king is extraordinarily difficult and rare. In planning out Hal's journey:

1. Shakespeare must have thought deeply about what constitutes a great king. Maybe he even compiles a list of the qualities one would find in an ideal king. He would also consider how this king would avoid the failings of his predecessors.

2. With these ideal attributes in mind, Shakespeare would have imagined the ways a character could develop or display them so the audience can see the hero's greatness unveil itself, and he identifies specific challenges to include across the plays.

3. Then Shakespeare works backwards, to decide on the best starting point for the journey. For maximum effect, he gives Hal an unpromising beginning—showing him as a carouser among bad company—so that the goal seems almost impossible to accomplish.

4. It would take many scenes in which to show the making of a great king, while also telling the rest of the period's relevant history, so Shakespeare spreads out the story across multiple plays. Because the plays are performed individually, and premiere over the course of several years, each installment must stand on its own as well.

5. This means he needs to show challenges and the achievement of milestones in each of the plays while periodically reminding the audience of Hal's overarching goal and what is at stake.

One reason we hear Henry IV express in *Part 2* how heavily the crown weighs on him, and his fears about what will happen once his son takes the throne, is to remind us what is at stake in Hal's journey. We see what awaits the new King and what would happen if he fails.

There are many other considerations Shakespeare had in structuring Hal's journey. He needed to intertwine the stories of other characters, including Henry IV and Falstaff and as Hal's antithetical father and father-figure. Shakespeare also needed to depict at least the decisive moments of this period of English civil strife. There are whole acts in the final three plays of the Henriad in which Hal does not appear.

But Shakespeare keeps a steady eye on where he wants to take his protagonist, and reminds his audiences from time to time where this character is heading, what this goal is costing him, what is at stake if he fails, and what will be gained if he succeeds.

Structuring the Journey: How Hal's Challenges Lead to Attaining His Goal

The three plays in which this protagonist appears show him facing a series of tests and successfully meeting them. Together they demonstrate from many angles a brilliant, inspiring, if sometimes ruthless, head of state.

It's apparent that Shakespeare plotted out Hal's arc carefully. The challenges are selected to show key aspects of a leader. There is little time spent exploring his personal desires. This character is virtually subsumed in his goal.

The journey to becoming a great king, which requires so many facets of expertise, must be a particularly steep path. Hence, Shakespeare give him challenges in a wide range of domains in which a king must show proficiency; in addition, they show him surmounting his past behavior and the skepticism others have about his fitness.

We can isolate these tests in a list to highlight how Shakespeare has Hal demonstrate himself as capable of being a great king. Hal/Henry V overcomes a sequence of challenges and temptations, through which he demonstrates mastery of these facets of kingship:

1. Although he did not seek out the role of king, he accepts it as his duty, and he prepares himself for the challenges ahead; we see he anticipates this from early on, and continues it in the scene in which he tries on his father's crown.
2. He can sacrifice personal pleasures and relationships. Falstaff is a father figure but above all represents a world of fun and indulgence; Falstaff and his world show what Hal is able to relinquish.
3. He respects and enforces the law fairly, even if that means disappointing his friends. He can even show restraint and fairness toward the Lord Justice, who had earlier punished him.
4. In his interactions with others, he is frank and likeable, with an easy manner, which engenders trust and goodwill from his people. (Never mind if he behaves this way out of expediency.)
5. To increase his understanding of others, he seeks out and learns from them directly. We see this of him in Eastcheap and again before the Battle of Agincourt when he moves incognito among his troops.
6. He can withstand others' criticism of him and not be swayed from his course.

7. Despite others' low opinion of him, he is confident and bold: he promises to his father he will defeat the great Hotspur, and fulfills that promise.

8. He proves himself in one-on-one combat with Hotspur and shows respect for his adversary in victory.

9. He is ruthless, even Machiavellian, in conducting the business of state (in contrast with Richard II, who was prone to wishful thinking); he plans the French war on fairly specious grounds, but in this he is doing as his father cannily advised: to cement the peace at home by waging foreign quarrels.

10. He is discriminating about others, including seeing through others' machinations. He is a good judge of character and of what motivates others.

11. He does not let personal bonds or preferences cloud his decision-making. He banishes his old Eastcheap friends without flinching. When he discovers the nobles' plot to assassinate him, he executes them without remorse; by contrast, he is merciful to the soldiers who criticized him before the battle.

12. Whether he is speaking with the common folk or his nobles, he can communicate winningly and speaks their language. On the battlefield, he can inspire confidence in others who may be losing heart. He announces to the French herald that he will not allow himself to be ransomed if he should be taken in battle, and he vividly depicts the glory his loyal soldiers will attain by winning at Agincourt.

13. Showing commonsense instead of fear or rashness, he tries to avoid the Battle of Agincourt, because the odds are not in his favor, but faces it bravely when it becomes unavoidable. He remains steady under pressure.

14. He shows piety—he calls on God for help before battle and publicly gives God credit for victories.

15. He makes helpful alliances and is able to show attractive traits to Catherine; in the wooing scene, he shows himself as affectionate, but not excessive. He marries to propagate an heir, which is a major responsibility of a king.

These are a lot of attributes that Shakespeare has painted for his protagonist. It's hard to imagine anything more a country could want in a king.

The cycle's conclusion comes shortly after the peak moment of Henry V's reign, with the remarkable victory at Agincourt and his marriage alliance with the Princess of France. We will learn in the post script that the French victory was short-lived, and the son would lose the territories. But this doesn't diminish what Henry V was as a ruler.

How Much Did Shakespeare's Protagonist Resemble the Real Henry V?

Was the historical King Henry V like this? Not necessarily. Shakespeare reflects many of the details he found in the English history books about Henry's reign. The Battle of Agincourt was indeed a surprise victory against tremendous odds, not something Shakespeare made up. And as the Prince of Wales, he was said to have been a carouser. But Shakespeare invented events and made other changes as well. The characters of Falstaff and Hotspur are significantly altered from their historical counterparts, changes which underscore Shakespeare's intentions.

The real Henry V was viewed in Shakespeare's era as a great king who brought pride to the nation by winning lands in France. After combing through the annals of English history, with its centuries of troubled reigns, Shakespeare must have gladly seized on Henry V as a rare example of a successful leader.

In constructing Hal's journey, Shakespeare imposes a heroic intentionality to this character's actions. He emphasizes the protagonist's dutiful acceptance of his destiny and his savvy calculations that he could appear more impressive if staged a sudden reformation of his past ways. We cannot say if the real Henry V had any such thoughts, but they help Shakespeare make sense of this otherwise inscrutable and ambivalent figure.

If there is one gap in this very full protagonist journey, it would be in the character's personal realm. We see how proficient Hal/Henry V is in touching the hearts and minds of others. But his own mind and heart seem mostly a blank to us. He is almost self-contained beyond what seems humanly possible.

Instead, it would appear that Shakespeare displaces the emotional center of this story on to Falstaff and his circle.

Role of Falstaff in Hal's Journey

Falstaff not only brings abundant hilarity to this otherwise serious depiction of English history, but he plays an integral role in Hal's journey. It's worth exploring how Shakespeare uses Falstaff to reflect on Hal's character and illustrate what Hal must give up.

Falstaff became a crowd favorite even in Shakespeare's day. He is a major character in *Part 1* and a protagonist in his own right in *Part 2*. He only appears by report in the final play, *Henry V*, when we learn he has died.

In *Parts 1* and *2*, Falstaff is exuberance incarnate. He indulges in all manner of excess: in eating, drinking, boasting, whoring. He lies and steals; he borrows with no intention of paying it back. Everything becomes a laughing matter in his presence. As Falstaff exclaims, "I am not only witty in myself, but the cause that wit is in other men" (1.2). He inspires others to joke about him, for which he takes credit.

While Hal's father, Henry IV, loses sleep over affairs of state, this other father-figure holds court uproariously into the night as the Lord of Misrule.

Some actors playing the part of Hal have, understandably, performed his rejection of Falstaff at the end of *Part 2* as causing the young man pain. There are, after all, moments in the series where Hal shows the old knight genuine affection. When Falstaff tries to take credit for the killing of Hotspur, Hal graciously goes along with it: "For my part, if a lie may do thee grace, / I'll gild it with the happiest terms I have" (1H4 5.4).

But a strict reading does not show Hal as sentimental about his friends, Falstaff included. He announces to the audience early in *Part 1* that he will reject all of them. When Falstaff jokingly warns Hal, "Banish plump Jack, and banish all the world," Hal avows, "I do, I will."

When Hal (now Henry V) fulfills this promise and repudiates Falstaff and his cronies, it nevertheless comes like a thunderbolt—both to Falstaff and to the audience. It is painful to see this larger-than-life old man deflated so thoroughly and with so little apparent sympathy from his old companion.

But as Shakespeare devised it, this popular comic figure is himself a function of Hal's journey. Falstaff encapsulates what a responsible king *must do without*. No matter how tempting, a king must not give way to indulgence, which has been the downfall of many a leader. Shakespeare uses Falstaff to show what Hal, too, could be indulging in, but voluntarily gives up. To make Hal's restraint all the more impressive, he makes Falstaff and his realm all the more enticing and hilarious.

Hal does not give up his friendly bonds or humor altogether. But he renounces hedonism and virtually everything that comes solely from *personal* desire. A good king lives for his country, not for himself.

This self-abnegation is not for everyone. Nor should it be. Shakespeare emphasizes the endearing camaraderie of the common people—of the Eastcheap denizens and of the English soldiers in France. They have their vices, they may even cheat each other, but all can be forgiven. When they die, they are deeply mourned by their friends. But it's a network of simple, deep, and domestic attachments that Henry, as king, must exclude himself from.

Falstaff will die, but his death is only described, not shown. That report, early in the final play, lets the audience know not to expect any further appearance of this most popular of characters. But the bittersweet way his death is announced is also telling. The old man, we are told, was broken in spirit after Hal rejected him and crushed his hopes. Mistress Quickly describes Falstaff's final moments: his feet were cold as ice, he babbled of green fields, and he fumbled with the edge of his blanket. He dies in pathetic circumstances, but his friends are surrounding him, and even those he provoked in the past affirm their love for him. It is extremely moving stuff. And Hal is not part of this loving circle. This scene depicts what ordinary people can experience and a world in which the king cannot partake.

Summary

The character of Hal, later Henry V, is exceptional among Shakespeare's protagonists. His journey is traced across three, self-contained but related works. Uniting all of these plays is the protagonist's central goal of becoming a great king. Everything he does—even the time he spends slumming in Eastcheap—serves this aim.

His inner nature, his personal preferences or desires, are of far less concern than we find in Shakespeare's other protagonists. Instead, Shakespeare focuses on his endpoint and the path by which this protagonist will get there.

All of the plays in the Henriad series deal with kingship and how the leader at the top affects the health of the country. Shakespeare starts with two monarchs, Richard II and Henry IV, of varying strengths and weaknesses, before presenting us with Henry V, who unites in himself virtually all the traits of an effective monarch.

Shakespeare begins and ends the journey for maximum drama. Hal begins unpromisingly, carousing with dubious characters; he concludes just after his greatest military triumph and a marriage that will unite two countries and produce an heir to the throne.

Hal's arc is typical for a Shakespearean protagonist in that he has a particular problem that compels to move in a certain direction, and which will require sacrifice from him. Unusually, though, Hal is a conscious planner of his own destiny. To show the stellar and convincing rise of this great leader, Shakespeare must give him sufficiently steep tests along the way. These tests, and his success with them, trace out the attributes of a great leader. They are what gives Hal's arc its particular form and demonstrate step by step how Hal transforms into a model king.

Takeaway for Writers

We outlined in the previous chapter the basic principles of a protagonist arc. Shakespeare follows these when constructing the **journey of his protagonist, Hal/Henry V,** across a three-play sequence:

- **A journey needs a destination:** Hal's goal is to "pay the debt I never promised" — to become a great king for his country; Hal becomes the highly successful King Henry V. Hal is somewhat rare as a Shakespearean protagonist in knowing clearly from the start what his aim is and consciously plotting his journey.
- **Challenges should propel the protagonist toward that goal.** Hal/Henry faces a series of challenges related to the traits a king must be proficient at, including personal restraint and humility (or, at least, piety); upholding of justice; adeptness in communicating with all levels of society; heroism in one-to-one combat; and serving as a brave and inspiring leader in battle.
- **Challenges need to be of sufficient difficulty and appropriate to reach the goal.** At the beginning, everyone takes Hal to be a roustabout, and at first, he seems highly unlikely to become a great king. But he meets and overcomes the challenges he faces, many of which involve personal sacrifice, and all of them formative of a king who will be a good and fair leader.
- **The journey concludes when the protagonist's problem is resolved.** Hal's problem is resolved after the final and most impressive of his challenges are met. He has demonstrated all the key attributes of an effective monarch, including marrying in order to propagate and an heir. There is a postscript that gives further context to the Henriad series, noting that in time, this King's son, Henry VI, would go on to lose the lands that were gained in France.

To become a great king is extraordinarily difficult and rare. In planning out Hal's journey, Shakespeare would have:

- Thought deeply about what constitutes a great king, perhaps he even compiles a list of the qualities one would find in an ideal king. He would also consider how this king would avoid the failings of his predecessors.

- Imagined the ways a character could develop or display them so the audience can see the hero's greatness unveil itself, and identifies specific challenges to include across the plays.
- Worked backwards to decide on the best starting point for the journey; for maximum effect, he gives Hal an unpromising beginning—showing him as a carouser among bad company—so that the goal seems almost impossible to accomplish.
- Spread out the story across multiple plays, because of the many facets he needs to show about the making of a great king,
- Shown the achievement of milestones in each of the plays, while periodically reminding the audience of Hal's overarching goal and what is at stake.

Extras

In *Henry V*, **the protagonist gives two rousing speeches** at critical moments of his war in France. They are among the most quoted speeches by Shakespeare in general, and in particular, are often invoked for patriotic ends.

Each an appeal to those fighting with him to redouble their efforts in battle or steel their courage for the upcoming fight. Shakespeare shows a critical skill of a great leader: how to reach the hearts of his people and rally them to a common cause, even at the cost of their own lives. He does this by showing personal courage and humility, and by appealing to the appropriateness of the cause, their manliness, the example of their forebears, the shame their mothers and fathers would feel if they fail, their pride in being English, and the divine support they have. He also implies a reward: the eternal glory they will earn, and the status of being an equal of the king: "For he today that sheds his blood with me / Shall be my brother; be he ne'er so vile, / This day shall gentle his condition..." (4.3).

The battle, and these speeches, encapsulate the penultimate, and most difficult, challenge Hal faces on his journey to achieving his goal of becoming a great king. He is facing tremendous odds, yet leads his forces with unshakable poise. (The final challenge is to achieve the peace through a marriage alliance with France, a relatively easy yet one for him, but perhaps no less gratifying for the audience.)

1. Henry V delivers this speech, which begins famously with "Once more unto the breach," during the battle for Harfleur.

Once more unto the breach, dear friends, once more;
Or close the wall up with our English dead.
In peace there's nothing so becomes a man
As modest stillness and humility;
But when the blast of war blows in our ears,
Then imitate the action of the tiger;
Stiffen the sinews, [conjure] up the blood,
Disguise fair nature with hard-favor'd rage;
Then lend the eye a terrible aspect;
Let it pry through the portage of the head
Like the brass cannon; let the brow o'erwhelm it
As fearfully as doth a galled rock
O'erhang and jutty his confounded base,
Swilled with the wild and wasteful ocean.
Now set the teeth and stretch the nostril wide,
Hold hard the breath, and bend up every spirit
To his full height. On, on, you [noblest] English,
Whose blood is fet from fathers of war-proof!
Fathers that, like so many Alexanders,
Have in these parts from morn till even fought,
And sheathed their swords for lack of argument.
Dishonor not your mothers; now attest
That those whom you called fathers did beget you.
Be copy now to [men] of grosser blood,
And teach them how to war. And you, good yeomen,
Whose limbs were made in England, show us here
The mettle of your pasture; let us swear
That you are worth your breeding, which I doubt not;
For there is none of you so mean and base
That hath not noble lustre in your eyes.
I see you stand like greyhounds in the slips,
[Straining] upon the start. The game's afoot!
Follow your spirit; and upon this charge
Cry, "God for Harry, England, and Saint George!" (3.1)

2. The speech, often called the St. Crispin's Day speech, is given by Henry V before the Battle of Agincourt, where his troops are vastly outnumbered.

WESTMORELAND   O, that we now had here
But one ten thousand of those men in England
That do no work to-day.
KING HENRY   What's he that wishes so?
My cousin Westmoreland? No, my fair cousin.
If we are marked to die, we are enough
To do our country loss; and if to live,
The fewer men, the greater share of honor.
God's will, I pray thee wish not one man more.
By Jove, I am not covetous for gold,
Nor care I who doth feed upon my cost;
It yearns me not if men my garments wear;
Such outward things dwell not in my desires.
But if it be a sin to covet honor,
I am the most offending soul alive.
No, faith, my coz, wish not a man from England.
God's peace, I would not lose so great an honor
As one man more methinks would share from me,
For the best hope I have. O, do not wish one more!
Rather proclaim it, Westmoreland, through my host,
That he which hath no stomach to this fight,
Let him depart, his passport shall be made,
And crowns for convoy put into his purse.
We would not die in that man's company
That fears his fellowship to die with us.
This day is called the feast of Crispian.
He that outlives this day, and comes safe home,
Will stand a' tiptoe when this day is named,
And rouse him at the name of Crispian.
He that shall see this day, and live old age,
Will yearly on the vigil feast his neighbors,
And say "To-morrow is Saint Crispian."
Then will he strip his sleeve and show his scars,
And say, "These wounds I had on Crispin's day."
Old men forget; yet all shall be forgot,
But he'll remember with advantages

135

What feats he did that day. Then shall our names,
Familiar in his mouth as household words,
Harry the King, Bedford and Exeter,
Warwick and Talbot, Salisbury and Gloucester,
Be in their flowing cups freshly remembered.
This story shall the good man teach his son,
And Crispin Crispian shall ne'er go by,
From this day to the ending of the world,
But we in it shall be remembered—
We few, we happy few, we band of brothers;
For he today that sheds his blood with me
Shall be my brother; be he ne'er so vile,
This day shall gentle his condition;
And gentlemen in England, now a-bed,
Shall think themselves accursed they were not here;
And hold their manhoods cheap whiles any speaks
That fought with us upon Saint Crispin's day. (4.3)

CHAPTER 7: PLOT STRUCTURE

A s an actor, Shakespeare would have felt the effects of good or bad plotting viscerally. Playing in front of an audience, he'd sense when their attention wandered or sharpened. He'd learn the value of hooking them early with a mystery or dilemma, and would sense when the audience was getting confused and needed more exposition. He'd discover that a plot needs to build the tension to keep them interested—but also, that it should have occasional respites, since constant excitement gets tedious. And he'd realize that an ending should come as a surprise, yet be prepared for, or the audience would feel cheated.

His audiences were his critics; from them and from studying his peers he learned how to shape an effective plot.

What Is a Plot?

A plot is not exactly the same as "the story." Plot refers to the way a story is structured. More precisely, it is the sequence of elements in a story and the relationship of these elements to each other. For example, is the story ordered chronologically? Or in flashback, or in some other kind of sequence?

A plot will raise a conflict, mystery, desire—let's call it the dramatic problem—and it will usually resolve that problem by the end. A plot will have a similar structure to the protagonist's arc, but be somewhat broader, providing a wider perspective on a story.

There are many common elements we find across skillful plots, but also variations that serve different purposes. Plot is the architectural plan of a narrative, and not every blueprint works for every story.

Plot: The Basic Concepts from Aristotle

Shakespeare's approach to plot was almost certainly practical—he did what worked, and he got feedback on what didn't work. But to see how he constructs plots, it helps to establish some basic terminology and concepts. For this we can do no better than go back 2400 years ago to Aristotle. His succinct explanations in *The Poetics* have been elaborated on over the centuries, but never bettered. *The Poetics* established much of how we still describe and analyze writing. Although the work focuses in particular on tragedy and performance, his concepts have wide application to other kinds of writing.

The "Complete" and "Whole" Action

Plot, says Aristotle, is "the arrangement of the incidents." He contends it is the most important part of tragedy, even more so than the protagonist or any of the other building blocks: "the incidents and the plot are the end [purpose] of a tragedy; and the end is the chief thing of all" (*The Poetics*, Part VI). We might infer he would say the same of comic works as well, but his treatise on comedy has unfortunately been lost.

So, how does a writer arrange these incidents in the best way? The first principle is knowing what to include and what to exclude. Aristotle speaks of a literary work as if it were a living organism. It must be unified—that is, "complete" and "whole," and not having missing, extraneous, or misplaced parts. Its plot should focus on one main action.

> Unity of plot does not, as some persons think, consist in the unity of the hero.... [T]he plot, being an imitation of an action, must imitate one action and that a whole, the structural union of the parts being such that, if any one of them is displaced or removed, the whole will be disjointed and disturbed. For a thing whose presence or absence makes no visible difference, is not an organic part of the whole. (Part VIII)

Creating an organic whole might sound like a tall order, but Aristotle's concept here is not that complicated. One way is to consider the whole action as equivalent to a problem and its resolution, or a goal and its achievement. In this view, plot is a series of incidents that begin with a particular problem (a mystery to solve, a duty to fulfill, a desire, an aim, etc.), and ends with that problem's resolution, much like the protagonist's arc. To decide where to begin and end the action, and to keep the structure unified, one provides only enough background information so that the audience understands what the problem is, and then ends the action when the problem has been resolved. No more, no less.

Any unnecessary incidents or information, such as redundant character background, is excluded because, in Aristotle's view, these aren't part of the organic whole. For instance, the audience doesn't need to see the protagonist progressing from childhood to adulthood, but only enough of their past in order to follow the upcoming action. This background information is commonly known as "exposition."

Rising and Falling Action (Tying and Untying)

In Aristotle's system, the whole and complete action in a tragedy falls in two parts: first is the rising action (also known as complication), and next, the falling action (or denouement). The actual terms Aristotle uses are *desis* and *lusis* ("tying" and "untying"). The complications of the first portion of a plot are like the tying of a knot; this phase ends with the turning point; after this, there is the untying phase, or falling action. The whole action consists of what we can visualize as a loop or arc, in which an action rises, turns, and falls.

More Useful Concepts on Plot

Later writers have refined or extrapolated on Aristotle's ideas. To expand our list of useful plot concepts, we'll review a few of those here.

In Medias Res

The Roman poet Horace offers more specificity than Aristotle about where to begin the plot. It should begin, Horace says, *in medias res* — in the midst of things. That is, begin at a point at which the whole action, the event to be treated, is already underway. Any necessary backstory, or exposition, can be provided soon after.

Pyramid Structure

Also influential is the nineteenth-century writer Gustav Freytag's conceptualization of plot. He proposed a pyramid shape to depict plot structure, and said it was composed of these parts: (a) introduction, (b) escalation, (c) climax, (d) fall or reversal, (e) catastrophe (The original terms in German are (a) Einleitung, (b) Steigerung, (c) Höhenpunkt, (d) Fall oder Umkehr, and (e) Katastrophe (Freytag 102).

Illustration from Freytag, *Die Technik des Dramas* (102)

(Note: The term *Höhenpunkt*, referring to the turning point between rising and falling action, has been usually translated in English as climax. This lends itself to some confusion, however, since the term "climax" is also used to mean the peak of emotional involvement by the audience at or near the story's end. To avoid this confusion, I will generally avoid this term and refer to this middle point, in which the rising action turns to falling action, as the "turning point.")

The term "catastrophe" simply means the final action that completes the denouement, and is often used to refer to the final events of a tragedy. The ending in tragedy is indeed often "catastrophic," in the sense that the hero dies or other terrible results comes to pass. But an equivalent term for a plot's ending would be "resolution," which works for all genres, whether its end is tragic or comic.

Inciting Incident

More recent writers refer to "inciting incident" or "inciting event" for a point early on that "incites" the protagonist's involvement in a course of action. It often coincides with the emergence of the protagonist's central problem or goal.

Hook

And still others describe the "hook" that gets us first intrigued by the story. A hook is not integral to the plot, but is an effective way of bringing an audience to attention. A hook may provide exposition, but not necessarily.

Typical Plot Structure

In sum, the key elements in a typical plot structure may be depicted in this pyramidal shape.

Common Elements of Plot Structure:

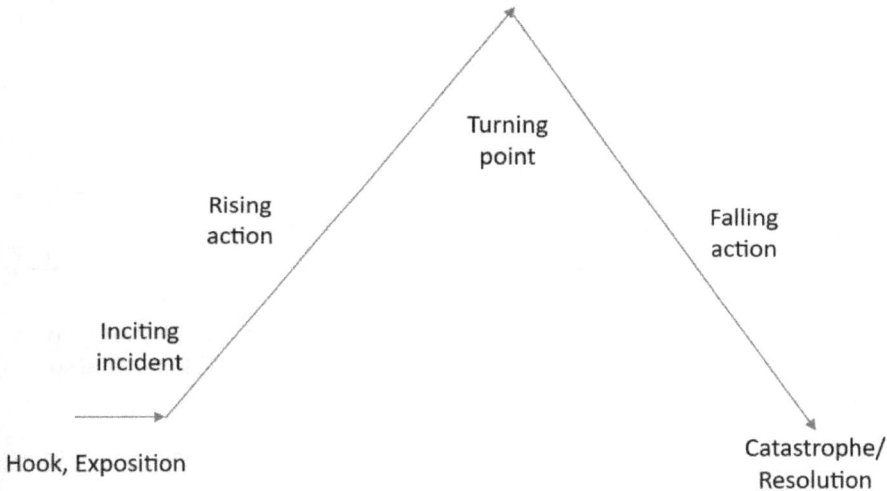

Value and Limitations of the Pyramid Structure in Depicting Plot

No matter what the genre he is writing in, Shakespeare's plots typically resembles this pyramid structure. And it's no surprise. This pattern is pretty universal.

This peak-shaped diagram can be a bit misleading, however. The falling action doesn't mean the tension is lessening. Things typically get even more tense as the plot enters this untying stage. But significant new information or entanglements (the complications) are no longer needed. The action from this point on is a working out of the complications that have already emerged.

That's why the last part of a plot will ideally feel faster and seem to cascade from previous events. We have all the kinetic energy we need. We have the justifications for why the characters do what they do, for example, and all that remains is to see how events play out from there. You will rarely see important new characters pop up in the latter half of Shakespeare's plays: if they are

141

important to the plot, they will usually be introduced in the rising section; Shakespeare will be speeding to resolution in the latter half, and doesn't want to slow things down with significant new material. (There are exceptions, though, which we will get to.)

The pyramid structure reflects these concepts fairly well. But in terms of *emotional* tension, this single-peaked shape may not be the best representation of how a particular play operates. The peaks of emotion may come in many different spots along the plot structure.

The Primacy of Plot over Protagonist

Aristotle insists that a work can be effective even with a mediocre protagonist as long as the plot is well constructed. So, although a protagonist is important (he ranks it second), it is less so than the arrangement of the action.

Is this true that a plot is more important than its protagonist? It might sound counterintuitive to modern readers. After all, isn't it Hamlet the character who interests us, and not so much the revenge story in which he takes part? But as we will see, *Hamlet* is exceptionally well plotted. Its plot is what enables us to be so fascinated by this character.

The Plot's Whole Action and Its Elements: *Julius Caesar*

So, let's see how these concepts play out so far in Shakespeare by analyzing *Julius Caesar* to identify its whole action and other key plot elements.

Where Shakespeare Begins: Shakespeare could have chosen almost any part of Julius Caesar's long and illustrious career and dramatized it, but he selects just a narrow band of his life—the very end of it. The play begins with the leader's ceremonial entrance to Rome. Tradesmen have left their work ""to see Caesar and to rejoice in his triumph," while two Tribunes deplore his growing popularity, fearing that Caesar might "soar above the view of men / And keep us all in servile fearfulness" (1.1).

Dramatic problem: Shakespeare establishes a dramatic problem early: If Julius Caesar seizes power, or if he is stopped, what will happen to Rome? We see this problem suggested in the opening scene and laid out by the conspirators, including the admirable Brutus. They rightly fear Caesar aims for total power and would destroy the Roman Republic. Brutus concludes they should assassinate Caesar now, before he gets too powerful and turns Rome into his dictatorship.

The overall plot, however, expands on this perspective. The conspirators think killing him will solve their dilemma. Their concern is to preserve the Republic. But we know that this is not to be. Brutus and his conspirators will fail in their goal. The plot explores the broader view of how Caesar's ambitions and downfall impacts Rome, at the time of his assassination and afterwards. Namely, the dramatic problem is: what will happen to Rome if Caesar lives, or dies?

Rising Action: Shakespeare develops this problem in the rising action, as Brutus and other less principled conspirators argue whether they should assassinate him and as Julius Caesar and his allies position themselves to help Caesar seize control.

Turning Point: The play's turning point occurs when the conspirators stab Caesar at the Capitol. This unleashes the mob's response as well as a backlash by Caesar's allies, including Mark Antony.

Falling action: The falling action is the chaos that ensues. Because of the assassination, the anti- and pro-Caesar forces battle each other; the fickle mob is incited first on the side of the conspirators, then against them.

Resolution: The endpoint of the whole action comes after the conspirators are defeated. Brutus gets an answer to his question, can we save the Republic by destroying Caesar? That answer is no. The plotters lose their battle against Caesar's allies and end up killing themselves. The plot finds a resolution of greater scope: Rome's Republic is now obliterated as Caesar's allies seize power. What the conspirators hoped to prevent they only accelerated and brought greater bloodshed to Rome in its wake. In its place, we see the rise of the next phase of Roman politics, with Mark Antony and other pro-Caesar allies taking control and ushering in the triumvirate, a three-man dictatorship.

Difference between Plot and Protagonist in Structuring Julius Caesar

It is easier to see in *Julius Caesar* than in almost any other Shakespeare play the difference between plot and protagonist in structuring a work.

Although he is not the title character, it is Brutus who functions as the protagonist. It is his journey we trace throughout the play—his central problem, or goal, is to prevent Rome from falling to a tyrant. He reasons that once Caesar is given greater powers, there will be no stopping him: "therefore think him as a serpent's egg, / Which, hatched, would, as his kind, grow mischievous, / And kill him in the shell" (2.1).

Brutus appears early (1.2), and dies near the end. He is a pivotal figure in the plot's turning point, the one whom Caesar singles out, saying, "Et tu, Brute?"

Brutus stands up for what he has done: "People and Senators, be not affrighted. / Fly not; stand still. Ambition's debt is paid" (3.1).

As the protagonist, Brutus is sympathetic and noble, a well-meaning patriot who agonizes over assassinating his friend and who pays dearly for his principles. Yet his fate forms just part of a greater question.

Even more compelling than Brutus is the larger picture. We are witnessing a unique and fascinating moment in world history. The *plot* examines this pivotal moment that Julius Caesar brought into being. It sets out how and why the great leader was assassinated. It depicts how the mob could be so easily seduced first by the pro-Republican conspirators, and then by charismatic rabble-rousers such as Mark Antony. It explores how the Roman Republic could falter, thereby setting the stage for the next bloody period of Roman history. These elements go beyond Brutus' own perspective, although he provides an integral central view on the events.

This is why Julius Caesar is the title character, even though he dies midway through the play. The *plot* is about him writ large—not just his personal fate but his effect on Rome. So powerful is Julius Caesar—as a threat to the Republic, as a potential tyrant, as a great figure around whom Mark Antony and so many others rally—that the plot is a working out of the problem he poses the great city of Rome. His assassination midway through the play doesn't put his threat to rest, but on the contrary unleashes a counter attack that puts an end to the Republic. This is the "whole action" with which the plot concerns itself.

Shakespeare uses Brutus as the protagonist so that we can have a primary perspective through which to see this historical event unfold. But the *plot* is greater than Brutus' concerns. It is about the political reality created by Julius Caesar, which is why this character gets top billing.

Plot Structure: *Hamlet*

In *Julius Caesar,* Shakespeare designs a plot about a famous event involving many historical characters and uses a relatively minor protagonist to take us through the plot. Within a couple years of completing that play, Shakespeare takes on a different kind of challenge: creating a protagonist who very much dominates his play. There is no question who is the protagonist of this story.

Hamlet is a long play—over four hours of running time if all the existing versions of the text are synthesized (though this is rarely done). And so much of the play consists of Hamlet himself, who has by far the greatest number of lines of

144

any character in Shakespeare. In addition to his dialogue with others, Hamlet spends a lot of time reflecting in soliloquy on his dilemmas.

So, how does this protagonist-centric plot work? Very much like a typical plot, in fact.

Let's lay out the bare-bones structure of the plot and then analyze it more closely.

- **Beginning point**: The play begins *in medias res*. It starts shortly after some major events in this story have occurred: Claudius has already killed his brother, taken the throne, and married his widow.
- **Hook**: The ghost of the late King appears to be haunting Elsinore. The atmosphere is uneasy and oppressive; something is rotten in the state.
- **Exposition**: We meet the main characters and learn of recent past events and current tensions.
- **Inciting incident**: The Ghost tells Hamlet to avenge his murder; Hamlet accepts, having already had suspected Claudius: "O my prophetic soul!" he cries.
- Rising action:
  - o Polonius meddles by using Ophelia to try to expose what is troubling Hamlet.
  - o Claudius spies on Hamlet through Hamlet's friends.
  - o Hamlet fears the Ghost might be a spirit attempting to entrap his soul.
  - o Hamlet is frustrated he can't bring himself to take revenge on Claudius.
  - o The arrival of the acting troupe gives Hamlet an idea of how to prove Claudius' guilt.
- **Turning Point**: The Mousetrap performance, in which Claudius betrays guilt, and soon after, the Closet scene, in which Hamlet kills Polonius.
- Falling action:
  - o Claudius sends Hamlet to England with a secret order to have him killed.
  - o Hamlet discovers the plot and escapes.
  - o Ophelia loses her already tenuous hold on sanity and drowns.
  - o Laertes seeks vengeance for his father's and sister's deaths.
- **Catastrophe/Resolution**: Hamlet finds peace within himself regarding his internal struggles; and in the final scene, after realizing he's been poisoned,

he kills Claudius. Hamlet himself then dies; another prince, Fortinbras, enters and is poised to take the throne.

Now let's unpack each of these plot elements to see what Shakespeare is doing with them.

Beginning Point

If you wanted to construct a plot about a son who is called on to avenge his father's murder, at what point in the story would you begin?

1. Would you show the father and son pre-murder, having some interactions in order to establish their bond, and then depict the murder, followed by the son's reaction?
2. Or would you start after the father's death, and let this backstory come out during the early scenes?

Either one could work. But the second, of course, is what Shakespeare chooses. He begins his story about two months after the death of the king. Since his death, the late king's brother has taken his throne and married his widow—much to the chagrin of her son, Hamlet.

Why begin here? One reason is that it keeps the focus of the play on the protagonist Hamlet and his burdens, not on the murdered king and his sufferings. We have little attachment to this king, and have not seen him alive. Perhaps this helps keep more open the question of whether the Ghost is a damned spirit sent by hell to entrap Hamlet, as Hamet later fears. But above all, it's not necessary to see Hamlet's father before his death, because the relevant information can be conveyed through exposition.

Hook

Even before we meet Hamlet or other major characters, we are given a hook. The play opens on a scene of confusion and fear.

The first very lines are tense: Bernardo asks, "Who's there?" and Francisco responds, "Nay, answer me. Stand and unfold yourself." It is nighttime, and these guards on the battlements are not sure who is approaching.

They fear the reappearance of a Ghost they have seen on previous nights. This Ghost resembles the late king in his war-like armor. In their anxiety, they have persuaded Horatio, a visiting gentleman and friend to the prince, to witness the event as well. At the expected hour the Ghost again appears, and they entreat it to say what it wants. They think he is about to speak, but then a cock crows to signal morning and the Ghost retreats. Says Horatio, "it started like a guilty thing / Upon a fearful summons." They fear the Ghost's appearance portends no good. "Something's rotten in the state of Denmark," concludes one guard.

This opening scene hooks us with the mystery: why is a Ghost who resembles the old king haunting Elsinore? The scene also provides some exposition about relevant past events.

Exposition

After the mysterious scene on the battlements, we meet the main characters of the play and get a lot more exposition. We witness Hamlet's distress over the fact that his mother has so quickly remarried to someone he considers unworthy.

Shakespeare has started *in medias res*. In this scene we learn the king has been gone some two months, and that his uncle is already enjoying the privileges that come with the position, including the king's widow, now his wife. This marriage had come so soon after her husband's death that her morose son bitterly remarks, "the funeral meats did coldly furnish forth the wedding feast" (1.2).

With this and the next scene, we have most of the exposition we need. Shakespeare has established the main characters and the outlines of their relationships with each other.

Inciting Incident and Dramatic Problem

Horatio informs Hamlet what they have seen on the battlements, so the prince joins them that night. We come to the first major plot point. The Ghost tells Hamlet he was murdered by the man who now wears his crown, and Hamlet, who has already distrusted his uncle, exclaims, "O my prophetic soul!": he already guessed this crime. The Ghost then asks him to avenge his foul murder. We can identify this as the inciting incident because it's from this point on that Hamlet has a particular goal, which he will follow until the end.

We get a succinct summary of Hamlet's problem in his comment to Horatio near the end of the scene: "The time is out of joint; o cursed spite / That ever I was born to set it right" (1.5). But even if that line were cut in production, the rest of the early scenes have established the same idea. There is something seriously amiss in Denmark. Hamlet has been given the weighty duty to avenge a wrong and thereby set things right.

This dramatic problem is what Shakespeare is using to demarcate the "complete action," as Aristotle would call it. The plot will be complete when the dramatic problem is resolved—which it will be at the end.

Rising Action, or Complications (or "Tying")

Hamlet knows what he must do, but complications—around him and within him—arise. His friends Rosencrantz and Guildenstern arrive at court, and Hamlet soon perceives they are spying on him for Claudius. Ophelia is being used by her father Polonius and the King as a means of finding out what is troubling Hamlet. This, too, makes him deeply suspicious, so he takes steps to put them off the scent. When the traveling players arrive, he concocts a plan he hopes will prove Claudius' guilt beyond doubt.

During this rising action, which continues until the middle of act 3, Hamlet tries to overcome his hesitations, protect himself from the machinations of others, and—which may seem surprising—pause to reflect on life and on his own weakness. (These introspective moments *do*, in fact, serve a purpose in the plot, but we'll leave that aside for now.)

Events in this "tying" phase hinder Hamlet from fulfilling his solemn vow and delay him from setting the diseased state right again. He berates himself for his failure.

Turning Point

The rising section ends when there is a decisive turning point. Where would you say Shakespeare constructs this peak? Where does the wheel of the plot pass over the crest and start careening down the other side?

Most plausibly, it's in the middle of act 3 when the Players enact a scenario showing a murder much like the one Claudius committed. Hamlet calls this performance the Mousetrap, and his plan works because Claudius does indeed betray guilty reactions. Hamlet is now sure he's caught the conscience of the King. We are sure, too, since Claudius confesses the murder soon afterwards in a soliloquy when he tries to pray.

But because of this development, Claudius now realizes Hamlet knows the truth, and this puts Hamlet in greater danger. It's a turning point because there is no turning back now. Hamlet sets in motion a cascade of reactions that will lead to an ultimate showdown.

But the turning point arguably continues in the Closet scene, when Hamlet charges into his mother's chamber and, startled by a noise, rashly stabs through a curtain, accidentally killing Polonius. This action gives Claudius even more cause to eliminate the threat posed by Hamlet, and now he can enlist Polonius's son Laertes as an avenger.

Consider if these two particular sections of the plot—the Mousetrap and the Closet scenes—were cut. There are many scenes before this point that could be (and have been) cut from productions, yet the plot's action will remain more or less intact. Not so these central scenes. They are de rigueur because of how pivotal they are to the plot: they set up an inevitable confrontation between Hamlet and the man he has vowed to kill.

Falling Action

Claudius now knows Hamlet is dangerous to him. He had already planned to send Hamlet to England, but now includes a secret order to have him killed. Ophelia's mental state decays further after her father's death and, distraught, she falls into a brook and drowns. Laertes seeks vengeance for the murder of his father and his sister's consequent death.

Some of the intrigue is kept offstage. From letters Hamlet sends Horatio, we learn Hamlet has discovered Claudius' plan to have him killed, and also that a pirate attack has conveniently enabled Hamlet to get back to Denmark. (A pirate attack could have been highly entertaining to see onstage, but Shakespeare is in the untying stage right now and probably judged it too distracting.)

On Hamlet's return from England, he happens upon Ophelia's burial and gets in a scuffle with her brother Laertes over who loved her more. Later, Hamlet apologizes and agrees to a friendly fencing match with him. We then see Claudius and Laertes preparing for this match, in which Laertes will use a rapier tipped with poison, and Claudius will have a poisoned drink on hand to ensure Hamlet's death.

Notice how the elements during this section derive from the turning point. Because of the Mousetrap performance, Claudius plans to kill Hamlet. Hamlet becomes exhilarated and manic at this confirmation of Claudius' guilt, which makes him rashly strike through the curtain, which kills Polonius. Ophelia loses what's left of her wits after father's death at the hands of her former suitor and drowns. Both of these deaths bring Laertes into the picture to seek to kill Hamlet in revenge. These acts are untying—falling from—the earlier turning point. There are no new complications added—hence no pirates onstage.

In fact, during much of act 4, Hamlet is out of the picture. This is common among Shakespeare's protagonists—they are often left off stage for long stretches in act 4. This helps to build anticipation for their return and the resolution in the final act. (Plus, it gives the lead actor a rest. With his hundreds of lines in the play, Richard Burbage no doubt welcomed it).

The Catastrophe / Resolution

The final scenes of the play resolve the problem established at the beginning: Hamlet's duty was to avenge his father's murder and to set right a world that is out of balance.

His vengeance comes about suddenly and without premeditation on Hamlet's part. As he is taking part in a fencing match with Laertes, Hamlet is scratched by the poisoned rapier tip, which Hamlet then turns against Laertes. Queen Gertrude drinks the poisoned cup meant for Hamlet. Once both Hamlet and Laertes are dying, the latter admits Claudius arranged this attempt on his life and asks to exchange forgiveness. It is at this point that Hamlet turns to his uncle, stabs him, and forces him to drink from the poisoned goblet.

Why would this be a satisfying resolution to the play's problem? The time has been out of joint, and many people have been complicit. It's not so much that they deserve to die, but they all participated in a court tainted by murder and conspiracy. Laertes was as justified in wanting vengeance for his father's death as Hamlet was, but Laertes also stooped to unjust means in using a poisoned-tip rapier.

And then there's Hamlet. Why should he die? Although he had justifiable motives, he, too, has killed: one was an innocent, albeit meddling counselor, Polonius, and another, a more deserving one, Claudius; he caused Rosencrantz and Guildenstern to die as well, which Hamlet considered fair recompense for their betrayal ("they did make love to this employment; / They are not near my conscience"). So, Hamlet, too, has blood on his hands. Hamlet did not want to be put in this situation, but fate gave him no choice—he was enmeshed in this corrupt court. He had been born to set it right, but not to rule afterwards.

Even in this protagonist-dominated story, the plot is still a bit larger than Hamlet's story. With this final slaughter, a sickness has been purged from the Danish body politic. At the very end, we see the beginning of a new era as Fortinbras the Norwegian prince is poised to take the throne. Hamlet gives his "dying voice" to him. Denmark will not be left rudderless, but the old corrupt world will have been purged.

Through Hamlet's death, a new world can emerge, but the ending is tragic in the classic sense. Denmark may be in good hands now that Fortinbras is set to take power, but we know how much has been lost by Hamlet's death.

The Impeccable Nature of Hamlet's Plot

Hamlet is a very effective plot. It works like the best-engineered of watches. It'll work under any conditions. It could be adapted to nearly any time period or place, because the problem Shakespeare poses and the emotional situations he depicts are so universal. Consider how much propulsive energy is generated in just this stripped-down summary of the dramatic problem:

A son is deeply depressed. The father he loved and respected, who was also an excellent king, has died suddenly. His mother, who hung on his father's every word, quickly remarries with his uncle. This uncle takes the throne the son had hoped for. A ghost resembling the old king is reported haunting the castle. Then the son encounters his father's ghost and finds out it was murder. Worse yet, his father is suffering in the afterlife because he was cut down unprepared. *What can the son do to get justice?*

That is a lot of stress for one person to bear and a lot of energy to resolve. There is so much riding on him, including the health of his country. Shakespeare has set up in the opening scenes an amazing amount of tension. An audience is going to wonder, how could this possibly be made right?

Hamlet knows early on what he should do. But he can't set things right immediately because new complications come up. He is betrayed by people he trusted. He suffers from doubts—it may be an evil spirit trying to lead him to his damnation. It is natural that a child will want to see justice for their parent's murder, maybe even take revenge. But killing is difficult. Even so, he does not understand what is preventing him from killing Claudius.

And then there is the mysterious element introduced by the ghost and the world beyond. What can we really know about what happens after death? How can Hamlet be sure this ghost is who he says he is?

There is a good reason revenge stories and ghost stories are so universally compelling. They respond to some deep needs and fears in all of us. And *Hamlet* taps right into those universal feelings.

So, the plot of *Hamlet* is based on perennially fascinating themes and is impeccably structured. I would suggest to any writer as an exercise to copy this plot structure and major events, adapting them to another time period and set of characters; the result should be a solid script.

However, there's an important element we aren't accounting for yet. What about Hamlet's soliloquies?

These are among the most famous features of the play. When someone is quoting *Hamlet*, there's a good chance it's from a soliloquy. And there are many of them throughout the play (depending which text version you use, up to seven soliloquies). Since these are private, inward-focused explorations, they will slow down the action. Why would Shakespeare choose that and risk the momentum of his plot?

This is a crucial question to address if we hope to analyze how the plot of *Hamlet* works. As we will see, the soliloquies, together with Hamlet's other private musings with Horatio, form a plot-like structure of their own. They pursue and resolve a problem that runs in parallel with the action of the main plot. But we will defer this analysis to a later chapter.

Other Aristotelian Elements of Plot

To round out, for now, our list of terms concerning plot, the following concepts from Aristotle are useful in explaining how an effective plot works:

- *Peripeteia*, **or Reversal:** A moment in the plot when the protagonist has a reversal of fortune; when events turn suddenly to their opposite (from high to low, or low to high)

- *Anagnorisis*, **or Recognition or Discovery**: A scene of recognition of another's or one's own identity; this can be extended to include recognition of a significant truth about a situation that had been hidden; when a major discovery changes our understanding of the relationships or events we've been seeing.

- *Pathos*, **or Suffering:** A moment that bring to a peak the physical or psychological suffering of the protagonist; by extension, this suffering engenders in the audience a sympathetic response. The term "pathos" is commonly used as more precise than suffering.

Each of the three elements can, by itself, provide a powerful moment in a plot and in a protagonist's journey. In practice, reversal and recognition (and sometimes even pathos) can coincide at the same moment. These are often among the most effective elements in any story and can make a strong impression on readers or viewers. In fact, Aristotle often describes them in terms of their effect on the audience.

All three of these elements appear regularly in Shakespeare's tragedies, not surprisingly, but they also show up in his other genres, including comedy. Even in his happiest of comedies there may be moments of pathos.

Adapting His Plots: Much Ado About Nothing

Whether through instinct or his own analysis, Shakespeare identified the contours of what we now call the pyramid plot structure and made regular use of it. But he does not hem himself in by that structure alone.

Nor, for that matter, does he usually build his plots from scratch. He seeks out others' stories and adapts them. For some of these he retains their general plot structure, but often he disassembles the parts and reuses them in novel ways.

His use of other sources and his career-long tendency to experiment with plot variations are among the most key features in Shakespeare's approach to plot.

We find a sterling example of this in *Much Ado About Nothing,* a romantic comedy written a few years before *Hamlet.* This comedy displays how Shakespeare makes use of another source and how he constructs a plot, largely anew. We can see how he improves on in the original, also makes incorporates in this comedy the Aristotelian elements of reversal, recognition, and pathos.

Much Ado: Overview and Plot Elements

Much Ado About Nothing, one of Shakespeare's most popular romantic comedies, was written in the late 1590s. It is best known for the lovers Beatrice and Benedick, who wittily spar with each other and profess to be indifferent to each other. They vow to remain single all their lives, but are easily hoodwinked by their friends, who contrive for them to believe the other is madly in love with them. This dissolves their own resistance: Beatrice and Benedick now realize they do, in fact, love the other.

But there are actually two romantic storylines developing side by side, and they closely track with each other. Each storyline includes similar the plot elements — exposition, rising action, turning point, falling action, and resolution — and these parallel events occur at roughly the same points in the play.

Shakespeare borrowed the story for the Claudio–Hero plot from a sixteenth-century novella by the Italian Matteo Bandello, but as best we can tell, Shakespeare invented the Benedick–Beatrice one, overlaying these together.

Before we explore how he adapted his source story and varied the standard plot structure, let's identify *Much Ado*'s plot elements for each storyline.

Exposition: The play begins as Claudio, Benedick, and the prince Don Pedro arrive in Messina, where the governor Leonato warmly welcomes them. They have been triumphant in their recent wars. Claudio encounters Leonato's daughter, Hero, whom he knew before, but now falls instantly in love with her. At the same time, Beatrice and Benedick renew their old acquaintance and resume an ongoing battle of wits. The relationships of these two pairs will develop in parallel throughout the play. The betrothal of Claudio and Hero is soon announced and all but one are joyful: Don John, the malcontent bastard brother of Don Pedro.

Inciting Incidents: Don John conspires with his henchmen to snuff out Claudio's happiness by making him believe Hero is false. The plot then shifts to the secondary story. Just after Don John arranges his trap for Claudio, another trick is set in motion, this one benevolent. Friends conspire to make Benedick and Beatrice fall in love by making them believe, each in turn, that the other is already madly in love with them.

Rising Action: Both tricks bear fruit. In the malevolent trick, Don John and his men convince Claudio that it is Hero they see entertaining a man on her balcony at night. In the benevolent trick, the sworn bachelor and maid acknowledge privately how desirable the other is, but each worries they will be mocked for reversing course.

In an interlude, we are introduced to Dogberry and his bumbling crew, who keep watch over the town at night. By chance they will overhear Don John's men confess their dark deeds and arrest them.

Turning Point: Then comes the turning point and a major reversal (*peripeteia*). Claudio, believing he saw Hero in the arms of another man, awaits her the next day at the altar only to publicly repudiate her. The Prince adds his own rebuke, and they depart. Leonato, fearing his daughter has been unchaste, rebuffs her as well. Hero swoons and appears dead. This is the most emotionally wrought part of the story, a scene of suffering (*pathos*) for Hero. Instead of the happy union she was expecting, she is harshly rejected not only by her bridegroom but by the Prince and her own father.

At Hero's lowest point, Beatrice rises to her defense. The Priest is also convinced of Hero's innocence, so he proposes to have her proclaimed dead until she can be proven guiltless or, if not, then quietly installed in a convent. This plotline now focuses on the working out of that plan.

The secondary plot's turning point happens soon after the first. Beatrice and Benedick drop their defenses and admit their love for each other. But Beatrice makes an almost unbearable demand of him. Since she cannot defend her cousin's honor herself, she demands Benedick do it by killing Claudio. Benedick recoils but at last agrees to challenge him to fight.

Falling Action: Benedick rebukes Claudio and the Prince for their cruel behavior to Hero, and he challenges his friend to a duel, proving his commitment to Beatrice and honoring her over his allegiance to his comrades.

Then news of Don John's treachery is made known and Hero's innocence is confirmed. Claudio and the Prince become deeply contrite and vow to endure whatever penance her father asks of them. Leonato demands that Claudio marry Leonato's "niece," whom Claudio has never met, and Claudio agrees without reservation.

Resolution: In the final scene, Benedick is granted permission to wed Beatrice at the same time that Claudio will marry his bride. After Claudio presents himself for the wedding, the veiled "niece" reveals herself to be Hero. This discovery that Hero is still alive is, to Claudio, a recognition scene (*anagnorsis*). It also represents a comic reversal (*peripeteia*) for Hero, bringing her from an unhappy state to a happy one, from low to high. As the couples and their friends celebrate this double wedding with a dance, news arrives that the evil-doer Don John has been arrested.

Much Ado *Plot Chart*

This chart helps illustrates how Shakespeare aligns the primary and secondary plots in ways that keep the play feeling essentially like a single story, not two competing stories.

Much Ado: Structure of Primary and Secondary Plots:

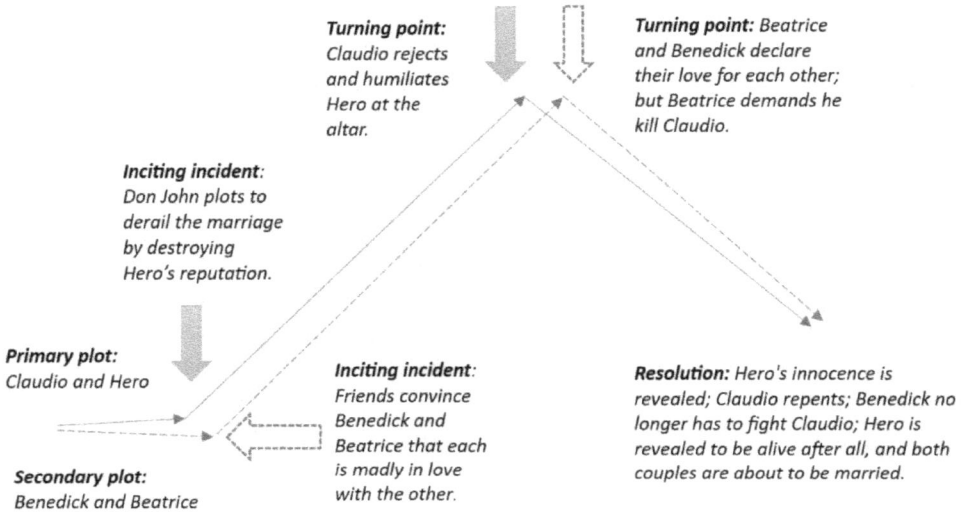

Turning point:
Claudio rejects
and humiliates
Hero at the
altar.

Turning point: *Beatrice
and Benedick declare
their love for each other;
but Beatrice demands he
kill Claudio.*

Inciting incident:
Don John plots to
derail the marriage
by destroying
Hero's reputation.

Primary plot:
Claudio and Hero

Inciting incident:
Friends convince
Benedick and
Beatrice that each
is madly in love
with the other.

Resolution: *Hero's innocence is
revealed; Claudio repents; Benedick no
longer has to fight Claudio; Hero is
revealed to be alive after all, and both
couples are about to be married.*

Secondary plot:
Benedick and Beatrice

Now consider how would it affect the flow if any of the plot elements in either plotline had been spaced out differently. What if Shakespeare had Claudio reject Hero at the altar, and then showed Beatrice and Benedick being tricked into believing the other is madly in love with them? It would clash tonally, of course, and the plot rhythm would be thrown off. We are primed to expect to see consequences flow from Claudio's rejection of his innocent fiancée, not to start up another complication. As it is, we now expect the consequences of Benedick's promise to challenge Claudio. The turning points of both plotlines are in sync.

To space these out differently would make it feel as if two different stories were competing with each other instead of peaking and flowing at the same time.

Similar to *Hamlet* and Shakespeare's other works, *Much Ado* has the classic pyramid-shaped structure, but with the distinct difference that there are two nearly overlapping pyramids: the Claudio–Hero storyline and the Beatrice–Benedick storyline.

Much Ado's *Primary Source and its Relation to the Plot Structure*

Those are the outlines of the double-plot as Shakespeare constructed it for *Much Ado*. With this structure in mind, let's see how Shakespeare got there—how he reshaped his primary source in building this plot.

Original Source Story

Shakespeare appears to have consulted at least three or four sources in creating *Much Ado*, but his main source is Matteo Bandello's twenty-second tale, about Signor Timbreo di Cardona and Fenicia, from his first volume of novellas.

Shakespeare ignores much of its opening section and borrows a plotline that begins several pages into the story. A noble young soldier Timbreo falls in love with Fenicia, but after being deceived into thinking she's been unchaste, he spurns her on the wedding day. Fenicia is then reported dead. Hearing this, the young man repents and agrees to her father's request that he marry another woman of his choosing. It's then joyfully revealed that this new choice is the spurned bride, who was not dead after all.

And here is what Shakespeare does with this original source:

1. Trims Background and Gets Straight to Romantic Plot

The novella has a long introductory section describing political struggles and a war between Italian city-states. These wouldn't add to his romantic comedy, so Shakespeare cuts all that and begins with Claudio (the Timbreo character) as he arrives in Messina with the Prince (Don Pedro) and others, having just triumphed in the war.

The novella also provides a longer courtship period, whereas Shakespeare gets straight to it: Claudio and Hero fall in love quickly and become engaged straightaway, because why stretch that out? It isn't the courtship that matters in this story, it's the twists and turns later.

2. Sharpens the Turning Point

In both the novella and in *Much Ado*, the bride is spurned on her wedding day by the groom, who has been deceived into thinking she has had a lover. But the Italian version is tamer compared to how Shakespeare manages it. In the original, the groom sends a messenger to tell the parents and bride he will not marry her because of her supposed offense; the woman's father discounts this, trusting his daughter. Shakespeare immensely increases the pain and harshness of Hero's rejection: Claudio waits for Hero to arrive at the altar before publicly humiliating her; the Prince joins in the shaming, as does Hero's father. As a result of Shakespeare's tinkering, this moment becomes a particularly acute turning point in the play, with Hero being harshly repudiated by three important men in her life.

3.   Curtails the Ending

Another change Shakespeare makes is to curtail the ending. This, like trimming Bandello's opening, was kind of a no-brainer. The Italian story has many pages after the happy double-wedding of Timbreo and Fenicia and of another couple (the bride's sister and the now-repentant villain). Bandello has them return to Sicily to inform the prince of their new marriages. The prince then gives the virtuous young woman and her sister generous dowries as well as restoring the fortune of the girls' father. Shakespeare would have seen this extended ending as anticlimactic, so he simply has Hero's father well-off in the first place—no need to restore their wealth. His play instead ends as they all join in a dance—an image of restored harmony and delight—just before the double wedding of Claudio and Hero and Benedick and Beatrice is about to take place.

4.   Adds a Parallel Plot and New Characters

The most important additions to the play are all Shakespeare's own, as best we can tell: he adds the parallel love story about Beatrice and Benedick, a pair who proudly claim to be impervious to love, but fail to resist their love for the other.

Here is where we can almost hear Shakespeare's critical mind clicking away. He would have recognized the novella's plot as being based on a simple folk-tale motif. Namely, a bride is unjustly spurned and is believed dead, the groom repents his mistake once her innocence is proven, agrees to marry another chosen by the "dead" bride's father, and all are delighted to discover she is still alive. It's entertaining in the way folk tales are—it provides a nice surprise at the end and the satisfaction of seeing an unfairly maligned maiden be restored to her rightful position.

But Shakespeare clearly wasn't happy with the plot as is. For one thing it would have seemed rather old-fashioned to his audience. But what must have seemed especially off to Shakespeare is how passive the bride Fenicia is in the whole proceeding. She is essentially a victim whose fate is decided by others. To judge from his other comedies, this clearly wasn't Shakespeare's kind of female protagonist.

He presumably asked himself after reading Bandello, what would more modern characters think about this event? And especially, how would a more spirited and confident female protagonist, the kind he clearly favored, react?

He realized the plot could be enhanced by a more sophisticated, parallel storyline that would reflect on the first story. So, he invents this witty pair and has them fall in love as well, while they aid and comment on the first pair of lovers.

And to make this all more comic, he adds the bumbling town watchmen, who help expose the evil scheme.

Value of Adding the Parallel Storyline

What does he gain by adding this parallel storyline of Benedick and Beatrice? Two of the most delightful characters in the whole canon, for starters. They add wit, romantic tension, and a particularly feisty protagonist in Beatrice. The play is far more well known for these two characters than for those of the main plot. Yet it is the main plot, with its more standard lovers, that allows Benedick and Beatrice to shine as being all the more spirited and independent.

Their romantic journey functions as a counterpoise to the main one, which would have appeared pretty conventional even in its own day.

Through the parallel storyline, Shakespeare can provide valuable commentary on the main plot. When Hero is publicly rejected, Beatrice and Benedick frame this as unambiguously wrong. Beatrice is livid over Claudio's cruelty and says she would "eat his heart in the marketplace" if she were a man. Shakespeare has Beatrice point out, as the novella never does, how outrageously the men have treated her cousin.

Why Not Simply Write *Beatrice and Benedick*?

Since Beatrice and Benedick ended up being the audience favorites, why didn't Shakespeare simply think to have a single plot revolving around that pair and call it *Beatrice and Benedick*? (The French composer Hector Berlioz did just that in his opera by that name.)

But these two sparring lovers are the more appealing precisely because of the contrast with the more conventional pair. Shakespeare does something similar in his early comedy *The Taming of the Shrew*, in which he contrasts the volcanic-tempered Katharina with her seemingly compliant sister Bianca, whom the suitors other than Petruchio prefer. Katharina's fiery nature stands out more against the backdrop of her more praised and petted sister.

Both Beatrice and Benedick show courage and loyalty in rising to Hero's defense, and they stand out all the more for their independence and their witty, teasing manner. With these parallel storylines, Shakespeare provides the spurned-bride folk tale of Claudio and Hero, but also calls into question the assumptions of the original story by showing this alternative, more modern couple, Beatrice and Benedick. Shakespeare gives us the put-upon young fiancée and adds another woman so unwilling to tolerate her cousin's humiliation that she would rather kill the offender than let the insult pass.

Recap of Source Alterations in Much Ado

The changes Shakespeare makes to Bandello's story are improvements to the original—certainly, they make sense in an adaptation for performance, but most of the changes would be beneficial even for a novel or short story adaptation. Shakespeare shapes his source by:

- Getting started *in medias res* (the pairs of lovers have already met each other; it's just that now, with the wars having ended, they are ready to fall in love).
- Ending the story sooner, right after the problem is resolved, for a tighter conclusion.
- Speeding up the action considerably (having a shorter courtship period).
- Eliminating elements that are irrelevant to the central problem, which is to bring the lovers together (the bride's family is not poor, since their financial status has no bearing on Hero's plight of being falsely accused).
- Adding the comic watchmen to lighten the tone, bring the villain to justice, and clear Hero's name (they catch the wrong-doers, which in turn exonerates Hero).
- Most significant of all, adding a parallel plot that offers a more modern, spirited alternative and reflects on the folk-tale-like primary plot.

From *Much Ado*, we see Shakespeare's dexterity in intertwining two parallel plots, while maintaining the classic plot structure. The secondary plot—that of Beatrice and Benedick—may draw more attention because of their witty, sparring nature, but structurally their storyline is not allowed to take precedence over the primary plot. They are more effective just as they are—as the foils to the primary lovers.

Summary

While it is protagonists who typically capture a reader's interest, it is thanks to plot structure that they have the chance to shine.

Hamlet, although very much a protagonist-centric work, follows the contours of the standard pyramid-style plot to great effect.

Much Ado About Nothing demonstrates Shakespeare's mastery in adapting a source and experimenting with plot structure. He takes a folk-tale-like story and turns it into something sophisticated and witty without losing the satisfying nature of the original. He does it by adding the parallel plot of Beatrice and Benedick, and shaping both of the romantic storylines so their major plot points unfold more or less in sync.

Shakespeare did not hesitate to adjust plot structure in other ways when it suits his purpose. As we'll see in the following two chapters, he finds many novel and creative ways to plot his stories.

Takeaway for Writers

Aristotle's *The Poetics* discusses what makes a skillful plot. In his system, the plot:

- is the most important element of tragedy (and, presumably, he would say this of comedy as well);
- depicts a whole action;
- often incorporates scenes of reversal, recognition, and pathos;
- provides necessary exposition and rising action;
- has a turning point that is followed by falling action (denouement); and
- ends with the completion of the whole action.

Theorists following Aristotle have identified other elements that often appear in effective plots. The plot:

- begins the action *in medias res;*
- often begins with a hook; and
- soon after the beginning, has an inciting incident that sets the protagonist off in a particular direction.

Taken together, these form a prevalent pattern in much storytelling.

In the examples we analyzed:

161

- *Hamlet* shows an impeccable plot structure, conforming to the classic elements of plot structure; it also has a series of soliloquies, whose function in the plot we will explore in a later chapter.
- *Much Ado About Nothing* displays complicated plotting and use of multiple protagonists—four of them—but the blending and similar timing of the two stories help to make them seem like a unified plot.

Terms

Anagnorisis [Recognition]: "Recognition, as the name indicates, is a change from ignorance to knowledge, producing love or hate between the persons destined by the poet for good or bad fortune. The best form of recognition is coincident with a Reversal of the Situation, as in the Oedipus. There are indeed other forms. Even inanimate things of the most trivial kind may in a sense be objects of recognition." (Aristotle Book XI)

Anagnorisis denotes "turning point in a drama at which a character (usually the protagonist) recognizes the true state of affairs, having previously been in error or ignorance." (Baldick)

"It is discussed by Aristotle in the *Poetics* as an essential part of the plot of a tragedy, although anagnorisis occurs in comedy, epic, and, at a later date, the novel as well. Anagnorisis usually involves revelation of the true identity of persons previously unknown, as when a father recognizes a stranger as his son, or vice versa…This recognition is the more artistically satisfying because it is accompanied by a **peripeteia ("reversal"),** the shift in fortune from good to bad that moves on to the tragic catastrophe. An anagnorisis is not always accompanied by a peripeteia…. Aristotle discusses several kinds of anagnorisis employed by dramatists. The simplest kind, used, as he says, 'from poverty of wit,' is recognition by scars, birthmarks, or tokens. More interesting are those that arise naturally from incidents of the plot. (Britannica https://www.britannica.com/art/anagnorisis)

Exposition: "the opening part of a play or story, in which we are introduced to the characters and their situation, often by reference to preceding events." (Baldrick)

Falling action [often called **Denouement**], arrives after the **turning point**; the section in a story "in which the complexities of the plot are unraveled and the conflict is finally resolved. In the denouement of a traditionally structured plot, the villain may be exposed, the mystery explained, misunderstandings clarified, or lovers reunited." In a tragedy, the conclusion is often called the catastrophe. (Britannica https://www.britannica.com/art/denouement)

Hook: A hook is an event or other element that occurs at the opening of a story and that provokes, or "hooks," the audience's immediate attention.

Inciting incident: The moment in a story in which the protagonist is "incited" to move in a particular direction.

Commonly described in relation to film, "the inciting incident… sets the story in motion; it is…what the story is about, and draws the main character into the story line." (Field 129)

In medias res: "the practice of beginning an epic or other narrative by plunging into a crucial situation that is part of a related chain of events; the situation is an extension of previous events and will be developed in later action. The narrative then goes directly forward, and exposition of earlier events is supplied by flashbacks." (Britannica https://www.britannica.com/art/in-medias-res-literature)

Pathos: "**The Scene of Suffering** [Pathos] is a destructive or painful action, such as death on the stage, bodily agony, wounds, and the like" (Aristotle Part XI).

Pathos is "the emotionally moving quality or power of a literary work or of particular passages within it, appealing especially to our feelings." (Baldrick)

Peripeteia [Reversal]: "Reversal of the Situation is a change by which the action veers round to its opposite, subject always to our rule of probability or necessity." (Aristotle Part XI).

Peripeteia is "a sudden reversal of a character's circumstances and fortunes, usually involving the downfall of the protagonist in a tragedy, and often coinciding with the **'recognition' or anagnorisis**. In a comedy, however, the peripeteia abruptly restores the prosperity of the main character(s)." (Baldrick)

Plot: "the Plot is the imitation of the action—for by plot I here mean the arrangement of the incidents" (Aristotle, Part VI).

Plot is "the pattern of events and situations in a narrative or dramatic work, as selected and arranged both to emphasize relationships—usually of cause and effect—between incidents and to elicit a particular kind of interest in the reader or audience, such as surprise or suspense.... Plots vary in form from the fully integrated or 'tightly knit' to the loosely episodic. In general, though, most plots will trace some process of change in which characters are caught up in a developing conflict that is finally resolved." (Baldrick)

Plot is, "in fiction, the structure of interrelated actions, consciously selected and arranged by the author. Plot involves a considerably higher level of narrative organization than normally occurs in a story or fable. According to E.M. Forster in *Aspects of the Novel* (1927), a story is a 'narrative of events arranged in their time-sequence,' whereas a plot organizes the events according to a 'sense of causality.'" (Britannica https://www.britannica.com/art/plot)

Rising action [also called **Complication**]: "Every tragedy falls into two parts—Complication and Unraveling or *Dénouement* [**Falling action**]. Incidents extraneous to the action are frequently combined with a portion of the action proper, to form the Complication; the rest is the Unraveling. By the Complication I mean all that extends from the beginning of the action to the part which marks the turning-point to good or bad fortune. The Unraveling is that which extends from the beginning of the change to the end. ...Many poets tie the knot well, but unravel it ill. Both arts, however, should always be mastered." (Aristotle, Poetics, Part XVIII).

Turning point (often called **Climax**): "In the structure of a play the climax, or crisis, is the decisive moment, or turning point, at which the rising action of the play is reversed to falling action. It may or may not coincide with the highest point of interest in the drama." (Britannica https://www.britannica.com/art/climax-literature).

Gustav Freytag uses the term *Höhenpunkt*, which means high point, for the turning point.

Extras

Perhaps no single work of literary criticism has been more influential in Western thought than **Aristotle's *The Poetics***. The Poetry Foundation has reproduced large excerpts of this work on their website at https://www.poetryfoundation.org/articles/69372/from-poetics. Consider reviewing the entire work, which is quite compact; Aristotle's pragmatic approach and clarity of thought still come through after 2400 years. The sections, or "Parts," that are most relevant to plot are Parts VI-IX, XI, XIII, and XVIII. Some key passages are below.

From Part VI:

Tragedy, then, is an imitation of an action that is serious, complete, and of a certain magnitude; in language embellished with each kind of artistic ornament, the several kinds being found in separate parts of the play; in the form of action, not of narrative; through pity and fear effecting the proper purgation of these emotions....

Again, Tragedy is the imitation of an action; and an action implies personal agents, who necessarily possess certain distinctive qualities both of character and thought; for it is by these that we qualify actions themselves, and these—thought and character—are the two natural causes from which actions spring, and on actions again all success or failure depends. Hence, the Plot is the imitation of the action—for by plot I here mean the arrangement of the incidents....

Besides which, the most powerful elements of emotional interest in Tragedy— Peripeteia or Reversal of the Situation, and Recognition scenes—are parts of the plot.

From Part VII:

A whole is that which has a beginning, a middle, and an end. A beginning is that which does not itself follow anything by causal necessity, but after which something naturally is or comes to be An end, on the contrary, is that which itself naturally follows some other thing, either by necessity, or as a rule, but has nothing following it. A middle is that which follows something as some other thing follows it. A well constructed plot, therefore, must neither begin nor end at haphazard, but conform to these principles.

Again, a beautiful object, whether it be a living organism or any whole composed of parts, must not only have an orderly arrangement of parts, but must also be of a certain magnitude; for beauty depends on magnitude and order....

From Part VIII:

But Homer, as in all else he is of surpassing merit, here too—whether from art or natural genius—seems to have happily discerned the truth. In composing the *Odyssey* he did not include all the adventures of Odysseus—such as his wound on Parnassus, or his feigned madness at the mustering of the host—incidents between which there was no necessary or probable connection: but he made the *Odyssey*, and likewise the *Iliad*, to center round an action that in our sense of the word is one. As therefore, in the other imitative arts, the imitation is one when the object imitated is one, so the plot, being an imitation of an action, must imitate one action and that a whole, the structural union of the parts being such that, if any one of them is displaced or removed, the whole will be disjointed and disturbed. For a thing whose presence or absence makes no visible difference, is not an organic part of the whole.

From Part IX:

But again, Tragedy is an imitation not only of a complete action, but of events inspiring fear or pity. Such an effect is best produced when the events come on us by surprise; and the effect is heightened when, at the same time, they follow as cause and effect. The tragic wonder will then be greater than if they happened of themselves or by accident; for even coincidences are most striking when they have an air of design.

From Part XI:

Reversal of the Situation is a change by which the action veers round to its opposite, subject always to our rule of probability or necessity. Thus in the *Oedipus*, the messenger comes to cheer Oedipus and free him from his alarms about his mother, but by revealing who he is, he produces the opposite effect....

Recognition, as the name indicates, is a change from ignorance to knowledge, producing love or hate between the persons destined by the poet for good or bad fortune. The best form of recognition is coincident with a Reversal of the Situation, as in the *Oedipus*. There are indeed other forms. Even inanimate things of the most trivial kind may in a sense be objects of recognition. Again, we may recognize or discover whether a person has done a thing or not. But the recognition which is most intimately connected with the plot and action is, as we have said, the recognition of persons. This recognition, combined with Reversal, will produce either pity or fear; and actions producing these effects are those which, by our definition, Tragedy represents.

Moreover, it is upon such situations that the issues of good or bad fortune will depend.

Two parts, then, of the Plot—Reversal of the Situation and Recognition—turn upon surprises. A third part is the Scene of Suffering. The Scene of Suffering is a destructive or painful action, such as death on the stage, bodily agony, wounds, and the like.

From Part XIII:

The change of fortune should be not from bad to good, but, reversely, from good to bad. It should come about as the result not of vice, but of some great error or frailty, in a character either such as we have described, or better rather than worse. Hence they are in error who censure Euripides just because he follows this principle in his plays, many of which end unhappily. It is, as we have said, the right ending. The best proof is that on the stage and in dramatic competition, such plays, if well worked out, are the most tragic in effect; and Euripides, faulty though he may be in the general management of his subject, yet is felt to be the most tragic of the poets.

In the second rank comes the kind of tragedy which some place first. Like the *Odyssey*, it has a double thread of plot, and also an opposite catastrophe for the good and for the bad.

From Part XVIII:

Every tragedy falls into two parts—Complication and Unraveling or *Dénouement*. Incidents extraneous to the action are frequently combined with a portion of the action proper, to form the Complication; the rest is the Unraveling. By the Complication I mean all that extends from the beginning of the action to the part which marks the turning-point to good or bad fortune. The Unraveling is that which extends from the beginning of the change to the end....

Many poets tie the knot well, but unravel it ill. Both arts, however, should always be mastered. Again, the poet should remember what has been often said, and not make an Epic structure into a tragedy—by an Epic structure I mean one with a multiplicity of plots—as if, for instance, you were to make a tragedy out of the entire story of the *Iliad*. In the Epic poem, owing to its length, each part assumes its proper magnitude. In the drama the result is far from answering to the poet's expectation.

CHAPTER 8: PLOT VARIATIONS

Apyramid-plot structure is a sturdy, effective thing. And plots don't come any sturdier or more effective than the one in *Hamlet*. It builds steadily in energy from its *in medias res* beginning, through exposition and complications, until its turning point midway through the story, at which time it cascades to the ending, which resolves Hamlet's central problem.

This is the classic plot structure. But as we've also seen, Shakespeare is not afraid to vary this structure, which he does in *Much Ado About Nothing* by developing two storylines in tight parallel.

The use of an intertwined double plot (and quadruple protagonists) is just one of the variations on a standard plot structure that he uses. Far from being a formulaic writer, churning out work after work in the same template, he experiments with plots throughout his career.

In virtually all of his plays, Shakespeare includes some additional storylines—subplots—that intersect and reflect on the main plot or character. And he shifts where he places the peak emotional moments of the plot. These peaks of tension lend a certain rhythm to a plot, which the audience responds to. Shakespeare varies where he creates this tension according to the particular needs of his stories.

In this chapter, we will explore several of the plot variations Shakespeare uses. What they show, once again, is his pragmatic approach to literary "rules": he adjusts his usual pattern of constructing a plot when he can find a more effective way of doing it.

Subplots

A subplot is a related, yet largely independent, storyline within a larger storyline. The use of subplots is as fundamental to Shakespeare's instincts as anything.

Through his subplots, Shakespeare can emphasize something significant in the main plot. He shows a strong preference in general for what we might call theme and variations. In *Hamlet*, for instance, Shakespeare creates a situation in which the protagonist is responding to the death of his father, and then gives that problem as well to two minor characters, Laertes and Fortinbras. This has the effect of showing a breadth of human response, underlining the universality of the situation, but also the variety of reactions people have. While Hamlet turns inward to explore existential questions, Fortinbras turns outward, waging battle over a plot of Polish land too small even to bury the dead. Laertes shows a third reaction, being so swept up with the desire for revenge that Claudius can manipulate him for his own ends. Each is responding to the same type of loss, but in different ways. Whenever Shakespeare can refract a question, to explore it from many angles, he usually seizes the opportunity.

His subplots can vary from very short to quite extensive. But each functions like a mini-plot, with its own main characters. And these subplots will be interwoven with, and reflect on, the main plot in a significant way. This is true even with minor subplots, such as we find in *Othello*.

Brief Subplot in Othello

The main plot of this tragedy traces how Othello, an outsider who holds a high position as Venice's military commander, can be provoked by his ensign, Iago, to lethal jealousy. The subplot involves Othello's second in command, Cassio, and how he dismissively treats the courtesan Bianca, who is in love with him.

In the main plot, Cassio plays a minor, but crucial role as the subject of Othello's misplaced jealousy. Iago has coaxed Cassio to banter coarsely about Bianca in Othello's hearing, but in such a way that Othello thinks Cassio is referring to Desdemona. Cassio jokes about her fondness for him and her deluded hopes that she'll marry him. Iago also contrives for Cassio to come into possession of an embroidered handkerchief, a precious gift from Othello to Desdemona; when Othello sees it, he takes it as further evidence of an affair with his wife.

Through this subplot, we gain brief glimpses of the courtesan Bianca's jealousy and humiliation. While this brief subplot consists of just a handful of speeches during the latter half of the play, it is enough to establish the two characters' unequal relationship. Cassio enjoys Bianca's company, but cares little for her feelings. When he asks her to embroider a copy of Desdemona's handkerchief, Bianca becomes madly jealous thinking she has a rival. In her suffering, we get an echo of Othello's misery.

What does Shakespeare gain by building out, however briefly, Cassio's and Bianca's relationship? He can underscore the theme of jealousy, showing that Othello's misery, though extreme, is not an anomaly. It is a common scourge. We see how deeply wounded Bianca is by Cassio's light treatment of her. Bianca as a courtesan is in a weaker social position than if she were a nobleman's daughter. (Othello, similarly, is a social outsider in spite of his powerful position.) And Cassio, however decent he seems in other respects, is flippant in his attitude toward Bianca's feelings. This contrasts with both Desdemona and Othello, who treat each other with great respect and appreciation of each other's qualities—that is, until Othello is overwhelmed with suspicion.

Nowhere does Shakespeare explicitly compare Bianca's and Cassio's relationship with that of Othello and Desdemona, or directly connect Bianca's and Othello's plights. Here, as with subplots in his other plays, Shakespeare simply interweaves this storyline in the plot, letting their themes resonate with each other. The effect is subtle and implicit, but adds at least a grace note.

Extensive Subplot in King Lear

The more extensive the subplot, the more challenging it is to integrate without overshadowing or distracting from with the main plot. *King Lear* has a masterful example of this in the Gloucester subplot.

The main characters from this subplot—Gloucester and his sons Edmund and Edgar—are key players in the main plot as well. But this subplot is nearly as developed as Lear's storyline, and it echoes the main plot on many points.

Gloucester's bastard son Edmund tricks him into believing his other son Edgar is plotting against him. To save himself, Edgar flees and disguises himself as a madman. Edmund, meanwhile, conspires with Lear's cruel elder daughters against his own father. After Gloucester aids the old King, he is punished by having his eyes gouged out and bring expelled from his own home. Like the King, Gloucester wanders in the wilderness. In his despair, he intends to cast himself off a cliff, but Edgar intervenes. The blind old man makes peace with his fate and reconciles with his good son, who has revealed his identity to him.

The Gloucester subplot recapitulates Lear's main challenges in many ways. Both characters:

- are fathers who unwisely reject one of their children, and are then victimized by their other offspring;
- are driven from their home;
- suffer greatly, both physically and emotionally;
- are "blind"' (Lear, metaphorically, and Gloucester literally): neither of them have seen clearly;
- deplore the gods' lack of justice; and

- ultimately find redemption through their own perseverance and the devotion of their good child.

One note of contrast between the men is that Gloucester begot his son Edmund out of wedlock, whereas Lear's children were all "got 'tween the lawful sheets." This makes this situation, again, more universal: children may be ungrateful, whether sons or daughters, legitimate or not. It is not simply the curse of parents who break the marriage vows who are plagued by cruel children. Legitimate children can turn on their parents as well.

By setting the characters side by side, Shakespeare highlights a number of differences between them. The most important is their contrasting outlook on suffering and the nature of the gods. They strive in different ways to make sense of a bewildering world.

Gloucester's response to his great suffering is to concede defeat and lose faith. After being blinded and learning his son Edmund was the cause, he seeks to end his life. He concludes the gods are arbitrary and cruel: "As flies to wanton boys are we to th'gods, / They kill us for their sport" (4.1). But Edgar stages a "miraculous" scene in which the blind man is persuaded he fell off a cliff but was spared from harm. This apparent miracle restores Gloucester's faith and he vows hereafter to bear up with patience. "Henceforth I'll bear / Affliction till it do cry out itself / 'Enough, enough,' and die" (4.6). It's a moving and insightful depiction of how we perceive the role of a higher power in our lives, and shows how faith can give us the courage to carry on.

The protagonist, by contrast, takes a more active and confrontational approach to his sufferings. Lear demands justice and truth, seemingly a futile quest, but he cannot do otherwise. Even when his wits are frayed, he attempts to bring his wrongdoers to trial. He engages with the madman Poor Tom (Edgar) as if he were an antique philosopher who can answer his questions about life's mysteries. And Lear wages an existential battle with "the heavens" during the storm. But he cannot compel the gods to answer him. Unlike Gloucester, he doesn't perceive any benevolent intervention on their part. But Lear does come to see it is up to humans to "show the heavens more just" — to enact the justice on earth that we wish the divine force would enact.

In his efforts to reach existential truths, which he pursues to the limits of his physical and psychological abilities, Lear appears as even more heroic than Gloucester. He never ceases to try to resolve his untenable condition.

But the fact that Gloucester has taken another way doesn't invalidate either response. It simply shows the variety of human nature.

171

What does Shakespeare accomplish with this extensive subplot? With the Gloucester storyline echoing the main plot, Shakespeare:

- emphasizes the pathos of old age; Lear is not alone in being vulnerable because of his age, infirmities, and dependence on others to safeguard him;
- reinforces the theme of "blindness"; Gloucester's gouged-out eyes will be a visceral reminder of Lear's fault in not seeing better when he was king;
- amplifies, through further examples, the nature of a father's relationship with his children, including the profound pain of having "a thankless child," but also the blessings they can bring; Lear is not alone in misjudging his children, nor in failing to see clearly in spite of having the benefit of advanced years; and he
- broadens the play's perspective on how humans interpret existential mysteries, such as the nature of the gods and how they believe their fates are determined.

Both Gloucester and Lear are pushed by extremity to find reasons for their suffering. Gloucester resigns himself to the inscrutable will of the gods, whereas Lear does not reconcile himself fully; in one of his last lines, about the death of Cordelia, he remains bewildered by life's mysteries: "Why should a dog, a horse, a rat have life, / And thou no breath at all?" (5.3). But Lear has also accepted that it is the duty of humans to show the heavens more just. His final line is, "Look there, look there!" apparently seeing Cordelia's lips move, something that no one else, onstage or in the audience can see. Like Gloucester, Lear seems to die in hope.

The Gloucester subplot is fascinating in its own right. But it also serves to shine a light on the protagonist's situation. By providing an audience with a character who shares the same kind of frailties as Lear, we can see in Lear a more universal figure of suffering; and in contrast with Gloucester, Lear can appear even more heroic in his determined search for answers and justice.

Plots with Dual Protagonists and Their Separate Storylines

In his plays with a romantic pair at their center—such as the tragedies *Romeo and Juliet* and *Anthony and Cleopatra* or the comedies *As You Like It* and *Much Ado About Nothing*—the plot will deal with the attempts of the dual protagonists to be together. But plotting with two protagonists can be more complicated to structure than with just one.

Shakespeare usually fleshes out each romantic protagonist individually, giving them, in a sense, an independent life outside of their romantic interests. This choice is not self-evident; many non-Shakespearean love stories focus on one member a romantic pair, framing a story primarily through this character's perspective.

But when Shakespeare has a romantic plot, he tends to provide perspectives from each lover. He builds out their lives individually and shows each one engaging in their own challenges. This entails that each romantic protagonist has their own quasi-subplot. (This is not quite the same as a subplot, which usually involves non-protagonists; instead, this is a consequence of treating two protagonists individually.)

In Romeo's individual "subplot," we see a youth among his close friends. They console him, spar with him, get in trouble together. He experiences the tragic loss of Mercutio as a consequence of his alliance with a Capulet. And we see him mature quickly, having to leave behind his ties with friends and kin in order to embark on a union with Juliet.

In Juliet's segments, we see a girl who is initially pliable to the wishes of her parents about their choice for a husband; then she comes to rebel and takes matters of love in her own hands. We witness her outgrow her strong ties to the Nurse and distance herself from her confidence once the Nurse advises her to commit bigamy by marrying with Paris.

In *Antony and Cleopatra,* the protagonists each have their own political fortunes they want to preserve, their own web of intrigue to cope with. They try, with little success, to reconcile their ambitions with their desire to be with each other. Through Antony's interactions with his fellow Romans, we are reminded of his illustrious past and his current precarious power. To repair his uneasy alliance with Octavius Caesar, his co-ruler of the empire, Antony goes so far as to marry with Octavius' sister. But this alliance will not hold long; as Enobarbus notes, "in the East his pleasure lies" — that is, Antony will return to Cleopatra.

For Cleopatra, Shakespeare takes care to sketch out something of her life in Egypt, her pursuit of pleasure and the maintenance of her power. She attempts to make her own self-preserving deal with Octavius, although this expediency, like Anthony's, also fails. Each of these protagonists was, in real life, historically prominent; Shakespeare found it all the more vital to depict their individual lives as fully as possible, and not simply focus on their love story.

These segments — Cleopatra's efforts to remain in power in Egypt, and Antony's to remain in power in Rome — do more than flesh out their individual characters.

The central problem—their desire to be together—is more tension-filled precisely because their individual priorities exert such a great pull on them.

Purpose of Building Out Individual Storylines of Pairs

What does Shakespeare gain by building out the independent stories of his romantic protagonists? With these extensions of the main plot:

- Shakespeare can make each character more rounded, since we see more of their life outside of their romantic relationship. They become more vividly real by being seen in the world of their family, friends and adversaries, and not as simply one half of a whole.
- When the story turns back to their relationship, and each individual is more fleshes out, the love story itself is more interesting for being a union between two more interesting individuals.
- The challenges that are represented in the individual storylines can build greater tension between the individual's and the pair's interests. The individual's subplot can establish more thoroughly the challenges to the main plot's goal of bringing the lovers together.

Whereas some love stories are told from the perspective of one of the two lovers, or frame the lovers only in terms of their relationship with each other, Shakespeare rarely does that. In his romantic comedies as well as tragedies, he tends to give prominence to each of the lovers of a pair. To construct such a plot, he builds out something like to a subplot for them, a plot segment about their life separate from the life they share with the other.

Other Plot Variations through Tension and Emotional Peaks

To change up the rhythm or other effects on the audience, Shakespeare will vary how he treats the standard elements of a plot. We see this in how he alters where emotional peaks land in the course of the story. The turning point and the end of a plot are normally where the two greatest points of tension or excitement fall. But Shakespeare will place highly charged moments elsewhere, and multiply the effects through stretches of repeated or unrelenting tension.

The effect on the audience can be significant. Shakespeare adapts these elements, as needed, in pursuit of a plot structure that best tells the kind of story he wants to tell.

Farcical Structure

One plot variation we find in Shakespeare is what we'd recognize as the structure of farce. The rhythm of pure farce is distinct from that of other genres. In farce, there tends to be a steady series of humorous complications—such as mistaken identity, accidents, threats, or other broadly physical actions. One mistake or accident provokes a response based on partial knowledge of a situation—a person slaps another by mistake, for instance, and the slapped person takes offense—and from this, the complications cascade. The protagonist character's development, let alone subtleties about their inner world, take a back seat if any seat at all. You will not find many soliloquies in farce.

Farce depends on a chain of complications with almost no let-up until the end. As John Cleese defines it: "The perfect farce script is like clockwork: the writer winds it up by carefully establishing certain credible premises, and then lets the whole thing unwind, with inevitable but startling logic" (Cleese, *The Guardian*).

This notion of a clockwork mechanism pushing the plot along puts farce somewhat at odds with a standard structure. In a pyramid plot, the first half typically builds the complications steadily (the tying section), with the protagonist's challenges taking an irrevocable turn around the midpoint. In the second half, the complications are untied. In farce, there is generally no significant turning point at the midpoint—this is protracted until just before the end. The driving force is not so much the protagonist's goals but rather, the initiating circumstances that play out, building up like a head of steam, until tension is released suddenly at the end.

The Comedy of Errors *as Farce*

The Comedy of Errors, from very early in Shakespeare's career, falls squarely in this genre. The play premise is more or less credible, if far-fetched.

Egeon, a Syracusan merchant, with his wife Emilia and two sets of twin baby boys have been separated during a shipwreck at sea. One set of twins, each named Antipholus, are the sons of the Syracusan couple; the other set, identically named Dromio, have been adopted to become companions and servants to the other boys. After being dispersed by the storm, one Antipholus and one Dromio return with Egeon to Syracuse, while the other twins land elsewhere and will grow up in Ephesus. When Antipholus of Syracuse reaches adulthood, he embarks on a quest to find his brother, and is accompanied by his servant Dromio. After years have passed with no word back from them, Egeon himself goes in search of them, even venturing to Ephesus, where Syracusans are banned on pain of death.

But this is all backstory and is relayed through exposition. The play itself begins just as Egeon has been arrested and is explaining his unlucky history to the Duke of Ephesus. Egeon is given till the evening to raise the ransom money or he will be executed. Unbeknownst to Egeon, both of his sons and both Dromios are also currently in Ephesus.

With this complicated premise now in place, the clockwork mechanism can begin.

There are two related problems that are set early on. Will old Egeon be able to save his life? And will the pair from Syracuse discover their long-lost twin brothers? We don't get the answer until the very end (and yes, he does, and yes, the twins reunite along with Egeon and Emilia, the long-lost wife and mother).

Shakespeare starts the complications immediately, and only keeps building. There is little sense of a turning point midway through the play because, as typical of farces, the tying, or complication, section continues in a steady torrent. Complications are the *prima materia* of farce.

Consider this chain of events that is set off when a particular mistake triggers a conflict, which triggers further conflict. It begins in act 2, scene 2 with an instance of mistaken identity:

Initial trigger: Adriana, the wife of Antipholus of Ephesus, accosts Antipholus of Syracuse on the street, thinking he is her husband. She forces him to come home to dinner.

> ↪ When Adriana's actual husband shows up, he is turned away at his own front door, which infuriates him.

> ↪ So, he promises to give the gold chain he has ordered for his wife to a courtesan of the city instead.

> ↪ The jeweler later meets Antipholus of Syracuse on the street and delivers this expensive chain to him, instead of the brother who ordered it.

> ↪ When the courtesan sees it around this Antipholus's neck and she asks for it.

> ↪ But Antipholus of Syracuse rebuffs her, asserting he promised no such thing and doesn't even know her.

> ↪ This leads the courtesan to complain to Antipholus's wife Adriana that her husband is mad.

↪ And this prompts Adriana to have her husband captured by a quack doctor to try to bring him back to sanity.

And so on.

The play carries on in this vein, with only occasional pauses of relative calm, until the big climax at the end as the identities are revealed and mysteries resolved.

Like many other farces, the play depends almost not at all on character drawing or the protagonist's arc. There are no lessons these characters are learning. Nor does the plot depend much on the *nature* of the protagonists. In this farce, unlike in other kinds of comedy, we don't usually find the protagonists at their lowest or most hopeless point about midway through the story, nor do we see them commit themselves to a particular course of action. This kind of turning point is missing in *The Comedy of Errors*.

Shakespeare does vary the tone occasionally. We get a pause when we hear about the suffering of Adriana, or when Antipholus of Syracuse woos Adriana's sister. These can feel like moments of rest, where we catch our breath from the mayhem. But there is little sense that we have passed a point of no return or shifted course; there is no midpoint change of direction or redoubled commitment to a goal.

Instead, the complications keep unspooling till they are played out in full.

The plot structure might be depicted like this.

The Comedy of Errors: Farcical Plot Structure:

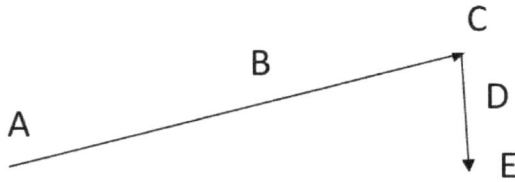

A. **Exposition** of characters, relationships, and past and current situations
B. **Rising Action** through continual series of complications
C. **Turning Point** comes near the end
D. **Falling Action** very rapid untying of complications through several scenes of recognition
E. **Resolution** as long-lost family members find each other

The play provides standard landmarks of a plot. The multiple protagonists—in this case, the Antipholi and the Dromii—are shown as heading toward a goal, although they are not aware of it. The family has been dispersed, and their implicit goal—the goal toward which the audience inevitably expects the story to go—is to reunite them. This is the endpoint toward which Shakespeare takes his characters.

The protagonists do not "achieve" the goal—the results drop in their lap, as if by a deus ex machina. There is no need to have a turning point midway through the story, because the protagonists' choices or decisions don't really play a role in the outcome. The mechanistic cause-and-effect is leading them there.

Horror/Thriller Structure

Another way in which Shakespeare experiments with plot is by placing moments of great intensity at points we normally wouldn't expect. In one play, he even anticipates the rhythm of modern horror/thriller stories by placing a shocking event early in the story, with other violent or extremely tense events occurring repeatedly thereafter. There is no gradual building of tension through complications to the midpoint, but rather a series of sudden peaks and releases throughout the play.

This proto-thriller, of course, is *Macbeth*.

Macbeth as Horror/Thriller

In some ways, this tragedy does conform to a standard dramatic structure. It has an intriguing hook. The play opens with the three witches plotting their next evil actions. It has efficient exposition, through which we learn of Macbeth's loyal service to the King. And midway through the play, Shakespeare provides a scene that qualifies as a turning point at just about the spot we'd expect it. This is the a highly charged moment at the banquet in act 3, scene 4, when he alone, among a group at the table, sees the ghost of Banquo, and shouts at it, "Thou canst not say I did it; never shake thy gory locks at me."

This can be called the turning point because Macbeth is now exposed to his nobles as likely guilty of murder. Macbeth's evident guilt triggers some of them to flee to England and leads to an inevitable confrontation on the battlefield later. Everything can untie from this exposure of Macbeth's guilt at the banquet.

So, the underlying structure of *Macbeth* can be depicted this way:

Macbeth: Basic Plot Structure

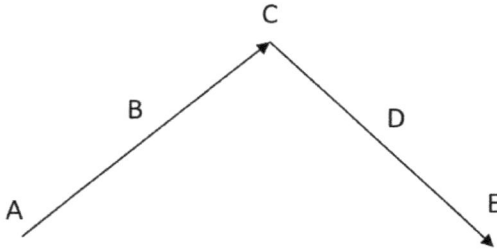

A. **Exposition** establishes Macbeth loyal service to the king.
B. **Rising Action** Macbeth murders Duncan and later Banquo.
C. **Turning Point** At the banquet (3.4), he alone, among a
   group at the table, sees the ghost of Banquo, exposing
   himself to his nobles as likely guilty of murder. Everything
   can untie from this point.
D. **Falling Action** Macbeth continues to kill to maintain his
   power; his opponents prepare to fight back; Lady
   Macbeth loses her hold on sanity.
E. **Resolution** Macbeth loses the will to continue, but dies
   fighting as the warrior he is; Macduff kills Macbeth,
   revenging his family's murder and restoring the murdered
   king's son to throne.

But what is the most tense and shocking moment of the entire play? Not the
banquet scene, though it certainly is tense. Nor it is near the end with Macbeth's
final showdown.

Without question, it is the murder of King Duncan, which comes a quarter of
the way into the work. Shakespeare prepares carefully for this scene, building up
tension before the murder and stretching out its discovery with strokes of suspense
that Alfred Hitchcock no doubt envied. There's a shrieking owl, a hallucinated
dagger leading Macbeth in the direction of the king, and Macbeth's anguished
observations before and after his fatal actions. This sequence is replete with
moments that foreshadow and keep us anticipating the murder. After the deed has
been done, we get a darkly comic scene with the Porter. This lulls us to relax again
just before Macduff makes the horrified discovery of the bloody body. With this
murder, Macbeth obviously crosses a point of no return. He has murdered his own

king who was also a guest sheltering under his roof, a doubly unthinkable betrayal.

In the way that Shakespeare meticulously prepares for and extends the reaction to Duncan's murder is, this plot element is equivalent in intensity to the turning points he provides in other plays at about the midpoint, such as in *Hamlet* (the Mousetrap scene and Closet scene) and *King Lear* (Lear on the heath). Yet in *Macbeth* Shakespeare brings this most energetic and consequential event of the play considerably earlier.

Repeated Peaks of Tension or Violence

But Shakespeare is just getting started. Peaks of tension, followed by relative calm, occur again and again.

Any plot analysis of *Macbeth* should account for this unusual pattern. Shakespeare's use of an early peak of tension and violence, followed by relative calm, and then repeated escalations and releases of tension. This pattern distinguishes *Macbeth* from Shakespeare's other tragedies. Although his other works will have moments of tension, there are more in Macbeth and those are more violent or otherwise terror-filled. Following are some of these peaks of tension.

In the **inciting incident,** Macbeth meets the witches, who predict he will be king. This is a highly tense scene, in no small part because the witches themselves are grotesque and describe revolting deeds they have done. From the start we are already put on edge.

The **rising action** includes an emotional peak more tense than any other in the play. Duncan's murder has a long set-up that builds suspense, the murder itself, which occurs offstage, a scene of comic relief with the Porter, and then another scene of horror as Macduff discovers the King has been murdered.

Also during the **rising action** is another act of violent and suspense, as Banquo is murdered but his young son manages to escape.

The plot's **turning point** occurs when Banquo is killed on Macbeth's orders, and shortly afterward when Macbeth sees his ghost during a banquet. The Scottish nobles flee him after seeing his evident guilt.

The **falling action** includes Macbeth visiting the gruesome Weird Sisters again where his hopes are dashed that a child of his will inherit the throne.

There are further scenes of violence or psychological tension during the **falling action** that almost match the previous emotional peaks:

- the abrupt murder of Lady Macduff and her son just after a touching domestic scene between them;
- Lady Macbeth being observed by others as she sleepwalks and betrays her guilty preoccupations with a blood-spotted hand;
- the later report of her death; and
- the moment when Macbeth sees the impossible happening—the forest of Dunsinane marching toward him—and he realizes he was led astray by the witches' pronouncements.

Just before the **resolution**, Macbeth shows himself utterly depleted ("Life's but a walking shadow"). There are no shocks left, just his determination to go out fighting: "I'll fight till from my bones my flesh be hacked. / Give me my armor" (5.3). His flesh will indeed become hacked, with Macduff displaying the tyrant's head at the end of the play.

The chart of *Macbeth*'s plot structure might be further refined by indicating relative peaks of tension (shown here by dashed vertical lines) along moments of Macbeth's pyramid shaped plot. An audience's response will be subjective, of course, and these are just estimates of the relative peaks of tension throughout the story.

Macbeth: Plot Structure with Peaks of Tension

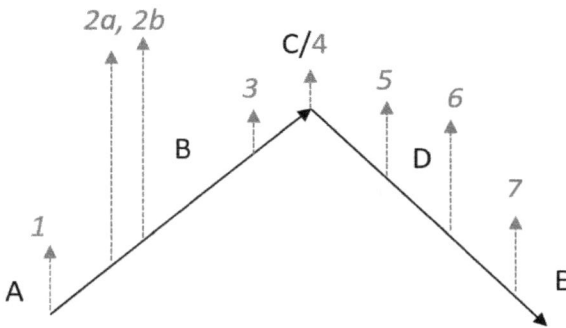

(1) Macbeth meets the witches, who predict he will be king; highly tense scene that is also the inciting incident.
(2) The greatest emotional peak, coming in two parts: Duncan's murder (2a), followed by comic relief with the Porter, and another scene of horror (2b) as Macduff discovers the King's murder.
(3) Banquo is killed on Macbeth's orders; his son escapes.
(4) Macbeth sees Banquo's ghost during a banquet and exposes his probable guilt to the Scottish nobles.
Other scenes of violence or psychological tension, including Macbeth visiting the witches again and seeing a depiction of the future (5), the murder of Macduff's family (6), and Lady Macbeth revealing her deep psychological distress, and soon after, dying (7).

Why An Early Peak of Tension?

Why would Shakespeare make the most terrifying scene of all come early in the play? Why not prepare for this moment gradually and peak later?

The answer has everything to do with how Shakespeare wants the audience to feel. This is a story about the uncanny—about evil and humans' susceptibility to it. In telling this story, Shakespeare wants to throws the audience into an uneasy, tense state of mind. An early and shocking event sets this up. Even though the act 2 murder takes place offstage, the audience is brought through Macbeth's tense, atmospheric preparation for it, and then witnesses his horrified reaction. Shakespeare next lulls the audience into relaxing a bit with the Porter's drunken, darkly comic interlude, and then ratchets up the tension with Macduff's shocked discovery of the murder. An audience will be on guard for the rest of the play, since at any moment there might be a new outbreak violence or terror. And so there is.

Shakespeare repeats this valley-and-peak pattern later in the sequence in act 3. Banquo's murder is followed by the banquet scene, in which Lady Macbeth and Macbeth give warm welcomes and gracious toasts to their guests, a mood that is abruptly interrupted when Macbeth shouts in terror at the appearance of Banquo's ghost. Similarly, Lady Macduff and her son are shown in an affectionate, if strained, conversation in their home just before Macbeth's men enter and kill them.

Macbeth's plot structure doesn't lend itself to traditional analysis, in which we'd expect tension to build gradually, with an emotional high point about midway through the work and again at the end. Shakespeare was going after a different effect on the audience. He is trying to frighten us, again and again, to make us feel terror or dread, and he accomplishes it through techniques we have come to recognize in later horror/thriller genres.

Macbeth's structure, and its effect on audiences, is quite different from that of *The Comedy of Errors*, in which farcical conflicts keep building, with almost no let-up, until just before the end, when there is rapid and complete release. For *Macbeth*, it is a series of highly tense, sometimes violent scenes interspersed with more relaxed scenes. To thrill and terrify his audiences, he found an effective alternative to standard plot structure.

Episodic Structure

An episodic plot structure is rare in dramatic works, although it can often be found in longer formats, such as epic poems, serial stories, and novels.

In an episodic plot, there is a series of adventures, with each adventure self-contained to a degree. A sequence of episodes may use the same central characters while adding new ones and discarding others along the way.

Each episode will have its own focus or dramatic problem to solve, but these segments will generally be linked by some kind of through-line or common theme. In Homer's epic poem *The Odyssey*, Odysseus falls into adventure after adventure, often due to his irrepressible curiosity. But uniting these, as the narrative's through-line, is Odysseus' quest to get home.

An episodic plot provides variety, which can be quite appealing to an audience. But as new circumstances, such as a new locale or new characters, are introduced, more exposition is needed to get the audience up to speed. And to the extent that the segments are self-contained, they can also seem detachable from the rest of the story. This runs the risk of losing cohesion among the segments and of slowing momentum. In *The Poetics,* Aristotle cautions against the episodic form, particularly when "episodes or acts succeed one another without probable or necessary sequence" (Part IX).

None of Shakespeare's plays is entirely episodic, but *Pericles, Prince of Tyre* is distinctly more episodic than his other works. In fact, he leans into the episodic format in this play, experimenting with how to make it work onstage. It's worth analyzing to see how he handles the challenge of writing a largely episodic plot while keeping it seem unified. There are obviously elements in this plot structure that he found appealing.

Pericles, Prince of Tyre

Pericles is an unusual work on many counts. Its most defining structural features are:

- the long gap of time that elapses midway through the play (14 years), and
- the fact that there are two protagonists whose stories are treated more or less sequentially until the very end, when they combine.

The first half of *Pericles* focuses on the title character's adventures and travails, while in the second half, our attention turns to his daughter Marina, who was given as a newborn to be fostered at the end of act 3, but in act 4 is now grown and faces travails and adventures of her own.

Also notable are the circumstances of its composition: Shakespeare collaborated with another writer, which he rarely did. Scholars think the co-author (possibly George Wilkins) wrote act 1, and Shakespeare the rest.

To see how Shakespeare (and his co-author) handled the episodic structure, let's briefly survey its main events. Notice how the action falls into distinct episodes, particularly in the first half.

Pericles: *Plot Overview*

Part 1 (acts 1–3)

In Part 1, Pericles sails from location to location and from challenge to challenge.

Prince Pericles arrives in Antioch to seek its princess for his wife, but he uncovers her terrible secret of incest with her father. He flees, but now has an assassin on his trail.

Pericles then saves the city of Tarsus from famine by bringing them grain, after which he must again flee the assassin.

As his ship nears Pentapolis, he is shipwrecked, but reaches land; there he wins a royal bride, Thaisa, who in due course becomes pregnant.

Called home to handle a crisis, Pericles sets sail with Thaisa to Tyre, but another storm arises and he loses Thaisa in childbirth. He must consign her coffin to the waves.

He then relinquishes his newborn daughter to the governor of Taurus and his wife Dionyza to raise to adulthood.

Unbeknownst to him, Thaisa's coffin lands ashore and she is brought back to life by a gifted physician. She dedicates herself to serving as votaress in the nearby temple to Diana.

Part 2 (acts 4–5)

Part 2 also features rapid changes of locale, rescues from dangerous situations, and other fortuitous events, but these focus mainly on Pericles' daughter.

The beautiful Marina, now a teenager, incites the jealousy of her foster mother in Tarsus, who plots to have her killed. But pirates accost them just in time to save her. They carry Marina off as a prize, intending to sell her to a brothel.

When Pericles arrives in Taurus to recover his daughter, he is told she has died. Utterly bereft, Pericles will sail aimlessly and cease to speak or to take care of himself.

We next see Marina as she is installed at a brothel in Mytilene. Before she can be sold to the highest bidder, she eloquently shames the clients for their illicit intentions and they depart. The brothel keepers lose so much business because of her defense of chastity that they intend to have her raped to make her more submissive. But she surmounts this danger as well; with gold the governor Lysimachus has given her, she ransoms herself and sets up as a teacher of music and other arts.

When Lysimachus learns that a prince, anchored nearby, is suffering from grave melancholy, he arranges for Marina to sing to him in hopes of a cure. This prince is Pericles, who at first rejects her, but eventually they discover who the other is: father and daughter are joyously reunited.

Then, in a dream, Pericles hears the goddess Diana bid him visit her temple. He travels there with his daughter, where they discover Thaisa is still alive. The family is restored at last. Pericles and Thaisa will spend the rest of their lives ruling in Pentapolis, while Marina will marry Lysimachus and rule in Tyre.

Pericles: *Plot Analysis*

There are numerous changes of locale, dangerous threats, fortuitous rescues, even a new protagonist added halfway through. All of this is exciting, fast-paced stuff. But how does it hold together? Does it meet Aristotle's standards and avoid "episodes or acts [that] succeed one another without probable or necessary sequence"?

The first two episodes—in Antioch and Tarsus—can certainly appear detachable from the rest of the plot. They create little rising action for the rest of the story (the characters from Antioch never reappear, for instance). Any relevant details, such as the generosity Pericles shows the city of Tarsus, or the reason that Pericles keeps fleeing by ship, could have been depicted more briefly as exposition.

The events in the second part, focusing on Marina, are less disjointed, because they do build on each other and show a plausible progression. Namely, Marina is taken from Tarsus by pirates, who sell her to a Mytilene brothel; that is how she has arrived there. She is able save herself from the brothel by her own gifts. Her gifts are why Lysimachus sends her to sing for Pericles. Through this encounter, they discover each other's identity. These events, in spite of shifting locales, succeed each other in a probable sequence.

If there is a sense of disjunction in the second part, it comes when Shakespeare introduces this new protagonist and cast of characters. But this, too, is a natural kind of progression: the baby born at the end of act 3 has grown up, and in act 4 we follow the consequences of her unlucky start in life.

Strategies to Unify an Episodic Plot

Not coincidentally, the episodes that most lack what Aristotle warned about—a "probable or necessary sequence"—are those in Act 1, which were likely written by Shakespeare's collaborator. We don't know what kind of planning sessions the two authors had. Shakespeare may have simply been handed the draft of act 1 and carried on from there.

In any case, the senior writer would have seen that to make this episodic plot work, he needed to do more than pile on one adventure after another.

And so, here's what Shakespeare does:

- He adds an explicit framing device, in which the narrator provides information and a sense of continuity.
- He shapes the two protagonist arcs along similar themes with the same ultimate (if implicit) dramatic goal.
- And he unites the storylines at the end.

Explicit Framing Device

The framing device is an explicit effort by Shakespeare to overcome the inherent disadvantages of this episodic plot style. Shakespeare begins each of the five acts begin, and ends the plot, with a narrator, John Gower. The narrator helps to set the scene, move the action along, and generally provide a sense of continuity from episode to episode. (Scholars pretty unanimously identify Shakespeare as the author of the Gower speeches.) This sets up a clear "storytelling" framework.

This narrator is identified as the medieval poet John Gower, who harkens back to the old times: "To sing a song that old was sung, / From ashes ancient Gower is come" (1.Chorus). With this ancient and famous storyteller, the audience is prepared for a more narrative format. The narrator obligingly returns to orient us to sudden shifts of time, place, and characters.

Unifying the Protagonist Arcs and Goals

More subtly, Shakespeare also shapes the two protagonist arcs along similar themes.

It's an unorthodox choice to introduce a new protagonist halfway through the piece. But one way Shakespeare holds these two halves together is by making the storylines of each protagonist echo each other.

Each of them is given great trials, including betrayals and physical threats. Both protagonists are betrayed by Dionyza of Tarsus. Pericles must flee an assassin and endure grave losses. Marina is seemingly orphaned, nearly murdered, and then is sold into a brothel, where she must use her wits to preserve her virginity and escape captivity. At the end, she must persist when her nearly catatonic father, whom she assumes is a stranger, pushes her away and refuses to respond to her.

What is the play's central problem? We have to infer it, and it is not especially clear at first. The hand who wrote Act 1 sets up Pericles' first goal as that of finding a wife, and next, when he draws the wrath of the King of Antioch, to save his own life. Saving his own life is the premise that sets him across the seas where his adventure continues.

But when Shakespeare takes over, probably in Act 2, he resolves that first goal (by having Pericles gain his wife Thaisa), and dispenses with the other goal (the incestuous King, who sent the assassin after him, dies, as does his daughter). With the turning point in Act 3, in which the family is dispersed, we finally have a sense of what the dramatic goal will be: how can this family be reunited? This, too, is a theme that unites Pericles' and Marina's arcs. Even though neither of them is aware of this goal, each is heading in the same direction: to find again the other members of their family.

This goal is not something either Pericles or Marina actively pursues. Pericles believes both his daughter and wife are dead. But the audience knows the truth, and as with *The Comedy of Errors*, we want to see this imbalance righted and the family together again.

Uniting the Storylines at the End

The two main storylines of the plot come together near the end, when Pericles' will to live is restored by his long-lost daughter's intervention. But this fortuitous reunion is not all. In the final episode, as Pericles and Marina arrive at the goddess' temple, they discover Thaisa: all are united as the final strand of the plot is woven in. Pericles, Marina, and Thaisa each endured great loss, persevered, and were restored to each other at the end.

Pericles' structure is unorthodox in terms of classic structure because:

- The first act is more or less removeable. It mainly establishes a reason why Pericles must embark on further journeys. (And assuming act 1 was the piecemeal creation of another playwright, we can absolve Shakespeare of this.)
- In the traditional "untying" section (the second half of the story), we are, in fact, introduced to new significant characters—the grown-up Marina, the brothel keepers, and Lysimachus. A second plotline is starting up while the first plotline, of Pericles, is more or less in suspension until near the end.

But Pericles' love—first, for wife, then his daughter, and his suffering over their loss—remain a continuous thread from the second act on. The dramatic questions are: How can Pericles endure? Will the family be reunited? Marina's story, in the fourth and fifth acts, echoes that of her father.

So, although this play is more episodic than in a classically built plot, it also features some continuity of the protagonist's central problem, which is resolved at the end.

Summary

Although in most of his works, Shakespeare structures his plots in a the standard, pyramid shape, he adapts it when he can find a more effective way of constructing the stories he wants to tell.

In the next Spotlight chapter, we will see another example of this creative approach to plotting: he threads a kind of "inner plot" throughout the otherwise classic plot structure of *Hamlet*.

Takeaway for Writers

Shakespeare follows a pragmatic approach to plotting adapting the standard structure of plots to suit his purposes. In the previous chapter, we saw Shakespeare doubled the plot in *Much Ado About Nothing*, developing the Benedick–Beatrice plot to run in parallel with Claudio–Hero story. In this chapter, we explored further variants:

- In many works, Shakespeare creates a **subplot** that reflects on the main plot. These range from very brief—such as the Cassio-Bianca subplot in *Othello*—to major subplots, as in the Gloucester storyline in *King Lear.*
- In many of his romantic comedies as well as tragedies, he develops quasi-subplots in which he **examines each co-protagonist individually**, as he does for Romeo and Juliet.
- Shakespeare alters where he places the turning point falls when he uses a **farcical structure**. This kind of plot has an extended and continuous series of complications, as we find in *The Comedy of Errors,* with the turning point and falling action happening only near the end in a greatly compressed timeline.
- For a **horror/thriller structure,** Shakespeare may follow the standard pyramid plot, but includes numerous peaks of emotional tension along the way; in the case of *Macbeth*, the greatest peak of horror and tension happens a quarter of the way through the story.
- An **episodic structure** link several more or less self-contained brief stories together, using certain common characters or themes to unite them. *Pericles* is not entirely episodic, but comes closest to this format. Shakespeare draws attention to its narrative-like format by using a narrator, John Gower to introduce each act and conclude the play and to fill in the audience on the passage of time or place, or other developments that happen off-stage.

Terms

Episodic plot: An episodic plot is "constructed as a narrative by a succession of loosely connected incidents rather than by an integrated plot. Picaresque novels and many medieval romances have an episodic structure in which the only link between one episode and the next is the presence of the same central character." (Baldrick)

Farcical plot: The plot of a farce, which is "a kind of comedy that inspires hilarity mixed with panic and cruelty in its audience through an increasingly rapid and improbable series of ludicrous confusions, physical disasters, and sexual innuendos among its stock characters." (Baldrick)

Subplot: A subplot is "a secondary sequence of actions in a dramatic or narrative work, usually involving characters of lesser importance (and often of lower social status). The subplot may be related to the main plot as a parallel or contrast, or it may be more or less separate from it. Subplots are especially common in Elizabethan and Jacobean drama, a famous example being that of Gloucester and his sons in Shakespeare's *King Lear*." (Baldrick)

CHAPTER 9: SPOTLIGHT: THE "INNER" PLOT OF *HAMLET*

Shakespeare, as we've seen, creatively reformulates plot structure for the needs of a particular story, which inevitably shapes the way audiences respond to it. With this in mind, let's return to *Hamlet* and explore the question of why it includes so many soliloquies. How do these philosophically searching speeches fit into an otherwise classic plot structure? Why would Shakespeare pause the action at numerous points to have Hamlet alone on the stage, focusing inward as he talks to himself (and to the audience)?

And why is it that these speeches are some of the most revered and quoted of all of Shakespeare's writing?

The Subgenre Shakespeare Uses

First, it helps to recognize the model Shakespeare was adopting. *Hamlet* is not just a tragedy, but a revenge tragedy, a very popular subgenre in Shakespeare's day. In it, the protagonist vows to commit revenge on behalf of a loved one and may even declare they are acting as God's scourge. This is what makes the act of taking another's life different from murder. It is a quasi-righteous act because they are bringing a wrongdoer to justice, and the avenger undertakes it knowing it may cost them their own life. In that sense, it can be seen as heroic, a self-sacrifice for a higher good.

Shakespeare decides to write in this popular form but he takes it much further, of course, exploring what it means to take revenge. How can a decent, sensitive person kill another, no matter how righteous the cause? What fears and doubts might arise in taking on the role of avenger? What does this cost a person psychologically or spiritually?

These questions are posed and largely answered through Hamlet's more private speeches, namely, his soliloquies and a few confessional speeches with his confident Horatio.

Rather than simply sprinkle in the occasional reflective speech, Shakespeare addresses the questions in a progressive and dramatic way. While the revenge plot is unfolding along its classic contours, Shakespeare traces out the psychological drama Hamlet undergoes.

In effect, Shakespeare creates an "inner drama." This plays out in parallel with the outer, revenge plot, similarly to how the two closely aligned romantic storylines play out in *Much Ado About Nothing*.

Hamlet's desperate search for the answers to some of life's most central questions is what makes *Hamlet* so much more than a mere revenge tragedy. We become as curious to see how Hamlet can make peace with himself as to how he can revenge his father's murder.

The Story of *Hamlet*'s Inner Plot

When the story opens, Hamlet already feels out of balance and has been contemplating suicide. His inner dilemma comes into focus, however, at the same moment that his outer challenge does—when he is called upon to revenge his father's murder. The time is out of joint, he says, and he must set things right. What does that mean for him personally? Spiritually? This is the "inner" plot that Shakespeare explores.

Because these speeches are long, I'll just summarize their content for our analysis. This does no justice to their depth, of course, and they more than repay careful study. The full soliloquies and other relevant passages are reproduced below in the Extras section of this chapter for easy reference. (Consider reading these together now, separate from the rest of the play, to get a sense of the common preoccupations running through these passages and the drama that builds and resolves through this philosophical "parallel plot.")

Here we aim just to show the movement in Hamlet's thoughts. Taking the speeches together, we can discern the outline of a plot progression, complete with a kind of exposition, a central problem, rising action, turning point, falling action, and resolution.

Exposition

During our first view of Hamlet, in Act 1, scene 2, we are plunged into Hamlet's already existing despair. (This is the soliloquy we have already analyzed a couple of times.)

193

Soliloquy 1: O that this too too [solid] flesh ... (1.2.129-59).

Summary: Hamlet finds the world "weary, stale, flat, and unprofitable," and regrets that the Almighty has "fixed his canon 'gainst self-slaughter." This refers to the religious law against suicide. He is disgusted that his mother married his father's brother—so inferior to the late king—and so soon after his death. "O God, a beast that wants discourse of reason / Would have mourned longer!" Hamlet compares humanity's failings to beasts.

Function: Already we see his inner turmoil. And what an image: he wishes his body would just melt and be absorbed into the air. This speech functions as an **exposition** of his spiritual distress, filling us in on what is causing him distress. He cannot bear life as it is, but he also cannot end his life or he risks damnation.

It is rare for Shakespeare to frame his plays along explicit theological or philosophical concepts, but in *Hamlet*, he does just that. Shakespeare invokes a Christian and stoical (philosophical) framework. This puts into relief Hamlet's dilemma over the revenge he must take and his spiritual misgivings: he is invoking the canon law that obliges humans to endure even a miserable life. He alludes to the costs to one's soul if they commit suicide and to the fear of what awaits us in the next life.

Inciting Incident

Later in Act 1, Hamlet encounters the Ghost who says he could share harrowing tales of afterlife, but that is not allowed to. The Ghost departs, bidding Hamlet: "Adieu, adieu, adieu! remember me." Hamlet promises a swift revenge, but feels a terrible shift in his usual world.

Soliloquy 2: O all you host of heaven! O Earth! What else? / And shall I couple hell?… (1.5.92-112).

Summary: Now that he knows of his uncle's crime, he vows he will wipe everything else from his mind except his vow for revenge. He's willing even to "couple hell"—that is, engage intimately with the darkest forces; there is nothing, not in heaven, Earth, or hell, that will dissuade him from fulfilling his duty.

Function: The functions as an **inciting incident** for the main plot as well as the inner plot: Hamlet commits to a course of action to take revenge (main plot) and to dedicate all of his thoughts henceforth to achieving this, no matter the cost. Yet however manic he sounds at this point, Hamlet recognizes his task is of the gravest spiritual nature (inner plot), which may involve engaging with, or coupling, hell. It's an undertaking the poses external challenges as well as metaphysical ones. This

194

moment incites him down the path of revenging his father's murder, but also, he grasps this may bring his soul into danger (by coupling hell). It is a harrowing task he is taking, and he will return in later soliloquies to the questions it raises.

Rising Action

In act 2, scene 2, Hamlet has just met with the Players and witnessed one of them enact a tragic speech.

Soliloquy 3: O, what a rogue and peasant slave am I!... (2.2.550-605).

Summary: Hamlet reproaches himself at the contrast between the Player and himself. The Player can display such passion over a fiction, while Hamlet has not yet revenged his father's actual murder. He wonders if he is a coward. He then shifts to formulating a plan to gain complete assurance that Claudius is guilty, since the Ghost might have been a spirit sent to ensnare his soul through lies. He will ask the Players to perform a play similar to his father's murder, and thereby detect if Claudius displays guilt.

Function: This contributes to the **rising action** in that he introduces a plan to solve his problem. As such, it addresses the main plot (in getting revenge), but also raises another existential question that involves his inner plot: he wonders about the nature of the Ghost and whether he should trust it. He is acknowledging, again, the threat this task poses his eternal soul. To save his soul from being ensnared by a false spirit, he will test Claudius' guilt with this stratagem of what he calls the Mousetrap. This is a "complication" because it adds a new situation that will need to be untied, or answered later.

Turning Point

The turning point of the main plot comes in act 3, scene 2 with the Mousetrap scene that exposes Claudius' guilt, and continues in the Closet scene in act 3, scene 4, which puts Hamlet in still more danger.

But earlier in act 3, in the most famous of soliloquies, Hamlet is at his most despairing. Along with his unhappy encounter with Ophelia that immediately follows, this soliloquy shows Hamlet's lowest point.

Soliloquy 4: To be, or not to be... (3.1.55-89).

Summary: Hamlet debates which path is "nobler in the mind": to patiently suffer or to fight to the death against one's troubles. Death would be a consolation, a sleep. But with sleep may come dreams. No one has returned from the dead to tell us what this is like. (His father's spirit, we are told, is in Purgatory, "Doomed for a certain term to walk the night / And for the day confined to fast in fires" [1.5], and as such has not yet crossed the bourn from which no traveler returns.) We put up with heartache and injustice in this life out of fear of what is to come. This fear also makes us falter in great enterprises we'd otherwise undertake—"thus conscience doth make cowards of us all."

Unlike the previous soliloquy, in which Hamlet devises a plan to put his fears to rest, in this speech he sees no path forward. He is at a total impasse. He is then distracted by the entrance of his erstwhile sweetheart: "Soft you now, / The fair Ophelia. Nymph, in thy orisons / Be all my sins rememb'red." The thought of his own sins is weighing on him. He sounds wistful toward her at first, even hopeful, but this encounter ends bitterly.

Function: In terms of Hamlet's emotional arc, this monumental soliloquy functions as a **turning point** of his inner drama. He is at his lowest and most hopeless. He again considers suicide, but is reflecting on more than "canon law." He feels stymied by the inscrutable unknowns of the next world. We may flee our current problems on earth for worse ones in the next. This makes him feel utterly stuck, even a coward. He has no more hopes or illusions.

Although he is at an impasse, this functions as a decisive point. By having reached rock bottom, he is stripped of hope. This will pave the way for the psychological/spiritual breakthrough that emerges by the end of the play. This soliloquy is the dark night of the soul that rids him of past illusions and readies him for a degree of enlightenment and peace of mind.

Recap of Inner Plot So Far

The soliloquies are not necessary for moving the revenge plot along. Most of their content relates to the emotional and spiritual dilemmas that Hamlet experiences. Let's recap what we learn from them.

In these soliloquies, Hamlet:

- is profoundly distressed, emotionally and spiritually;
- accepts a task knowing it risks the gravest spiritual consequences;
- cannot understand why he does not complete this task, which only deepens his melancholy;
- fears that the Ghost might be a demon sent to ensnare his soul;
- is wrestling with a series of existential questions:
  o Is it better to patiently suffer the wrongs done to us, or should we struggle, even to the point of death?

- o What is the next world like? What happens once we die?
- o Why am I unable to act when I know what I must do?
- o How can humans be endowed with angelic gifts, yet behave worse than beasts?
- o Why does this god-like ability to reason and reflect also turn us into cowards?

These questions are universally compelling on their own. *We* want to know the answers to these as well. And they considerably deepen the drama. They are not even directly related to the question of whether or not it is justified to kill Claudius. They are the questions of an intelligent and sensitive individual who is struggling to make sense of a world that is out of kilter.

The "to be or not to be" soliloquy shows Hamlet's inner drama at a critical point—he has explored every angle and can see no good way forward.

If this is the inner plot's turning point, then we should expect that what follows will be falling action—the consequences of this moment, and that subsequent events will "untie" his dilemmas and lead to their resolution.

And this is what happens. But he no longer expresses his turmoil solely through soliloquy. We see it also expressed through interaction with his sole confidant Horatio.

Falling Action

In act 3, scene 2, Hamlet has a private speech with Horatio, the only character in the play he fully trusts. The speech is virtually a monologue, since Horatio speaks little. What Hamlet say here is indispensable in framing how he will resolve his inner dilemmas. We detect in this speech that an answer is starting to dawn on him.

Speech to Horatio: "For thou hast been / As one in suffering all that suffers nothing…" (3.2.67-78).

Hamlet expresses his admiration for Horatio's stoical approach to life. He calls Horatio "as just a man / As e'er my conversation coped withal." He is not a slave to passion, because his emotions and judgment are evenly balanced.

> Since my dear soul was mistress of her choice
> And could of men distinguish, her election
> Hath sealed thee for herself. For thou hast been
> As one in suffering all that suffers nothing,
> A man that Fortune's buffets and rewards

Hast ta'en with equal thanks; and blessed are those
Whose blood and judgment are so well commeddled
That they are not a pipe for Fortune's finger
To sound what stop she please. Give me that man
That is not passion's slave, and I will wear him
In my heart's core, ay, in my heart of heart,
As I do thee. (3.2.67-78)

Summary and Function: This presents a new tone: instead of focusing on his suffocating despair, Hamlet now sees a way of coping. The philosophical ideal that Hamlet invokes in his praise of Horatio is stoicism, the classical philosophy that holds that rational thinking, and restraint from passion or emotional reaction, are necessary for happiness and for the fulfillment of one's duty. As the Stoic Marcus Aurelius wrote in *Meditations*, "Accept the things to which fate binds you" (6.39). This stoical ideal encompasses not passivity, but rather acting from wisdom rather than from impulse or personal desire.

Hamlet's ideal is someone like Horatio, who can accept hardships and good fortune "with equal thanks." In Horatio, Hamlet can see a way out of his own suffering, and not be a pipe for Fortune to play on.

Following this are two brief soliloquies that come in quick succession. These are not especially inward focused, but serve as narrative about what Hamlet plans to do next.

Soliloquy 5: Tis now the very witching time of night... (3.2.419-432).
Summary: Having seen Claudius betray his guilt at the performance, Hamlet is highly roused, even violently manic: "Now could I drink hot blood / And do such bitter business as the day / Would quake to look on." His mother requests to see him. The Ghost has warned him to leave her to heaven, and Hamlet cautions himself to only *speak* daggers to her, not use them.

Soliloquy 6: "Now might I do it pat..." (3.3.73-96).
Summary: Hamlet sees Claudius at prayer and is on the verge of killing him, but resists, thinking it would send him to heaven. His father, after all, is suffering in Purgatory because Claudius cut him down unprepared. Hamlet vows to catch him later, when "his soul may be as damned and black / As hell, whereto it goes."

Function: These two brief soliloquies (5 and 6) are focused more what he plans to do, and only indirectly address Hamlet's inner struggles. But they show that Hamlet is now ready to take action to accomplish his revenge.

They also help to establish Hamlet's ethical frame of mind: he is capable of killing now, but is striving to master his impulses. To truly take revenge, Hamlet must catch Claudius when his soul is at risk, and so Hamlet vows to wait for the proper moment. He also commits himself to leaving his mother to God's will, as the Ghost asked him. But it is a struggle, and as we will see, he will rashly strike out in the Closet scene with his mother, killing Polonius.

Both speeches, invoking God and the afterlife, remind us that the duty of an avenger involves matters of the gravest spiritual nature.

But Soliloquies 5 and 6 more clearly serve as **falling action** to the main plotline: he confirms he is willing to take revenge, now that Claudius' guilt is clear, and he intends to do it in the right way.

Soliloquy 7: "How all occasions do inform against me..." (4.4.32-66).

Summary: In act 4, Hamlet delivers another soliloquy. He again notes the "capability and godlike reason" of humans, and wonders if his delay in killing Claudius is "Bestial oblivion or some craven scruple / Of thinking too precisely on th' event." He reiterates he's willing to fulfill his duty, but cannot fathom why is not doing it.

Function: Although it more or less repeats what he has said earlier in the play, the soliloquy reestablishes Hamlet's frustration at not having completed his task, even though he has the will and strength to do it. (Note that this soliloquy is found only in the Second Quarto of *Hamlet* and does not appear in the Folio version of the play; some scholars suggest it may represent a deletion Shakespeare made later. From the perspective of this "inner" drama, it is, in fact, fairly redundant.)

Resolution

In the final act, there are two important moments during which Hamlet recapitulates his concerns about death's unknowns—a central theme in his inner drama. These moments show his progress in finding a more accepting stance towards life's mysteries. They are expressed not through not soliloquies, but in conversations.

Monologue with Yorick's Skull: "Alas, poor Yorick! I knew him, Horatio..." (5.1.183-95).

Summary: Hamlet engages in a one-sided "conversation" with the skull of his old jester Yorick, with Horatio at his side. But just before this, we see the Gravedigger at work and hear him opine, in black humor, on matters of death and theology. He explains why the person whose grave they're digging—a suspected suicide—is being allowed a Christian burial. The Gravedigger's twisted logic seems a parody of the god-like reason Hamlet admires as one of humans' finest potentials. This conversation sets the scene for Hamlet's own musings on death by reminding us of the physical results of death and of the dire spiritual consequences of suicide.

When Hamlet then contemplates Yorick's skull, he observes that everyone comes to this end. He bids him go to his lady's chamber and tell her: "let her paint an inch thick, to this favor (the skull's face) she must come." Even Alexander the Great's decomposed body might end up as loam that stops a beer barrel.

Hamlet is looking death right in the face, as literally as can be. He accepts the reality of what happens to our body at death. Even the young and beautiful will decay and turn to dust. All will die. He strikes a note of equanimity. Soon after, though, he turns distraught when he learns that the grave is for Ophelia. He fights with Laertes over who is suffering more because of her death. In his mind he can accept death's finality, but he cannot maintain this poise when faced suddenly with the death of a loved one.

A final critical moment in Hamlet's inner drama comes in act 5, scene 2, in an exchange with Horatio just before his fatal duel. Here we see Hamlet has made peace with his own troubled spirit and with the questions that tormented him. It represents the resolution to Hamlet's inner drama.

Dialogue with Horatio: "There's a divinity that shapes our ends…. The readiness is all…. Let be" (5.2.6-11, 212-24).

Summary: Hamlet begins by telling Horatio that during his sea voyage to England, he rashly opened a letter from Claudius meant for the King— "and praised by rashness for it." For he discovered it was his secret death warrant. He revised it to spare himself and have Rosencrantz and Guildenstern put to death instead. He credits a higher force for this "indiscretion," saying it shows that "There's a divinity that shapes our ends, / Rough-hew them how we will." With this image, Hamlet is saying we can do only so much on our own; the divinity shapes the results.

A short section follows in which Hamlet accepts a challenge sent by the King for a fencing match with Laertes. Hamlet then turns again to Horatio to confide an uneasy premonition: "thou wouldst not think how ill all's here about my heart. But it is no matter."

Horatio implores him to put off the duel: "If your mind dislike anything, obey it." But Hamlet refuses to back down—not from pride or a passion to fight. Rather, he says that even if his premonition is correct, he accepts his part in a greater, providential scheme.

> Not a whit. We defy augury. There is a special providence in the fall of a sparrow. If it be now, 'tis not to come; if it be not to come, it will be now; if it be not now, yet it will come. The readiness is all. Since no man of aught he leaves knows, what is 't to leave betimes? Let be.

Why turn away from fate? If it doesn't come now, it will later; if not later, then now. All that matters is being prepared.

There is a lot of meaning packed in these lines, and especially in the short phrases: "the readiness is all" and "let be." We cannot avoid what must be. We can only choose how to meet our fate. What is most important is to be ready for what life brings us.

His words "let be" show how far he has come from his earlier tumult and restless searching. Here Hamlet shows he has achieved what he admired in Horatio, a stoical acceptance of what is. He is now facing the possibility of his own death—his uneasy premonition about the fencing match—and accepts whatever fate will bring. He is no longer reactive as he was when he learned of Ophelia's death.

Hamlet has attained a stoical acceptance of his fate and his position within a larger scheme. This stoical ideal encompasses not passivity or impulsiveness, but rather acting from wisdom. In stoicism, one is taught to accept the world as it is and act accordingly. This means even if humans, capable of such greatness, behave worse than beasts, one accepts that as reality. Struggling against what one cannot change is pointless.

Hamlet has come to realize by the end of the play that we must rise to whatever challenges life presents us and fulfill our duties, and this is all we can control.

This represents Hamlet's *anagnorisis*, his recognition of a significant truth. This insight also suggests why he couldn't act earlier. As much as he wanted to take revenge against Claudius, it was not yet the right time. *If it be not now, yet it will come.* But he must make himself ready.

201

In this light, it now becomes clear he has not been a coward. He could not act earlier because, if one is serving as a divine instrument of justice, which is what revenge is supposed to be, one is not acting out of personal choice, but as an agent for a higher cause. This was one more lesson he needed to learn: he cannot control the timing of a fateful event such as revenging his father's death. He must simply make himself ready to fulfill it. We can only make ourselves ready to act when we must act. For the rest? Let be.

In this speech, we see that Hamlet has at last broken through his inertia. It required more wisdom and stoical acceptance on his part. His inner drama resolves when he accepts that "the readiness is all" and to act when circumstances are right for him to act. That is what happens shortly afterward, when he is in a position to revenge his father's murder to killing Claudius.

Final dialogue of Hamlet with Horatio: "…the rest is silence" (5.2.352-360).

Hamlet's final words, as he is dying show him entreating Horatio to tell his story aright, and therefore not to join him in death. He ends in silence.

HAMLET   O, I die, Horatio,
The potent poison quite o'ercrows my spirit.
I cannot live to hear the news from England,
But I do prophesy th' election lights
On Fortinbras, he has my dying voice.
So tell him, with th' occurrents, more and less
Which have solicited — the rest is silence. *[Dies.]*
HORATIO
Now cracks a noble heart. Good night, sweet prince,
And flights of angels sing thee to thy rest!

Summary: Hamlet pleads with Horatio to live so he can tell his story aright; he also endorses Fortinbras to succeed as ruler.

Function: His final exchange recapitulates Hamlet's concern to set the state of Denmark right again. He is silenced by death, but the last words, "the rest is silence," has more than one meaning. They remind us of the mystery that lies beyond death: *the rest of his journey, to us the survivors, is silence.* Horatio has the last word, invoking the notion that Hamlet has indeed surmounted his spiritual dangers and will be accompanied by angels to his rest.

How Is This an "Inner" Plot, and Why Construct It This Way?

Shakespeare must have known he had a sure-fire hit on his hands with the revenge plot of Hamlet, the prince who bides his time to take revenge by pretending to be mad. Had Shakespeare simply stuck with the main plot as we now have it, it would no doubt have been successful on the Globe stage and beyond.

But he saw how much more there was to this premise of a prince who must revenge his father's murder. And so, he explored the inner dimensions of how a highly intelligent and sensitive person might react in this situation.

Shakespeare might have included just one or two soliloquies setting out the nature of Hamlet's fears and dilemmas. But instead, he does something more ambitious. He treats Hamlet's inner struggles as a dramatic problem in its own right; he does this by constructing a quasi-plot that runs parallel to the main one, much as he did a year or two earlier with *Much Ado*.

And yes, as a consequence, Shakespeare makes the play a whole lot longer, almost too long to stage in full. That's a hurdle that directors have had to deal with ever since.

On the other hand, try to imagine Hamlet without this inward-focused exploration. Strip away most of Hamlet's soliloquies and confidential speeches with Horatio, and the main plot would hold together just fine. But add them, and we have a mesmerizing exploration of the protagonist's internal world: not just moments of introspection here and there, but a progression of thought from initiating problem to turning point to resolution.

Hamlet has sensed from early in the play that the time was out of joint, and that his cursed fate was to set it right. This means, of course, to bring justice to a corrupt kingdom. But his spirit was already troubled before he learns his father was murdered. Hamlet's psyche, too, was out of joint, grappling with the kinds of existential questions we all wrestle with at some point in our lives.

When Hamlet at last kills Claudius, and he and much of the remaining the Danish court die as well, this purgation makes way for the Norwegian prince Fortinbras to claim the throne and for Denmark to start anew. This brings a satisfying resolution to the main plot. But the play is especially rewarding because we also have followed how Hamlet has resolved his inner dilemmas, setting things right in his own troubled psyche and achieving a measure of peace in the midst of almost insupportable tension.

Takeaway for Writers

In *Hamlet,* Shakespeare constructs a kind of "inner" plot that traces Hamlet's emotional and philosophical journey.

- This play's main plot follows a classic structure and focuses on Hamlet's goal to get revenge for his father's murder.
- In addition, there is a quasi-plot that explores Hamlet's inner turmoil. This is conveyed through the play's many soliloquies and some private dialogues with his confident Horatio.
- In this "inner" plot, we see Hamlet wrestling with spiritual and philosophical questions, reaching an impasse, having breakthroughs, and finally reaching acceptance; this storyline unfolds in a coherent way that runs parallel to the main plot.
- The value of this "inner" plot is to considerably deepen the stakes of this protagonist's situation.

Extras

The following speeches depict **the drama of Hamlet's inner life:** what he grapples with, what he's afraid of, how much this duty is costing him.

There is a progression in Hamlet's musings about his inner experience and ideas, and these run parallel to the main action, but are more or less independent of it. The character Hamlet could have simply been a revenger, but he is much more than that.

1. O that this too too [solid] flesh… (1.2.129–59); this follows the scene at court in which we first meet Hamlet, Claudius, and Gertrude.

O that this too too [solid] flesh would melt,
Thaw, and resolve itself into a dew!
Or that the Everlasting had not fix'd
His canon 'gainst self-slaughter!
O God, God, How weary, stale, flat, and unprofitable
Seem to me all the uses of this world!
Fie on't, ah fie! 'tis an unweeded garden
That grows to seed, things rank and gross in nature
Possess it merely. That it should come [to this]!

But two months dead, nay, not so much, not two.
So excellent a king, that was to this
Hyperion to a satyr, so loving to my mother
That he might not beteem the winds of heaven
Visit her face too roughly. Heaven and earth,
Must I remember? Why, she should hang on him
As if increase of appetite had grown
By what it fed on, and yet, within a month—
Let me not think on't! Frailty, thy name is woman!—
A little month, or ere those shoes were old
With which she followed my poor father's body,
Like Niobe, all tears—why, she, even she—
O God, a beast that wants discourse of reason
Would have mourn'd longer—married with my uncle,
My father's brother, but no more like my father
Than I to Hercules. Within a month,
Ere yet the salt of most unrighteous tears
Had left the flushing in her galled eyes,
She married—O most wicked speed: to post
With such dexterity to incestious sheets,
It is not, nor it cannot come to good,
But break my heart, for I must hold my tongue.
[Enter Horatio, Marcellus, and Barnardo.]

2. O, all you host of heaven... (1.5.92–112); this soliloquy immediately follows
   the departure of the Ghost, from whom Hamlet has just learned of his
   father's murder by Claudius and readily takes on the duty to revenge him.

O all you host of heaven! O Earth! What else?
And shall I couple hell? O fie! hold, hold, my heart,
And you, my sinews, grow not instant old,
But bear me stiffly up. Remember thee!
Ay, thou poor ghost, whiles memory holds a seat
In this distracted globe. Remember thee!
Yea, from the table of my memory 105
I'll wipe away all trivial, fond records,
All saws of books, all forms, all pressures past,

205

That youth and observation copied there,
And thy commandment all alone shall live
Within the book and volume of my brain,
Unmixed with baser matter. Yes, by heaven!
O most pernicious woman!
O villain, villain, smiling, damned villain!
My tables—meet it is I set it down
That one may smile, and smile, and be a villain.
At least I am sure it may be so in Denmark.
[He writes].
So, uncle, there you are. Now to my word:
It is "Adieu, adieu! remember me."
I have sworn't.

3. O, what a rogue and peasant slave am I! (2.2.550–605); this long soliloquy
    follows his meeting with the troupe of actors and shows him castigating
    himself for his own failure to act; he ends by developing a plan to expose
    Claudius' guilt.

Rosencrantz and Guildenstern exit.
Now I am alone.
O, what a rogue and peasant slave am I!
Is it not monstrous that this player here,
But in a fiction, in a dream of passion,
Could force his soul so to his own conceit
That from her working all his visage wanned,
Tears in his eyes, distraction in his aspect,
A broken voice, and his whole function suiting
With forms to his conceit—and all for nothing,
For Hecuba!
What's Hecuba to him, or he to Hecuba,
That he should weep for her? What would he do
Had he the motive and the cue for passion
That I have? He would drown the stage with tears,
And cleave the general ear with horrid speech,
Make mad the guilty, and appall the free,
Confound the ignorant, and amaze indeed

The very faculties of eyes and ears. Yet I,
A dull and muddy-mettled rascal, peak
Like John-a-dreams, unpregnant of my cause,
And can say nothing; no, not for a king,
Upon whose property and most dear life
A damned defeat was made. Am I a coward?
Who calls me villain, breaks my pate across,
Plucks off my beard and blows it in my face,
Tweaks me by the nose, gives me the lie i' th' throat
As deep as to the lungs? Who does me this?
Hah, 'swounds, I should take it; or it cannot be
But I am pigeon-livered, and lack gall
To make oppression bitter, or ere this
I should have fatted all the region kites
With this slave's offal. Bloody, bawdy villain!
Remorseless, treacherous, lecherous, kindless villain!
Why, what an ass am I! This is most brave,
That I, the son of a dear father murdered,
Prompted to my revenge by heaven and hell,
Must, like a whore, unpack my heart with words
And fall a-cursing like a very drab,
A stallion. Fie upon't, foh!
About, my brains! Hum—I have heard
That guilty creatures sitting at a play
Have by the very cunning of the scene,
Been struck so to the soul, that presently
They have proclaimed their malefactions:
For murder, though it have no tongue, will speak
With most miraculous organ. I'll have these players
Play something like the murder of my father
Before mine uncle. I'll observe his looks,
I'll tent him to the quick. If he do blench,
I know my course. The spirit that I have seen
May be a devil, and the devil hath power
T' assume a pleasing shape, yea, and perhaps,
Out of my weakness and my melancholy,
As he is very potent with such spirits,

Abuses me to damn me. I'll have grounds
More relative than this. The play's the thing
Wherein I'll catch the conscience of the King.
Exit.

4. To be or not to be... (3.1.55–89); the soliloquy precedes the staging of the
    Mousetrap performance, which will confirm for Hamlet the guilt of
    Claudius. But here, Hamlet is at his lowest, most hopeless point.

To be, or not to be, that is the question:
Whether 'tis nobler in the mind to suffer
The slings and arrows of outrageous fortune,
Or to take arms against a sea of troubles,
And, by opposing, end them. To die, to sleep—
No more, and by a sleep to say we end
The heartache and the thousand natural shocks
That flesh is heir to; 'tis a consummation
Devoutly to be wished. To die, to sleep—
To sleep, perchance to dream—ay, there's the rub,
For in that sleep of death what dreams may come,
When we have shuffled off this mortal coil,
Must give us pause; there's the respect
That makes calamity of so long life:
For who would bear the whips and scorns of time,
Th' oppressor's wrong, the proud man's contumely,
The pangs of despised love, the law's delay,
The insolence of office, and the spurns
That patient merit of th' unworthy takes,
When he himself might his quietus make
With a bare bodkin; who would fardels bear,
To grunt and sweat under a weary life,
But that the dread of something after death,
The undiscovered country from whose bourn
No traveler returns, puzzles the will,
And makes us rather bear those ills we have,
Than fly to others that we know not of?
Thus conscience does make cowards of us all,

And thus the native hue of resolution
Is sicklied o'er with the pale cast of thought,
And enterprises of great pitch and moment
With this regard their currents turn awry,
And lose the name of action.—Soft you now,
The fair Ophelia. Nymph, in thy orisons
Be all my sins remembered.

5. Tis now the very witching time of night (3.2.419–432); this follows the
    springing of Hamlet's "mousetrap" and Rosencrantz and Guildenstern
    delivering a message to him that his mother wishes to see him.

'Tis now the very witching time of night,
When churchyards yawn and hell itself breathes out
Contagion to this world. Now could I drink hot blood
And do such bitter business as the day
Would quake to look on. Soft, now to my mother.
O heart, lose not thy nature! Let not ever
The soul of Nero enter this firm bosom,
Let me be cruel, not unnatural;
I will speak daggers to her, but use none.
My tongue and soul in this be hypocrites—
How in my words somever she be shent,
To give them seals never my soul, consent.
Exit.

6. Now might I do it pat. (3.3.73–96); this soliloquy comes just as Hamlet spies
    Claudius attempting to pray.

Now might I do it pat, now he is a-praying;
And now I'll do 't —and so he goes to heaven,
And so am I revenged. That would be scanned:
A villain kills my father, and for that,
I, his sole son, do this same villain send
To heaven.
Why, this is hire and salary, not revenge.
He took my father grossly, full of bread,

With all his crimes broad blown, as flush as May,
And how his audit stands who knows save heaven?
But in our circumstance and course of thought
'Tis heavy with him. And am I then revenged,
To take him in the purging of his soul,
When he is fit and seasoned for his passage?
No!
Up, sword, and know thou a more horrid hent:
When he is drunk asleep, or in his rage,
Or in th' incestuous pleasure of his bed,
At game, a-swearing, or about some act
That has no relish of salvation in 't—
Then trip him, that his heels may kick at heaven,
And that his soul may be as damned and black
As hell, whereto it goes. My mother stays,
This physic but prolongs thy sickly days.
Exit.

7.   How all occasions do inform against me… (4.4.32–66); this soliloquy comes
     while Hamlet is en route to the ship bound for England, just after seeing
     Fortinbras pass through territory,

How all occasions do inform against me,
And spur my dull revenge! What is a man,
If his chief good and market of his time
Be but to sleep and feed? A beast, no more.
Sure He that made us with such large discourse,
Looking before and after, gave us not
That capability and godlike reason
To fust in us unused. Now whether it be
Bestial oblivion or some craven scruple
Of thinking too precisely on th' event—
A thought which, quartered, hath but one part wisdom
And ever three parts coward—I do not know
Why yet I live to say "This thing's to do,"
Sith I have cause, and will, and strength, and means
To do 't. Examples gross as earth exhort me:

Witness this army of such mass and charge,
Led by a delicate and tender prince,
Whose spirit with divine ambition puffed
Makes mouths at the invisible event,
Exposing what is mortal and unsure
To all that fortune, death, and danger dare,
Even for an egg-shell. Rightly to be great
Is not to stir without great argument,
But greatly to find quarrel in a straw
When honor's at the stake. How stand I then,
That have a father killed, a mother stained,
Excitements of my reason and my blood,
And let all sleep, while to my shame I see
The imminent death of twenty thousand men,
That for a fantasy and trick of fame
Go to their graves like beds, fight for a plot
Whereon the numbers cannot try the cause,
Which is not tomb enough and continent
To hide the slain? O, from this time forth
My thoughts be bloody, or be nothing worth!

8. Monologue with Yorick's Skull: "Alas, poor Yorick! I knew him,
    Horatio..." (5.1.183–95); this speech arrives just after Hamlet and Horatio
    have chanced upon the Gravedigger digging a new grave and unearthing
    the skull of a jester that Hamlet played with in childhood.

Alas, poor Yorick! I knew him, Horatio, a fellow of infinite jest, of most
excellent fancy. He hath bore me on his back a thousand times, and now how
abhorr'd in my imagination it is! my gorge rises at it. Here hung those lips that I
have kiss'd I know not how oft. Where be your gibes now, your gambols, your
songs, your flashes of merriment, that were wont to set the table on a roar? Not one
now to mock your own grinning—quite chop-fall'n. Now get you to my lady's
[chamber], and tell her, let her paint an inch thick, to this favor she must come;
make her laugh at that.

211

9. Dialogue with Horatio: "We defy augury....there's a divinity that shapes our ends.... The readiness is all.... Let be" (5.2.6–11, 211–24); the resolution to Hamlet's inner dilemma is expressed in this conversation with Horatio.

HAMLET Sir, in my heart there was a kind of fighting
That would not let me sleep. Methought I lay
Worse than the mutines in the bilboes. Rashly—
And praised be rashness for it—let us know,
Our indiscretion sometime serves us well
When our deep plots do pall; and that should learn us
There's a divinity that shapes our ends,
Rough-hew them how we will—
....
HORATIO You will lose, my lord.
HAMLET I do not think so. Since he went into France, I have been in continual practice. I shall win at the odds. Thou wouldst not think how ill all's here about my heart—but it is no matter.
HORATIO Nay, good my lord—
HAMLET It is but foolery, but it is such a kind of gain-giving as would perhaps trouble a woman.
HORATIO If your mind dislike anything, obey it. I will forestall their repair hither and say you are not fit.
HAMLET Not a whit, we defy augury. There is a special providence in the fall of a sparrow. If it be now, 'tis not to come; if it be not to come, it will be now; if it be not now, yet it will come—the readiness is all. Since no man, of aught he leaves knows, what is 't to leave betimes? Let be.

10. Final dialogue: (5.2.352–360); this final exchange shows Hamlet entreating Horatio to live so that he can report his story aright. He gives his dying voice for Fortinbras to succeed to the throne in Denmark. But then, he is silenced by death. Horatio has the last word, invoking the notion that Hamlet has surmounted his spiritual dangers and will be accompanied by angels to his rest.

HAMLET As th' art a man,
Give me the cup. Let go! By heaven, I'll ha't!
O God, Horatio, what a wounded name,

Things standing thus unknown, shall I leave behind me!
If thou didst ever hold me in thy heart,
Absent thee from felicity a while,
And in this harsh world draw thy breath in pain
To tell my story.
[A march afar off and a shot within.]
What warlike noise is this?
[Osric goes to the door and returns.]
OSRIC Young Fortinbras, with conquest come from Poland,
To th' ambassadors of England gives
This warlike volley.
HAMLET   O, I die, Horatio,
The potent poison quite o'ercrows my spirit.
I cannot live to hear the news from England,
But I do prophesy th' election lights
On Fortinbras, he has my dying voice.
So tell him, with th' occurrents, more and less
Which have solicited—the rest is silence. *[Dies.]*
HORATIO
Now cracks a noble heart. Good night, sweet prince,
And flights of angels sing thee to thy rest!

CHAPTER 10: ANTAGONISTS

IAGO: Divinity of hell!
When devils will the blackest sins put on,
They do suggest at first with heavenly shows,
As I do now.
　　　—Othello, act 2, scene 3

Iago's scheming and amoral nature is only one reason that Iago has come to be seen as an all-time great villain. Shakespeare has created in Iago a character who sets out to do harm—committing "the blackest sins" while disguised by his "heavenly shows." But he also functions in the plot as an effective antagonist *to* the hero. He serves as the shadow to Othello's light. We care about Othello's fate in large part because of how Shakespeare strategically constructs this antagonist.

An antagonist takes Shakespeare into a different territory than his protagonists do. With Iago, Shakespeare can probe the darker side of human nature: why would someone want to intentionally destroy another, and how they could bring down even a noble character like Othello?

Antagonists are rarely as prominent in stories, or as malevolent, as we find in *Othello*, but here Shakespeare pulls out all the stops. He invests Iago with cunning and wit, and draws the audience into his confidence. Shakespeare intends Iago to be nearly as central to the story as the protagonist.

We don't want to see antagonists triumph, but there can be something paradoxically appealing about them. They transgress, destroy, and take what they want without a second thought. Their audacity and unleashed egos can provide us a degree of guilty pleasure. But when these forces of destruction are at last curtailed, as they usually are, we can also feel the satisfaction of seeing them brought to account, and order and goodness restored.

The potential of the antagonist character clearly fascinated Shakespeare; it gave him a channel for portraying aspects of humanity that wouldn't easily suit a protagonist (Richard III and Macbeth are notable attempts at this). The malevolence we find in characters like Iago or Lear's daughters can be disturbing, but Shakespeare shows it as no less part of human nature than the finer attributes he portrays in heroic protagonists.

Antagonists are by definition secondary characters, but they can be nearly as crucial as the protagonist in the overall dynamic of a story. Certainly, Shakespeare makes good use of this type of character.

What Is an Antagonist?

The Greek roots of the word clarify the role's function: anti (against) + agonist (the one who acts or strives). The antagonist works against the main actor. This character will be the primary cause of the hero's troubles or will thwart the hero in some significant way.

Functionally, the antagonist is the next most important character in a story after the protagonist. It is thanks to dangers the antagonist poses that we see the protagonist reach heights of resourcefulness, insight, and endurance they would not have otherwise. You can't have a great hero unless the hero has something formidable to fight against.

Antagonists often represent a threat to more than just the protagonist. In many of Shakespeare's works, we see they threaten the community as well, and raise the stakes of the central conflict: what will happen to others if the hero fails to overcome the antagonist?

Thematic Function of Antagonists

Antagonists will sometimes serve another role in a story: as a counterpoint of some kind to what the protagonist represents. They are not necessarily wrong versus the protagonist's right, but are an alternative to what the protagonist believes or values. In *Antony and Cleopatra,* Octavius Caesar is not wrong in opposing the protagonist Antony, who is neglecting his duties to Rome. But for Antony, "in the East his pleasure lies." The Roman values that Caesar represents— self-discipline, temperance, rationality—are antithetical to the sensuous, extravagant, supra-rational world of Egypt. Caesar would have no trouble resisting the charms of Cleopatra, but in Shakespeare's telling, this doesn't make Antony any less majestic. Neither approach to life is inherently wrong, but they are incompatible. This is why it's not always correct to call the kind of role Caesar plays a "villain."

Similarly, in *Richard II*, the antagonist Bolingbroke, who will depose the king, operates in the world of *realpolitik*. He knows how power works. He knows he must woo the common people to take his side; he knows that flesh-and-blood soldiers will win out over the angelic hosts whom Richard desperately invokes to save him.

With this protagonist–antagonist pair, Shakespeare can play out dialectical views of kingship: the idealistic one, promoted in propaganda, about the divine right of kings; and a more harshly pragmatic one, in which we see that might can find a way to appear right. In *Richard II*, there is a clash not only of two opponents and their armies, but of important political ideas.

Classic Outlines of an Antagonist

The primary function of the role is to block the hero's path and to give the hero a focal point against which to battle. At times, an antagonist may be functional and scarcely interesting in their own right. An antagonist need not be fully fleshed out to serve their function well.

But we will find an antagonist active in one way or another in most of the major plot moments. If a figure doesn't operate in at least some the plot's major stress points — its initiating incident, turning point, and resolution — this character is probably not fulfilling the antagonist function.

Claudius as Antagonist in Hamlet

With Claudius, Shakespeare has created a classic antagonist. This is a major figure against whom the protagonist must battle through much of the plot.

Although Hamlet is the character he lavished the greatest care on, Shakespeare would have thought carefully about how to use his antagonist to tell Hamlet's story.

Claudius fulfills the role of antagonist effectively because:

- He is the cause of the protagonist's central problem.
- He is a formidable adversary: powerful, suspicious, willing to kill Hamlet to safeguard his position. Because of him, the protagonist must strive even harder, show himself even more heroic, in order to save himself and accomplish his goal.
- Claudius is also the efficient means by which the protagonist's problem can be resolved. By vanquishing Claudius, Hamlet gets revenge for his father's murder and sets the state right again.

- Although is he a forceful character, Claudius does not take away too much attention or sympathy from the protagonist to throw off the balance of the audience's sympathies.

Just as the plot structure of *Hamlet* is classically structured, so is the main antagonist. Claudius will, in fact, figure in all of the key plot points:

Central Problem: Claudius appears at the start of the play as a polished and seemingly gracious king, but we are soon put on alert by Hamlet, who expresses disgust for him. Hamlet is troubled by many things—his father's death, his mother's hasty remarriage, his dashed ambitions. But as we will soon learn, his uncle is the root cause. Claudius killed the previous king, maneuvered his way to the throne, and quickly married the king's widow. All this is established in the exposition during act 1, scenes 2, 4 and 5.

Inciting Incident: The inciting incident comes in act 1, scene 5, when Hamlet learns from his father's spirit that Claudius murdered him and the Ghost implores him to revenge it. This squarely places Claudius as his antagonist. Hamlet sets his sights on his hated uncle and will set things right in Denmark by purging it of this killer.

Complication/Rising Action: As king, Claudius has the power to curtail Hamlet's movements and to set spies on him; we see this operating in the rising action. Claudius is on alert for any dangers from Hamlet, and constantly maneuvers to contain him. To that end, he forbids Hamlet from returning to university, and he summons Hamlet's old friends Rosencrantz and Guildenstern to report on him. Although Claudius is skeptical of Polonius's plans, he lets his counselor rope in Ophelia to try to draw out why Hamlet appears distressed.

In this stretch of the plot, Claudius throws up various hurdles to Hamlet, including alienating him from previous allies—his mother, two of his old friends, and his one-time sweetheart. His torment increases with his sense of being betrayed. But Hamlet also rises to the challenge. He displays a formidable intelligence in quickly smoking out Rosencrantz and Guildenstern as working for Claudius and concocting a plan to confirm his uncle's guilt.

Turning Point: Claudius reveals guilty behavior during the Players' performance, which convinces Hamlet of his guilt; the audience, too, is no longer in doubt, since Claudius confesses it during his attempt to pray shortly afterwards.

Untying/Falling Action: Now that he realizes Hamlet suspects the truth, Claudius starts working actively to kill Hamlet. First, he sends him on a mission to England with a letter asking that the letter-bearer be killed; and when that fails, he convinces Laertes to wound Hamlet with a poisoned rapier tip during a fencing match.

These threats again allow Hamlet a chance to show his own superior attributes, as when he instinctively decides to open the letter that would have him killed and replace it with other instructions. "Praised be rashness for it," he declares. The fencing contest shows Hamlet one last time as a noble prince, the "mould of fashion," as Ophelia described him. In addition to all his other gentlemanly talents, Hamlet is a fine fencer and plays fair. This is the flower of youth who will be cut down shortly. By contrast, the plotters—Claudius and Laertes—use subterfuge. Claudius' unscrupulously makes his downfall all the more welcome to the audience.

Resolution: Claudius rigs the fencing match so that Hamlet is poisoned by Laertes' unbated sword. This spells Hamlet's doom, but it also propels him to complete his long-intended aim—to kill Claudius. This was Hamlet's original quest: to avenge his father's murder, and by doing so, to return the state to wholesomeness. By killing the antagonist, the protagonist brings about a resolution to the plot's original problem, though at the cost of his own life.

Claudius as the antagonist functions as an integral cog in *Hamlet*'s impeccably structured plot. Without Claudius, there would be no heroic Hamlet. Claudius is there at every critical moment of the plot. His antagonism forces Hamlet to reach the utmost of his own abilities to counter the threats posed by his adversary.

How Much to Flesh Out the Antagonist?

As Shakespeare was deciding how his antagonist would operate in the plot structure, he had another choice to make. How much to flesh him out? Should he simply play a functional role, or be a figure of interest in his own right?

Shakespeare would not want to give to the multidimensional Hamlet a papier-mâché opponent to fight against. So, he draws Claudius realistically, indicating his motives and capacity to thwart Hamlet. But there's not a whole lot more flesh than that.

Claudius is eloquent and charming enough to make it seem plausible Gertrude and others would bend to his wishes. He's astute in his assessments of Hamlet and Polonius, and cunning in his plotting against Hamlet, so that he can seem a truly formidable adversary.

Shakespeare even gives us brief windows into Claudius' vulnerabilities—when he betrays his guilt by suddenly calling off the Mousetrap performance, and shortly after, when he attempts to pray (3.3).

During this prayer scene, we get his only soliloquy. Shakespeare shows us what's beneath the surface, and he's not a complete monster. "O, my offence is rank, it smells to heaven," Claudius admits (3.3). He loves Gertrude. He even makes an attempt at praying for forgiveness, commanding himself, "Bow, stubborn knees," but then gives up. There is no point since he knows he won't give up the fruits of his crime: "Words without thoughts never to heaven go." He admits he isn't truly penitent.

This soliloquy is enough to shed light on what motivated him to kill his brother and why he is trying to eliminate Hamlet. But it's not enough to engender a lot of sympathy for him.

The rest of the time, he is smoothly duplicitous and usually has the upper hand. If Claudius were any less threatening, less hypocritical, Hamlet would not need to be pushed to the limits of his own ability. He would not need to examine his own beliefs as deeply as he does, nor call up his own clever strategies to confirm the truth or protect himself.

Claudius represents a straightforward model for an antagonist. He's powerful and motivated to block the hero; we get insights into his motives for thwarting the hero; and if he succeeds, not only will the protagonist fail, but the world of the play will remain diseased because the regicide will be unavenged.

But is this style of antagonist right for all stories? No, clearly not, when you consider the wide range of antagonists that Shakespeare used.

Suiting the Antagonist to the Story

Shakespeare tailors the antagonist to the needs of the particular story he's telling. What matters is that there is some antagonistic force pushing against the protagonist. But the exact nature of that force will depend on the genre or other aims of the work.

Very early in his career, for his first attempt at tragedy, Shakespeare creates two over-the-top villains, Tamora, Queen of the Goths, and her lover, Aaron the Moor. *Titus Andronicus* is a exceptionally over-the-top revenge tragedy, replete with murder, rape, mutilation, insanity, cannibalism, torture, and still more murder. The young playwright leaves out almost nothing sensational in his quest to make an impression. (It worked. *Titus Andronicus* was a hit in its day, though, on the whole, has languished ever since.)

Not just his antagonists, but many of the other main characters show an inordinate proclivity toward violence and revenge. Aaron, however, is the mastermind behind the worst atrocities, and is unrepentant when captured at the end. He wishes only that he could have done more villainy:

> But I have done a thousand dreadful things
> As willingly as one would kill a fly,
> And nothing grieves me heartily indeed
> But that I cannot do ten thousand more. (5.1)

What are the roots of Aaron's sadism? Shakespeare does not go down that path. But in a play in which the gore's the thing, Shakespeare needs a truly outsized villain, one who will set terrible events in motion and transgress even beyond the horrors the other characters commit (and that's a steep challenge). Aaron achieves that.

In his later tragedies, Shakespeare will strike a far more subtle and realistic balance. He will develop naturalistically fleshed out antagonists whose inner workings we are made privy to, as he does with Claudius. But even the villainous ones will usually have enough traces of humanity that we can relate to them at some level. Edmund in *King Lear* is deceitful and murderous, yet Shakespeare also establishes some cause for his bitterness (he has been dismissed all his life as a bastard).

In comedies, the antagonistic threats often come from minor characters—they pose just enough of a threat to get the ball rolling in a certain direction and provide some challenges along the way. Their motives for doing harm, again, might be barely sketched in. Some characters, like Don John in *Much Ado About Nothing,* or Malvolio in *Twelfth Night*, are depicted simply as killjoys.

And it may be circumstances, not characters, that challenge the protagonists. Mistaken identity serves this purpose in many of the comedies. Shakespeare varies his style of antagonist depending on how they are needed in a story and its tone or genre.

Positioning the Antagonist Vis-à-vis the Audience

Even if he makes his antagonists' motives understandable, Shakespeare takes care how far he invites us into the antagonist's worldview. He positions these characters differently vis-à-vis the audience than he does the hero.

The more time we spend with a character, seeing things through their eyes, the more we tend to bond with them. Shakespeare's antagonists are almost never allowed to upstage the protagonists they oppose. It would throw off the balance of a story to have them attracting more attention and interest than the protagonist. Whom would you want to prevail if you became more intrigued by the antagonist than by the putative hero? Shakespeare comes close to doing this in one play—*Othello*—and it's an excellent case study of just how far to take an antagonist.

So, it's a balancing act to makes the antagonist as plausibly threatening as the situation requires, while also not stealing the hero's thunder. Claudius fulfills that role admirably in Hamlet.

Types of Antagonists in Shakespeare

There are countless ways to construct this kind of character. In Shakespeare, the antagonists tend to fall into these categories:

1. **Major characters**, such Claudius and Aaron, who pose an ongoing and active threat to the protagonist through much of the story. The adversaries may be nearly as powerful as the protagonist, or in some respects, more so.
2. **Minor characters**—that is, they don't appear often in the story—but they are usually formidable in some respect, and may wield power over the protagonist.
3. **Good or neutral characters** who oppose the protagonist. These antagonists may be nearly as sympathetic or heroic as the protagonist they oppose. They may be foil characters who help to put the protagonist's nature in sharper relief.
4. **Protagonists** may even serve as a significant source of antagonism to themselves or to their co-protagonists.
5. Rather than individual characters, the antagonist might **be groups of people, forces of nature, or other circumstances** that the protagonist must confront.

Shakespeare sometimes uses a combination of these antagonist types in a single work. Their nature will be tailored to fit the genre and other circumstances. With Claudius, we have reviewed the way a major antagonist operates. Now let's consider the other categories.

Minor but Formidable in Some Way

At their most functional, antagonists put problems in the way of the hero. Minor characters, who appear only rarely in the story, can fulfill this function. Their personal qualities matter little.

In *Much Ado About Nothing,* the main antagonist is Don John, the bastard brother of the Prince. We learn through exposition that Don John has just been taken back into his brother's circle after some unspecified falling out. Shakespeare signals right away this character has a depressive, miserable nature, and means no good. "I am a plain-dealing villain," Don John admits. Shakespeare has a lot of other characters to introduce, so he cuts right to the chase here.

When Don John learns Claudio is to be married, he welcomes the chance to ruin his happiness and thwart his brother's efforts to bring about the union. There's little to justify the lengths Don John goes to cause harm, except jealousy: "That young start-up hath all the glory of my overthrow. If I can cross him any way, I bless myself every way" (1.3).

Don John then sets in motion an effective ruse, enacted by two of his henchmen, and makes Claudio believe his betrothed, Hero, has been unfaithful. This antagonist is behind the events occurring at the key plot points: the inciting incident when Claudio is told Hero is false, and the turning point when Claudio rejects her at the altar.

The falling action shows the untangling of the false accusation.

Don John has no position of authority; instead, his power over his victims comes from his cunning and malice. He is minor character, appearing in only a few scenes. Don John doesn't even appear at the end—we just hear that he's been captured and will get his comeuppance. Shakespeare has no more need of him. The comedy simply needs someone to set the problems in motion for the protagonists.

The lighter and more comic the story, the less weighty the antagonist. This is true of *Much Ado,* but even more so of *As You Like It,* which is probably the most light-hearted of all of Shakespeare's comedies.

There are two antagonists, Duke Frederick and Oliver, one for each of the protagonists (Rosalind and Orlando). Duke Frederick has only about 20 speeches, while Oliver has roughly double that.

The usurping Duke Frederick banishes his brother, the rightful duke, causing him and many courtiers to take refuge in the Forest of Arden. Among these exiles is Rosalind. He will send his troops to pursue these refugees.

Oliver, meanwhile, has deprived his younger brother Orlando of his inheritance and now intends to kill him. This causes Orlando to flee into the forest as well.

Here in the forest is where the main heroes' adventures and self-discovery begin. Duke Frederick and Oliver serve as the initial triggers for this flight. We occasionally get notice of their ongoing pursuit and danger they pose, but otherwise we scarcely hear of them till late in the play. Oliver will reappear in act 4 and reconcile with his brother after Orlando saves his life. Duke Frederick doesn't even appear at the end—we simply hear he has converted. In keeping with the tone of this light comedy, both antagonists have sudden and complete changes of heart.

Why Not Provide Compelling Backstories?

Why not give Duke Frederick or Orlando, or *Much Ado*'s Don John, more compelling backstories that justify their cruel actions? One could guess at Shakespeare's pragmatic reasons—that there really wasn't enough time. Both of those comedies have overflowing character lists, with double sets of lovers in each and assorted subplots involving clowns and additional romantic entanglements.

But let's say Shakespeare fleshed out Don John's story more by establishing that his half-brother the Prince had mistreated him. What would be gained? Don John's function in *Much Ado* is to cause problems for the protagonists, and he does it.

In these comedies, we are in a realm where love can spark suddenly and rescues come from unlikely sources. We are far from the psychological realism of *Othello* or Shakespeare's other tragedies. In these lighter works, Shakespeare reckoned audiences needed only a perfunctory reason for why the antagonists choose to cause mischief. Once they provide that mischief, the plot can unfold under its own momentum.

Antagonists, in these instances, may be minor and their motives might be just scarcely plausible, and yet serve their purpose well.

Good or Neutral Characters Who Oppose the Protagonist

In *Richard III* and *Macbeth*, Shakespeare creates protagonists who themselves do horrible things, like having children killed. So, what kind of antagonist is best to oppose an anti-hero protagonist? For these, Shakespeare constructs antagonists who are good or neutral in comparison to the protagonist.

Macduff and Malcolm function as antagonists to Macbeth because they thwart and ultimately defeat Macbeth to save Scotland from his tyranny. Macduff in particular displays a heroic nature, dedicating himself to restoring the late king's son to the throne, even at the cost of his family's life. He reminds us of the great warrior and loyal Scot that Macbeth might have remained had he resisted the temptation for power.

There can be extra poignancy when the protagonist–antagonist pair is of almost equal merit; one will inevitably fall to the other, and this defeat can seem bittersweet. One of the great examples in Shakespeare comes with Prince Hal and Hotspur.

Hotspur as a Sympathetic Antagonist and Foil

Although an antagonist, Hotspur in *Henry IV, Part 1* is a highly appealing character. As his moniker suggests, Hotspur is passionate and headstrong, a great warrior. He is also blunt and witty, and is considerably humanized through his feisty, affectionate relationship with his wife.

Of all the rebels, he poses the greatest threat to Henry IV's rule, and will directly confront Prince Hal in battle. The king admires Hotspur's martial prowess, even declaring to Hal in a frustrated moment that he'd be glad to learn Hal and Hotspur had been switched at birth.

One might expect Shakespeare to set up Hotspur as the enemy, so we can take satisfaction in seeing our hero the Prince of Wales vanquish him. But Shakespeare makes this antagonist nearly as sympathetic as the protagonist. Hotspur could easily have been a protagonist in another play. When he is killed in battle, his demise is felt as tragic, even if necessary for the plot. His vanquisher, the Prince, speaks generously of him after his defeat.

Historically, the rebel-warrior that Hotspur is based on was much older than the Prince of Wales. Shakespeare takes liberties with history in order to set up a parallel between them, shaping Hotspur as a foil for Hal. The long-awaited showdown between these opponents offers a poignancy similar to when Achilles vanquishes Hector in Homer's *Iliad*.

As an antagonist, Hotspur must be defeated by the hero, but his death provides Hal—as well as the audience—a sense of loss as well. At the same time, as both Hal and Hotspur note, Hal's reputation will shine all the brighter because he defeated such a great opponent.

In this instance, Shakespeare creates an antagonist who is interesting in his own right, but also uses him to make the hero shine brighter still.

Protagonists as Antagonistic to Each Other

Another variant of antagonism comes in plays that have pairs of protagonists. They can serve as antagonists to each other, even if at other times they are united in a cause.

A prime example is *Antony and Cleopatra*. Octavius Caesar is the main antagonist: he first aims to compel Antony back to his duties in Rome, and then opposes both of them in battle, ultimately defeating them.

But the passionate lovers spend a good part of their time reacting to the hurdles they put in each other's way. Cleopatra possessively tries to distract Antony from his commitment to Rome. When Antony seeks a political rapprochement by marrying Caesar's sister, Cleopatra turns all her wrath on him. Antony cannot help but return to her. They reconcile and unite forces against Caesar. But when Cleopatra panics during the Battle of Actium and flees, Antony impulsively follows her, thereby committing a fatal military blunder. It is Antony's turn to rage against her. As formidable as Caesar is, he would likely not have conquered their joint forces. The lovers themselves undermine each other.

Antagonistic Groups, Situations, or Forces

Antagonism need not derive from a single character. The function is what matters—thwarting the protagonist in some way. This can come from a group, or circumstances, or even an inanimate source.

In the first half of *Coriolanus*, it is not only the enemy general Aufidius, but also Rome's plebeian mob, who serve as antagonists to Coriolanus. The mob poses more danger, in fact. On the battlefield, Coriolanus is preeminent. But alone against the horde, whom he has insulted and who have been kept close to starvation, he cannot win. They hound the great warrior out of the city he saved. This sets up a fatal showdown, in which he will join forces with his other antagonist, Aufidius, to threaten Rome.

With *Romeo and Juliet*, the warring families, who have put up barriers to the lovers' union, take the role of antagonists, rather than any individual character. There has been a long-standing animosity between the households. It is because of this vendetta that Romeo and Juliet must take dangerous steps to be together, ultimately leading to their deaths. Tybalt, Juliet's cousin, acts as an aggressive member of one of the families, and thus is an individual antagonist. But Tybalt dies by the middle of play. His death at Romeo's hands only exacerbates the feud between the families, and this continues to drive Romeo's and Juliet's actions until the tragic end.

Antagonistic Circumstances

In several of Shakespeare's comedies, the antagonistic force takes the form of mistaken or hidden identities.

In *The Comedy of Errors,* no one is wicked, everyone means well. But there are a *lot* of misunderstandings. This string of comical misunderstandings propels the plot along.

The premise is that two sets of identical twins are wandering the streets of Ephesus; separated as infants and now adults, these men do not suspect their twin's presence in town. Each one is mistaken for his twin brother, with abundantly farcical consequences, as when one wife compels the twin she supposes to be her husband to come in for a private dinner, which leads to the actual husband being denied entrance at his own home.

The antagonistic function—so necessary to push this comedy forward—comes from the circumstances, which provoke nearly everyone in the story to frustration and some to retaliation. When the mystery is resolved at the end, all is happily forgiven, and the antagonism evaporates as well.

Antagonism arising from circumstances also comes in *A Midsummer Night's Dream.* The mischievous sprite Puck puts magical love juice on the eyes of the wrong youth, causing him to fall in love with a woman who's in love with someone else: it's an accident that sets up a major comic hurdle for the two pairs of lovers wandering in the Athenian forest. Puck doesn't much regret his error, delighting in seeing "what fools these mortals be." But he didn't set out to harm anyone.

Twelfth Night also shows antagonism caused by circumstance, specifically, the fact that protagonist Viola is masking her true identity. She falls in love with her master Duke Orsino, who loves Olivia, but Olivia falls in love in Viola (disguised as Cesario). This engenders misunderstandings and conflicts, even leading to Orsino's threats to kill Viola/Cesario out of jealousy.

And then there is Olivia's puritanical steward Malvolio, whose name translates as "bad will." Isn't he an antagonist? Malvolio is a self-important striver who tries to thwart the carousing of Olivia's ne'er-do-well uncle Sir Toby Belch and others in her household. But Malvolio's power over them is limited, and he serves mainly as contrast to their merriment and a butt of their jokes.

Because Malvolio doesn't cause hurdles for the protagonist, he isn't technically the play's antagonist. If his part were cut altogether, the main plot could proceed along intact. But he is the antagonist in the Sir Toby subplot. More than that, his killjoy spirit adds a somber note to the entire story.

The transience of youth and joy is a major theme in *Twelfth Night*. As the wise fool Feste sings:

What is love? 'Tis not hereafter.
Present mirth hath present laughter.
What's to come is still unsure.
In delay there lies no plenty,
Then come kiss me, sweet and twenty.
Youth's a stuff will not endure. (2.3.47–52)

The bad-willed Malvolio represents one of the forces that would clamp down on the exuberance of youth and joy. He is an antagonist, we might say, to the brighter spirit of the play.

Accidental or Impersonal Antagonistic Elements

In *Pericles*, a storm figures as an antagonistic force at the play's turning point. Pericles and his pregnant wife Thaisa are crossing the sea by ship when a storm rises that sends her into labor, and she dies in childbirth. This causes Pericles to entrust his baby daughter Marina into the care of people who later try to kill her. Without the storm causing Thaisa's death, there is no turning point or later important challenges.

In *The Tempest*, Prospero is a powerful magician. Who or what are his antagonists? He is capable of commanding the elements and has a troupe of spirits ready to enact his will. He knows what others are thinking. How much can he be threatened? There are some who try to oppose him—Caliban and his new allies, who plot to kill Prospero to take over the island—but they are comically inept. His old enemies from Milan did indeed cause him harm in the past, but he has arranged for them to come ashore on his island and are now under his control. Even the recalcitrant spirit Ariel must obey him.

No person or spirit can withstand Prospero's magic. This protagonist is seemingly omnipotent. But there is one thing that threatens him. This antagonistic force is the clock. As he explains:

by my prescience
I find my zenith doth depend upon
A most auspicious star, whose influence

If now I court not, but omit, my fortunes
Will ever after droop. (1.2)

There is so much he must stage manage to make final use of his magic; he must tie up all his affairs during this brief window of time. If he fails, his fortunes will falter ever after.

Antagonism from Within

Shakespeare searches in unexpected corners for sources of conflict. Particularly in his tragedies, antagonism might arise from within the protagonist, and this internal battle can be the most intractable of all.

We see this with Hamlet as he battles with himself over why he does not take action against Claudius. And we see it in Lear, fighting against his imaginary foes and struggling with his own insanity. Macbeth and his wife are perhaps the clearest examples, with overwhelming torment arising from their guilt. In Macbeth's case, he is literally haunted by the ghost of Banquo, whom no one else sees; Lady Macbeth's mind disintegrates as she becomes prey to her own compulsions.

This is a particularly insightful aspect of Shakespeare's character drawing—that our psyches can serve as our own worst enemies. We'll expand on this topic in the next chapter on antagonists in the major tragedies.

Resolution of Antagonistic Forces

"The end crowns all." So says Ulysses in *Troilus and Cressida* (4.5). How a story ends puts everything preceding it into perspective, and this includes the end that the antagonist meets. We don't necessarily care about that character's fate as much as the state in which this world is left. Will truth and justice prevail and malevolence be overcome? We want to see what has been gained or lost, what lessons have been learned, as a result of the antagonist's threat.

Resolution of Antagonists in the Comedies

In comedies, the resolutions of the antagonistic threats can be as simple as dispelling the mistakes that were leading to conflict. When the threats have come from individuals, they usually are brought to account and their power over the heroes is extinguished. This need not be enacted in a particularly realistic way, but they still need resolution or the story will feel unfinished.

The ethos of comedy usually shows that we are luckier than we know. Everything can turn out well, even when we think all is lost. To restore the world's balance, the antagonistic force will typically be punished, purged, or converted.

Dark Elements Banished

In Shakespeare's romantic comedies, there is often a dark element introduced with the antagonists—an injustice or a malevolent spirit. This is usually purged at the end. The rest of society can return to a more wholesome, unified, or balanced state with these forces contained. This happens with Don John in *Much Ado*, whose ploy to vilify Hero is exposed and he himself is captured and due to be punished.

In *As You Like it*, Duke Frederick had usurped the dukedom, sending the rightful duke and his court fleeing into the forest. Near the end, as he is about to attack them with his army, he meets with a religious figure and is persuaded to follow a more peaceful life as a hermit. (This all happens offstage. It must have been a very eloquent hermit!) The Duke's conversion allows the banished courtiers and the rightful duke to return to their former lives. Oliver, who intended to kill Orlando, has had a complete change of heart after his brother saves his life. He falls in love with Celia, the cousin of Orlando's betrothed Rosalind, thus linking the brothers further through marriage to two cousins. So, both repent, and one antagonist removes himself, while the other can be reintegrated to society. The imbalance in the world of the plot has been restored. The sudden transformation of the two evildoers would indeed seem implausible in a more realistic story, but not in this idyllic, comic world.

Mistaken Identity Revealed

In those comedies where mistaken identity has caused antagonism, it's as simple as revealing the characters for who they are.

This happens in *The Comedy of Errors*. The wife who fears her husband is mad, the bruised and harassed servants, the merchant dumbfounded at his friend's ingratitude, and so on—all conflicts are resolved in a trice once they realize they have been dealing with a *different* Antipholus and Dromio. All is forgiven. It's the payoff the audience has been waiting, and the knot unties like a magician releasing an entangled silk scarf.

Similarly, at the end of *Twelfth Night*, the most jovial of coincidences will resolve the conflict. When Olivia meets Viola's look-alike male twin, this brother is agreeable enough to go along with Olivia's wish to marry instantly. Soon after the wedding, Olivia and Orsino happen upon Viola/Cesario and fight over him, until

Viola's twin arrives and Cesario is revealed to be a she, not a he. This smooths the way for Orsino to shift his affections immediately to Viola. The animosities from the previously unrequited love triangle are instantly dissolved, and there are twins enough to make both Olivia and Orsino happy.

Again, the genre and prevailing tone matter. Resolutions to the antagonistic forces don't have to be all that plausible, especially not in comedy. Sometimes, far-fetched, deux-ex-machina solutions are funnier than those that are meticulously justified.

The point is to tie up what would otherwise feel like loose ends. But that doesn't mean that every problem is glibly swept away.

Malvolio, who serves as an antagonist in the subplot in *Twelfth Night,* is not converted or contained. His resolution strikes a harsh note. After Malvolio realizes he was the victim of a cruel prank by the carousers, he lashes out with the vow: "I'll be revenged on the whole pack of you" (5.1).

(Although Shakespeare couldn't know this, the Puritans would eventually get their revenge on the whole pack of them. Some forty years later, when the Puritans took control of government, they banned all theater. It would seem Shakespeare was exceptionally prescient here.)

This resolution illustrates that Shakespeare does not see the need to end even his comedies in uniform happiness. Some elements of society resist the urge toward harmony. Malvolio is purged from the scene in the sense that he voluntarily departs, leaving behind the happy lovers and pranksters. But his departure is discordant nonetheless.

Resolution of Antagonists in Tragedy and Histories

In the tragedies and more serious works, the stakes are different. There has usually been a serious loss and dangerous threat posed by the antagonists. They may have breached what seems decent and morally acceptable. How they wind up will impact how satisfied we are with the story's conclusion.

Romeo and Juliet

In *Romeo and Juliet*, the tragic lovers are together at last in death. This brings their main goal to a bittersweet end (they are united forever in the grave). But Shakespeare doesn't conclude the play there. There are the antagonistic forces to deal with: Shakespeare provides a final scene in which the Capulet and Montague patriarchs pledge to end their strife.

The young protagonists were nearly helpless within their social milieu. The more powerful elements—the warring families, as well the Prince, whose own kin has succumbed—will learn at the end the costs of their enmity. Only from their children's deaths will they gain the will to put an end to it. Consider how different the demise of Romeo and Juliet would seem if their families did not bury their animosity. Their tragic end would seem bitter and almost pointless, rather than cathartic.

The Antagonist May Prevail

On some occasions, Shakespeare does not show the antagonist as contained or transformed. It may be that this threat simply cannot be altered from its course.

Antony and Cleopatra

In *Antony and Cleopatra,* it is the antagonist Octavius Caesar who ends up prevailing. But this antagonist is a special case. The audience realizes he will go on to become the great Augustus. He does not represent an evil that must be purged from the land to bring the state back to health (as Claudius does in *Hamlet*). Octavius is not a destructive force that the audience would want to see defeated. On the contrary, he will in time prevail over the golden age of the Roman Empire.

In Shakespeare's play, the antagonist Caesar represents pragmatic Roman values, which Shakespeare doesn't dismiss. This is the worldview that will become the normative culture for the Western world. But in contrast to the heights and depths of the lovers' journey, Caesar's world seems far more tepid and unimaginative.

Still, Caesar has lost as well: he fails to entrap Cleopatra in order to parade her in Rome as a trophy. But primarily, he loses in comparison to the lovers due to what they have gained through each other. Although they die, they are far more fascinating and shown to have lived more deeply than the level-headed Caesar, who is cautious even about taking one drink too many. Shakespeare uses this antagonist as a powerful contrast to them: this antagonist prevails in some respects, but not in all.

Ebb and Flow of History

In his English history plays, Shakespeare is similarly bound (more or less) by the facts of historical record. In these works, we are made aware of a broader historical perspective—the ebb and flow, the cyclical nature of time's passage. Whether the protagonist triumphs at the end, or falls tragically to his antagonist, life continues on with new battles ahead. Shakespeare knows, as does his audience, how things will turn out for the famous kings and queens and their troubles. Sometimes darkness does prevail, sometimes light, but neither prevails forever.

Shakespeare suggests this cyclic nature of history at the end of *Henry V*, the final play of his second tetralogy. The valiant young king triumphs over his antagonists—the Dauphin and his French forces—and wins France's princess as his bride. All concludes gloriously, and peace is established at last. This is a thoroughly satisfying resolution to the four-play sequence about a period of strife in England and the strengths and weaknesses of its leaders. Henry V, who has learned the lessons of his more fallible predecessors, unites his country and triumphs over its foreign adversary.

But Shakespeare adds an elegiac postscript at the end of the play to remind us that, in time, Henry's son Henry VI would lose the lands back to France. Shakespeare might have left that out and ended on a happier, jingoistic note. Instead, he leaves the audience with a broader perspective of the triumphs and defeats of their country's past. Antagonists and protagonists are perennially engaged with each other. There are more battles ahead.

Summary

Shakespeare shows us that making a character unlikeable or hateful isn't what makes them an antagonist. They need to have sufficient power to hinder and, potentially, to defeat the protagonist. They aren't necessarily highly individualized, but if they are, they will not be more appealing or compelling than the protagonist, or it sets up a competition for the audience's loyalty.

Antagonists usually figure in the plot resolution, too. Claudius, Iago, Regan, Goneril, Edmund, Don John—all die at the end, or are captured and destined for punishment; the families of *Romeo and Juliet* are reconciled at the end, and the antagonistic forces in *The Comedy of Errors* are dissolved once the true identities of the characters are unveiled.

Antagonists provide critical functions in the plot—as a means of giving the protagonist something to fight against, and through which they either succeed or die in the attempt, more or less nobly.

But as we will see in the next chapter, the antagonists in Shakespeare's four great tragedies can represent profound philosophical problems. To explore antagonism at its deepest and most threatening, Shakespeare embarks on a fascinating project of reinventing the antagonist's role.

Takeaway for Writers

- The antagonist's main function is to provide challenges for the protagonist.
- Shakespeare often uses antagonists, especially in his serious works, to present a viewpoint in opposition to the protagonist.
- Shakespeare uses a wide range of antagonist types, depending on the needs of the work;
    - Some are major characters, often wielding power over the protagonist.
    - Some are minor and rarely appear, but are formidable in some way.
    - Antagonistic forces might even be circumstances. For example, in *The Comedy of Errors*, the circumstances of mistaken identity serve as antagonistic force.
    - Joint protagonists may serve at times as each other's antagonist, as we find in *Antony and Cleopatra*.
    - Antagonistic forces may arise within the protagonist (Lear and Macbeth are their own formidable antagonists).
- The antagonist doesn't take so much attention or sympathy away from the protagonist to throw them out of balance, but there are examples where it comes close: Hotspur is a sympathetic foil to Hal. Iago is an unusual example in his relative dominance in the play and in the way he draws the audience in despite his repellent nature.
- Antagonistic forces are usually resolved at the end, much like a protagonist, by being brought to justice or another kind of stasis.

Extras

The **main antagonist in *Antony and Cleopatra*, Octavius Caesar**, delivers this speech to his entourage upon hearing of Antony's death. He draws attention to his own mourning of Antony, justifies why it was necessary that either Antony or himself had to die, but also breaks off this eulogy of "my brother…my mate in empire" for a more convenient time after an Egyptian messenger enters. Business first.

CAESAR What is't thou say'st?
DECRETAS I say, O Caesar, Antony is dead.
CAESAR The breaking of so great a thing should make

A greater crack. The round world
Should have shook lions into civil streets,
And citizens to their dens. The death of Antony
Is not a single doom, in the name lay
A moi'ty of the world....
O Antony,
I have followed thee to this; but we do launch
Diseases in our bodies. I must perforce
Have shown to thee such a declining day,
Or look on thine; we could not stall together
In the whole world. But yet let me lament,
With tears as sovereign as the blood of hearts,
That thou, my brother, my competitor
In top of all design, my mate in empire,
Friend and companion in the front of war,
The arm of mine own body, and the heart
Where mine his thoughts did kindle—that our stars,
Unreconciliable, should divide
Our equalness to this. Hear me, good friends—
Enter an Egyptian.
But I will tell you at some meeter season,
The business of this man looks out of him;
We'll hear him what he says.—Whence are you? (5.1.12-19 and 35-51)

CHAPTER 11: ANTAGONIST VARIATIONS IN THE FOUR GREAT TRAGEDIES

T he greater the hero, the stronger the adversary needs to be. In Shakespeare's hands, the antagonists can become nearly as fascinating as the heroic characters they oppose.

Nowhere is this truer than in the great quartet of tragedies from his middle to late period: *Hamlet, Othello, King Lear*, and *Macbeth.* Just as Shakespeare dives deeply into what animates and motivates of his protagonists, so he explores how they can be threatened, what can lead to their downfall.

In these four plays, Shakespeare varies the nature of the antagonists and shows an evolution in his concept of this character type. It's as if he made a project out of exploring all the ways that a character or other forces can threaten and destroy a protagonist. Shakespeare works out seemingly all possible kinds of antagonism in this quartet. He takes it from a straightforward opponent to something more subtly psychological to metaphysical threats that strain what humans can comprehend.

By reimagining the nature of the antagonist in each tragedy, Shakespeare depicts with greater breadth the challenges a protagonist may face.

Claudius in *Hamlet* (1600)

As we saw in the last chapter, Claudius functions as a classic type of antagonist. His character is rounded out enough so that we understand his motivation in having killed his own brother and wanting his nephew Hamlet dead. Shakespeare depicts Claudius's behavior in a way that makes sense to us.

Although uncle and nephew are mortal enemies, there is an important area in which they are in accord. They both know what Claudius did was wrong. Claudius does not try to excuse his crime. As he admits to himself, "O, my offence is rank, it smells to heaven, / It hath the primal eldest curse upon't, / A brother's murder" (5.3).

He even tries to pray over his guilt. He acknowledges that although he might be able to get away with his crimes here on earth, he cannot in heaven:

In the corrupted currents of this world
Offense's gilded hand may shove by justice,
And oft 'tis seen the wicked prize itself
Buys out the law, but 'tis not so above....

One could say that Hamlet and Claudius agree on a worldview, on what is right and wrong. It's simply that Claudius transgresses because he so strongly desires the fruits of his crime. To defeat Claudius, as Hamlet is called upon to do, is to punish that wrong and rectify the imbalance in this world.

In light of the next three tragedies, this common ground between the antagonist and protagonist is almost reassuring in its moral clarity, because Shakespeare will later make this picture far more complicated.

In the later three tragedies, opposing forces won't necessarily have the same ethical frame of reference. They may not agree on, or even care about, what's right and wrong. The antagonists will represent a worldview that is far murkier. And for the protagonist to curtail the threat, it will not be as straightforward as it is when Hamlet stabs Claudius.

Indeed, by the time he reaches *King Lear* and *Macbeth*, Shakespeare has moved far away from the notion of a single, readily graspable antagonist. Instead, we see some of the troubling antagonistic forces arising from within and projected outward from the protagonists themselves.

Iago in *Othello* (1603–04)

As with *Hamlet* of a few years earlier, *Othello* features a single major antagonist who thwarts the hero and causes his downfall. This antagonist, Iago, is Shakespeare's most hateable character. Although Iago is witty, it is an acid, mirthless wit.

This antagonist embraces his own evilness. In act 2, scene 3, after he has advised Cassio to do something he knows will make Othello more jealous, Iago turns to the audience in mock innocence and asks: "How am I then a villain / To counsel Cassio to this parallel course / Directly to his good?"

But then he confesses his strategy to us: "Divinity of hell! / When devils will the blackest sins put on, / They do suggest at first with heavenly shows, / As I do now" (2.3). Iago takes pride in how he can deceive others. And Shakespeare shows him as frighteningly adept at it.

Near Dominance of the Antagonist

At the beginning of the play, when the Venetians are threatened by the Turkish fleet, they turn to Othello to save them. Othello is respected and admired throughout Venice. He has a forceful, commanding presence, a gracious manner, and a poetic eloquence that outshines everyone else in the play. He makes for a strong protagonist.

No one would say that Iago is more heroic. But with his devious cunning, the antagonist at times shows himself as more powerful still.

This is one of the many curious features of this antagonist, the fact that he is so dominant in the play. Iago is actually given more lines than the protagonist, and it's by a longshot: he has more soliloquies (seven total) and 20% more lines to speak than Othello. Iago is the one pulling the strings, luring the hero into his trap. He looms over him—probably literally—in the scene in which Othello "falls into a trance" (4.1), usually interpreted to mean Othello has a seizure.

Yet, however major his part, Iago is not the central figure. He is not an anti-hero protagonist in the vein of Richard III or Macbeth. Instead, he fulfills the function of antagonist, just as Othello clearly serves as protagonist.

So, the question is, why would Shakespeare give Iago's such an extensive part?

Since this is Shakespeare's most fully developed and most famous antagonist, it's worth examining in detail how Shakespeare constructs the character and why he makes these choices.

How Does Shakespeare Construct this Antagonist?

In some respects, Iago operates in the same way that Claudius does in *Hamlet*. Just as Claudius is pivotal in all the major plot points in Hamlet, so is Iago in this work:

- Iago is the source of Othello's problems; he manipulates the hero into doubting his wife's fidelity, which is Othello's central problem.
- Almost all of the challenges Othello faces during the story are put in motion by Iago or are exploited by him. He goads the general into making his fatal errors, including at the turning point in act 3, scene 3, when Othello determines Desdemona must die.
- Iago is there at the end when the crime is brought to light; his machinations are exposed and Othello takes his own life in consequence.

This antagonist supports the plot in a structural way, as Claudius did in *Hamlet*. But clearly, Shakespeare went well beyond mere functionality in creating Iago.

To see what he was going for, it helps to see what this character was like originally in the source story Shakespeare used, and how Shakespeare adjusted the character to deepen the threats he poses.

Adapting the Source Characters

Shakespeare closely follows much of his source story, a novella by the Italian writer Cinthio. But he makes subtle, yet significant changes to the primary characters.

The Ensign (the Iago character) wishes to harm the Moor (Othello) out of revenge because he could not seduce the Moor's wife. Cinthio says he "fell passionately in love with Disdemona." The Ensign's hatred arises out of frustrated lust and jealousy.

Rather than proactively devising a scheme to destroy the Moor, the Ensign mostly responds to opportunities as they arise. The Moor's wife, on her own initiative, pleads to her husband on behalf of the Captain (Cassio). Only when the Ensign hears of this does he think to use it to make the Moor jealous.

The Moor, in Cinthio, also takes a more active role in planning his wife's murder, requiring less prodding and manipulation from the Ensign. He lies to the authorities later about his guilt and tries to escape the consequences.

Cinthio's Ensign and Moor are rather middling figures in comparison with what the later writer will make of them. Shakespeare puts greater space between them, creating Iago as more coldly malevolent and crafty in plotting the hero's downfall. And he makes Othello more noble, the victim of particularly devious manipulations by Iago.

Evidently, Shakespeare saw in these two characters an opportunity to explore a couple of related questions:

1. What could push a good character to do a terrible wrong? How could an accomplished, dignified, virtually impeccable protagonist be led to a crime as heinous as murdering his own wife?
2. What is the worst that a person could do to another? What would be the most dangerous and malevolent kind of antagonist, the closest to evil in human form?

From these questions, one imagines, Shakespeare's Othello and Iago were born. Iago would be constructed as the character to whom Othello would be most vulnerable; and Othello would be great hearted and noble except for the narrow vulnerability that Iago could exploit.

Making Iago Dangerous and Effective

So, in shaping his antagonist, Shakespeare would have had the nature of his protagonist clearly in mind, and vice versa. The challenge would be how to create a villain that is effective, powerful enough to make Othello's crime and downfall appear tragic to the audience, and not rather tawdry, as it is in Cinthio's version.

He had to construct a truly dangerous opponent, one who can convincingly bring a great man to his destruction. As so, Shakespeare endows Iago with these attributes:

- He has a strong desire to harm Othello; he thoroughly hates him and wants to destroy him at any cost.
- He has the skills to harm Othello. He is crafty and exploitative; he looks for others' weaknesses and is clever in figuring out how to exploit them.
- He hides his villainy well. He is close to Othello, trusted by him, so that the protagonist would let down his guard and heed what he says.
- He undermines through innuendo or other indirect means.
- He lacks any conscience, and even takes pride in his power to harm others.

In other words, Shakespeare endows Iago with traits that pretty closely match our modern definition of a sociopath.

Let's review in more detail how Shakespeare depicts an antagonist who could plausibly bring down a protagonist like Othello.

Strong Motivation to Harm

Shakespeare establishes that Iago's motivation to harm Othello comes from an intense, but irrational hatred of him. Coleridge described Iago as "motiveless malignity," but Iago does have motives of a certain kind. They're simply not what normal people would be ruled by.

Some of this hatred stems from his failure to get a promotion that Othello instead gave to Cassio. And part comes from a suspicion that Othello slept with his wife Emilia, though Iago concedes there's no proof of it. He doesn't care and says he'll proceed as if it is true. Unlike the Ensign in Cinthio, he shows no love or even lust for anyone. His character simply gets satisfaction from harming others. And he's decided to direct his efforts, at all costs, to destroying Othello.

This already takes us to a different world than in *Hamlet*, where Claudius' motivations are relatable, even if few would kill to get their desires. Hamlet and

Claudius are on the same page—both know that murder is wrong. By contrast, Iago's outlook is so malign, so remorseless, it is hard to fathom; there is almost no point in common in Othello's and Iago's worldviews.

Skills to Harm

Perhaps the most chilling part of this creation is Iago's skill at deception. Shakespeare shows how a sociopath operates. Iago sets traps for his victims by reading their weaknesses. He zeroes in on the particular vulnerabilities and trusting nature of others.

He does this with all of his victims. To Roderigo, who hopes to seduce Desdemona, he speaks smuttily, encouraging his illicit desires while extracting from him money and jewels he claims will seduce Desdemona for him. He knows that Cassio can't handle liquor, so he adopts a convivial tone and goads him into getting drunk, which, as Iago hoped, gets Cassio dismissed from Othello's service. And Iago convinces Desdemona to take Cassio's side, playing on her fair-mindedness and desire for her husband's best interests, and he does this knowing it will inflame Othello's suspicions all the more.

But he's especially astute in identifying where to attack Othello. What does he target? This is a brave and respected general. But he intuits that Othello's love for Desdemona, and the fact he's an outsider to Venetian society, are his weak links. And so, Iago reminds Othello that he is not familiar with how Venetian society works. He hints: *You don't know the adulterous games these Venetians play.* Othello is middle-aged and a dark-skinned African. *It's only natural she'll turn her eye back to her own kind. And isn't Cassio a fair young man with good manners?* She seems virtuous, of course. *But remember, Desdemona tricked her father when she eloped with you. Don't you think she'll trick you, too?*

A Seeming Ally

Shakespeare indicates that Iago has been dissimulating for a long time. "Honest Iago" is what nearly everyone calls him, because that is the façade he has cultivated. He is smooth enough to appear unguarded and jocular in social situations, as when he jokes with Cassio about his paramour and with Desdemona about women's chastity. At other times, he adopts a blunt manner, all the better for seeming an honest person. The mask slips a bit in his exchanges with his wife Emilia, showing him in private as cold and harsh with her.

Although Othello's long-time ensign, he declares to Roderigo, "In following him, I follow but myself; / Heaven is my judge, not I for love and duty, / But seeming so, for my peculiar end" (1.1). That is, he only appears to be following Othello for love and duty; it is actually for his own purposes. His apparent honesty and loyalty, of course, make it more plausible that Othello would confide in in him and be vulnerable to his deceptions.

Undermining Through Innuendo or Other Indirect Means

Iago's particular talent is for gaslighting, for innuendo that sows doubt. He is adept at dropping hints that provoke Othello's suspicion. After Othello demands to know what Iago has observed, Iago feigns reluctance, making Othello believe all the more that Iago is hiding something from him. This passage shows how Iago baits the hook:

IAGO. Did Michael Cassio, when you wooed my lady,
Know of your love?
OTHELLO. He did, from first to last. Why dost thou ask?
IAGO. But for a satisfaction of my thought. No further harm.
OTHELLO. Why of thy thought, Iago?
IAGO. I did not think he had been acquainted with her.
OTHELLO. O yes, and went between us very oft.
IAGO. Indeed!
OTHELLO. Indeed? ay, indeed. Discern'st thou aught in that?
Is he not honest?
IAGO. Honest, my lord?
OTHELLO. Honest? ay, honest.
IAGO. My lord, for aught I know.
OTHELLO. What dost thou think?
IAGO. Think, my lord?
OTHELLO. Think, my lord? By heaven, thou echo'st me,
As if there were some monster in thy thought
Too hideous to be shown. Thou dost mean something.
I heard thee say even now, thou lik'st not that,
When Cassio left my wife. What didst not like?
And when I told thee he was of my counsel
[In] my whole course of wooing, thou criedst, "Indeed!"
And didst contract and purse thy brow together,
As if thou then hadst shut up in thy brain
Some horrible conceit. If thou dost love me,
Show me thy thought. (3.3)

241

Here, Iago doesn't directly try to plant the venomous ideas in Othello's ear. He prods him in such a way that Othello demands the poison himself.

Lacking Conscience

It is Iago's lack of conscience that singles him out as especially dangerous; he is cut off from normal human compassion. A lack of conscience allows a character to do things others would find inconceivable to do. Iago's hate comes first, and he looks for justifications for it afterward—but he doesn't even require those to do harm.

> I hate the Moor,
> And it is thought abroad that 'twixt my sheets
> He's done my office. I know not if't be true
> But I, for mere suspicion in that kind,
> Will do as if for surety. He holds me well,
> The better shall my purpose work on him. (1.3.386-91)

Nowhere else in the play is it suggested that Othello would do something like seduce his ensign's wife. Shakespeare wants us to see through this paltry justification of Iago's. This character doesn't even care what is true or not.

Add these attributes together, and you have a dangerous antagonist. Much like Richard III, Iago is fascinating because he is so good at what he aims to do. The audience has to wonder whether they could withstand a similar concerted attack from an adversary like Iago.

"The Moor is of a free and open nature / That thinks men honest that but seem to be so," (1.3), observes Iago. Shakespeare creates Othello's nature as fundamentally trusting, and he pairs that with an Iago who is especially gifted at deception and harm.

But Shakespeare goes a step further with Iago, making a significant and surprising choice. He positions Iago vis-à-vis the audience much as he would a protagonist.

Involving the Audience

In *Hamlet*, Claudius has just one private moment, when he attempts to pray. In *Othello*, by contrast, we hear Iago's private thoughts regularly. In this speech in act 3, scene 1, he is pondering how he can get Cassio's position and destroy Othello. We witness his efforts to conceive of a plan that will lead to a "monstrous birth" (phrases bolded here for emphasis).

> Cassio's a proper man. **Let me see now:**

242

To get his place and to plume up my will
In double knavery—**How? how?—Let's see—**
After some time, to abuse Othello's ear
That he is too familiar with his wife.
He hath a person and a smooth dispose
To be suspected—framed to make women false.
The Moor is of a free and open nature,
That thinks men honest that but seem to be so,
And will as tenderly be led by th' nose
As asses are.
I have 't. It is engendered. Hell and night
Must bring this monstrous birth to the world's light.
[Exit.]   (1.3)

Iago hides his vicious nature from the other characters, but not from the audience. We are brought along for the ride as he concocts his hateful plans. Since we know what he is plotting, this increases our unease as we see Othello and others fall into his traps.

Aside from building tension, Iago's intimacy with the audience will have another effect. It's rather like being trapped in a conversation with someone speaking maliciously about others. It can make a listener feel complicit.

Again and again, Iago leads us to view Othello, Desdemona, and others through the antagonist's dehumanizing eyes. When Iago alerts Desdemona's father to his daughter's elopement, he paints lurid scenes of what she and Othello are doing on their wedding night:

IAGO Even now, now, very now, an old black ram
Is tupping your white ewe. Arise, arise!
Awake the snorting citizens with the bell,
Or else the devil will make a grandsire of you....
you'll have your daughter covered with a Barbary horse, you'll have your
nephews neigh to you, you'll have coursers for cousins and jennets for
germans. [Note: These phrases express the idea that Brabantio will have horses as
close relatives.]
BRABANTIO What profane wretch art thou?
IAGO I am one, sir, that comes to tell you your daughter
and the Moor are now making the beast with two backs. (1.1)

Iago here describes Othello and Desdemona in the most degrading terms. He tells Brabantio the devil will make him a grandfather. He depicts the newly married couple as animals—an old black ram covering a white ewe; their offspring as horses; their union as being a beast with two backs.

Elsewhere, Iago speaks of other characters in similarly coarse, but arresting ways. In his speech style, he is the antithesis of Romeo and Juliet: whereas the young lovers express themselves in idealistic, refined, yet novel turns of speech, Iago describes others in the most debased, yet no less novel terms. It is easy to reject an evil character when you feel distance from the character. It becomes more uncomfortable when the character is taking you into his confidence, sharing his acid thought thoughts in vivid, mordantly witty ways.

Why This Kind of Antagonist?

So, why does Shakespeare give Iago more soliloquies and more total lines than the hero? His counterpart in *Hamlet*, Claudius, has a much smaller role.

Clearly, Shakespeare was intrigued by the extreme kind of character he depicts in Iago. Human nature of all its varieties interested him. But he takes it much further than a character study of amorality.

Shakespeare is attempting a steep challenge in *Othello*: to depict how an otherwise good person might kill his wife and have the audience comprehend how he could be brought to that extremity.

For Aristotle, an effective tragedy will engender pity and fear towards the protagonist: "for pity is aroused by unmerited misfortune, fear by the misfortune of a man like ourselves" (Part XIII). Shakespeare clearly wants us to consider Othello's downfall as tragic, not deserved. His misfortune is not merited. (By contrast, in Shakespeare's source, the Moor tries to evade accountability and seems more deserving of his downfall.) We must be convinced that, were we put in Othello's position, we, too, might have fallen prey to Iago.

To achieve this, he invests Othello with a range of admirable traits and certain vulnerabilities—among them, is jealousy, which we see another character, Bianca, display. But the other and necessary half of the equation is the antagonist.

Shakespeare evidently judged that it wasn't enough to construct as his antagonist a wicked person skulking in the background, secretly laying traps (which is, more or less, what Claudius does in *Hamlet*). Instead, Shakespeare has Iago engage with the audience again and again to help us feel more viscerally how he operates. We follow along as he hatches his plots, as he justifies on thin pretexts his intended evil. Through his eyes, we see others in degrading and unjust ways. And on numerous times, we see Iago correctly predict how other characters will behave and engineer effective traps that they fall into. He is powerful and, in a sense, more intelligent than everyone around him. He's *almost* like a protagonist.

Through Iago's intimacy with the audience, Shakespeare helps us see and feel how malign and manipulative this antagonist is. We can hardly wonder how even a great man like Othello would succumb.

In *Othello*, Shakespeare constructs a virtual parity between two opposing characters, the antagonist and protagonist. He wants to show the dark as thoroughly, as viscerally, even, as the light.

One might wonder where Shakespeare could go next after creating this dominant and highly fleshed-out antagonist. The answer is, he would go on to create antagonists almost as cruel as Iago, but none in such detail. No one of them would come to dominate their own play as Iago does his. Instead, Shakespeare finds other incarnations, each one allowing him to explore in a new facet of antagonistic forces and the threats they can pose a protagonist.

Pervasive Antagonists in *King Lear* (1605–06)

In *King Lear*, which was probably the next of the four great tragedies, we see another highly unusual approach to antagonistic forces. Instead of the threat being posed by one individual, such as Claudius and Iago, we have multiple villainous people, and there are other, amorphous kinds of threats as well.

The primary antagonists are Lear's daughters Goneril and Regan, who turn against him, and Edmund, who assists them and betrays his own father Gloucester. The daughters first humiliate their father, then provoke him so that he flees from their homes. Eventually they threaten anyone who would help him. By the end, they seek to imprison him. These sisters are backed up by others. Regan's husband Cornwall takes part in the cruelty toward both Lear and Gloucester; and Oswald, a servant of Goneril, does whatever she bids him, including grossly disrespecting the old king.

The threats in this world are more widespread than in *Othello*, and if anything, more unsettling. In *Othello*, the threats arise only from Iago and his patsy Roderigo. In this dark world, children turn on fathers, subjects against their king. The loyal Fool acts as a kind of chorus who observes the widespread hypocrisy and self-serving nature of those sworn to serve. As Lear frequently reminds us, the gods seem to be indifferent to the injustice humans suffer.

245

This is one major way Shakespeare reconsiders the role of the antagonist in his tragedies. The antagonism can be systemic, and all good things—familial love, justice, loyalty, the benevolent force of the gods—may be in doubt.

How Does Shakespeare Construct the Antagonists?

Shakespeare begins straightforwardly enough with Lear's two elder daughters as the villainous antagonists. But there are other sorts of antagonists in store.

Goneril and Regan as Initial Antagonists

Lear, as the protagonist, takes the first major step in his own downfall by giving away his power to his two elder daughters, and banishing his one honest daughter, Cordelia, along with his loyal advisor, Kent.

Lear has thrown himself to the wolves. Goneril and Regan begin to treat him—till now, a king accustomed to being flattered and having every command obeyed—with disrespect and abuse. They refuse to house his knights, stripping away Lear's retinue and other marks of honor, and treat him as if he were an inconvenience.

Goneril and Regan are nearly interchangeable in what they say and do. They justify their harshness at first as being due to their father's insupportable behavior. But once they have power, they become increasingly cruel and tyrannical. When Lear reproaches Regan, "I gave you all," she curtly responds: "And in good time you gave it."

When he flees into the wilderness in a state of rage, they lock their doors to him and threaten with death anyone who would help him.

Wandering the heath in a storm, he feels their ingratitude gnawing at him and fears he will go mad:

> In such a night
> To shut me out? Pour on, I will endure.
> In such a night as this? O Regan, Goneril!
> Your old kind father whose frank heart gave all—
> O, that way madness lies. Let me shun that!
> No more of that. (3.4)

Whereas Cordelia triggered in Lear his first bout of fury, that anger arose from his wounded feelings. Goneril and Regan, by contrast, push Lear to a breaking point physically and psychologically.

Internalized/Projected Antagonists

The daughters who allow Lear to fend for himself in a storm are clearly menacing figures. But even after Lear has fled their homes, he remains tormented by their unkindness. At this point, the "antagonists" take on a new form.

He begins to address imaginary, threatening figures, among them entities he believes are Goneril and Regan. In the hovel in act 3, scene 6, he attempts to arraign his daughters for their crimes, and enlists the beggar Tom (Edgar) and the Fool as justices. The Fool plays along, addressing what might be an actual stool—or it could be anything—as if it's one of the daughters:

> LEAR: I'll see their trial first. Bring in their evidence.....
> Arraign her first, 'tis Goneril. I here take my oath before this honorable
> assembly, she kicked the poor king her father.
> FOOL   Come hither, mistress. Is your name Goneril?
> LEAR   She cannot deny it.
> FOOL   Cry you mercy, I took you for a joint stool.
> LEAR   And here's another whose warped looks proclaim
> What store her heart is made on. Stop her there!
> Arms, arms, sword, fire! Corruption in the place!
> False justicer, why hast thou let her 'scape? (3.6)

Shakespeare is showing that the daughters do not need to harass Lear in person to continue as his antagonists. Lear invokes them as if they were still with him. Their antagonism lives on in his painful reliving of their ingratitude.

In a similar vein, Lear carries on tormented arguments with "the heavens," which he associates with the storm and with the gods in this pagan world. He at first tries to appeal to them as allies, calling on them destroy the world: "Blow winds, and crack your cheeks! Rage, blow!" (3.2). He entreats the storm to drown the steeples and the thunder to flatten the earth, destroying all seeds "that makes ingrateful man."

But then he shifts and reproaches the elements as "servile ministers" for conspiring with his daughters against him. He is projecting his trauma onto the storm. The storm—or rather, Lear's experience of it—becomes an antagonistic force, an entity he pleads with, accuses, reproaches.

> I tax not you, you elements, with unkindness;
> I never gave you kingdom, called you children;
> You owe me no subscription. Then let fall
> Your horrible pleasure. Here I stand your slave,

A poor, infirm, weak, and despised old man;
But yet I call you servile ministers,
That will with two pernicious daughters join
Your high-engendered battles 'gainst a head
So old and white as this. O, ho! 'tis foul. (3.2)

Like the absent wicked daughters who continue to plague his thoughts, the storm presents him with a focal point against which he can project and battle his inner demons.

The gods are only vaguely invoked and often identified with "the heavens," but they are a central antagonist. Shakespeare doesn't establish whether the "gods" are there or not. Instead, we witness only a storm and see that Lear is projecting onto it his beliefs about the gods—that they neglect to enforce justice. Lear's one-sided battle with the heavens is one of the most important themes of the play, even though it emerges from Lear's fantasies; it is also echoed by Gloucester in his subplot.

With Lear's projected battles, Shakespeare shows that we can be our own worst enemies. The antagonist is within. But Shakespeare also uses this scene to explore a profound existential question: Where *are* the gods that they allow injustice to happen? Is there no divine entity that cares about the evil done on earth?

Although these "antagonists" are projected, they still serve the same basic purpose as a more standard antagonist: they give the hero something to fight against and a way to reveal or learn more about themselves. But they allow Shakespeare to explore with even more psychological acuity the struggles humans face. They are not just "villainous" opponents we battle against. They can be our own flesh and blood who lack a sense of loyalty. They can be a function of our own emotional and physical frailties. They can be philosophical or spiritual questions that cannot be answered but which torment us.

Shakespeare will take a similar approach in his next tragedy, Macbeth, but develop even further the ways that a protagonists can serve as their own antagonist. And he introduces another framework for the threats facing the protagonist: the overtly supernatural forces that go beyond what humans can clearly comprehend or battle against.

Supernatural and Psychological Antagonists in *Macbeth* (1606)

Macbeth is usually thought to have been the final of Shakespeare's great tragic quartet. Here, as in *King Lear*, we have multiple antagonists, not one major one.

And again, some are human while others are of another sort. We could say there are no conventional antagonists in the play at all, because Macbeth, who assassinates his king and wreaks terror on Scotland, is not a conventional protagonist.

Range of Antagonists in Macbeth

Macduff and Malcolm, as well as Banquo to an extent, are the human characters who put up hurdles to Macbeth's bloody ambitions. They are either good or neutral in moral terms. Macduff in particular is shown sympathetically, yet he fits the bill of antagonist, because he is the one who most directly thwarts what Macbeth seeks (to hold on to power). He deals Macbeth the fatal blow on the battlefield, finally putting Macbeth's reign of terror to an end.

Also acting as antagonists are the psychological forces of guilt and repression that torment Macbeth and his wife and prompt them to dire actions.

But Macbeth faces another, very peculiar set of antagonists. These are the supernatural Weird Sisters, who are a more insidious threat than those Macbeth meets on the battlefield. They plant the seed of his murderous ambition. He cannot discern their actual nature or deal with them in the open. When he goes to see them a second time to try to discover more about his fate, they only dig their hooks in deeper. They have, as their apparent goal, simply the desire to do harm. In that respect, they are like Iago. But as in *Lear*, this malevolence is an inchoate, yet pervasive reality. The witches have supernatural allies who wreak their evil deeds all over the world.

What made Shakespeare decide to use such an array of antagonists against the hero? Does Shakespeare want to suggest that witches really exist and cause us to do wrong? If so, why does he explore to such an extent the personal, psychological roots of Macbeth's and Lady Macbeth's actions?

To see what Shakespeare was aiming for, it's helpful to understand the larger framework in which he conceived this play.

Supernatural and Psychological Antagonist Forces

Upon Elizabeth I's death in 1603, James VI of Scotland inherited her crown and became James I of England. James was an avid believer that witches and sorcery plagued the world. He also became the official patron of Shakespeare's company, who, thanks to this honor, renamed themselves the King's Men. This brought the troupe great prestige, of course, as well as certain new challenges. Shakespeare had reason to cater to his benefactor, and he did so with *Macbeth*, which depicts witches doing their witchery, and portrays James' ancestor Banquo in a providential and more positive light than history has recorded.

But Shakespeare would have mulled over his royal patron's beliefs critically. He ended up treating them with an independent and fascinating twist. He accepts as his premise that there are forces of darkness and that their malign energies operate in the world. But Shakespeare probed further, asking himself:

- *How* do these evil forces actually work?
- And, where does that leave human free will?

Shakespeare explores these as radically as he explores questions in *King Lear* about whether the gods are just and how do they intervene in our world, if at all.

What we find in *Macbeth* is a psychologically complex exploration of the roots of evil, taking it to even murkier regions of the human psyche than he did with Iago.

Powers of Evil vs Freewill

His treatment of the supernatural creatures in the play is simple in one respect. The witches themselves are *real*. They appear several times during the play, confiding to each other and conjuring up their wicked plans. Macbeth does not hallucinate them, because Banquo also sees and hears them. So, Shakespeare accepts they are real, and yet they are definitely not human.

Shakespeare conceives of them as terrifying yet ambiguous creatures. As Banquo marvels:

What are these
So wither'd and so wild in their attire,
That look not like th' inhabitants o' th' earth
And yet are on't. Live you? or are you aught
That man may question? You seem to understand me,
By each at once her choppy finger laying
Upon her skinny lips. You should be women,
And yet your beards forbid me to interpret
That you are so. (1.3)

Banquo and Macbeth cannot even be sure they are women. Whatever seems most abhorrent to humans brings the witches delight, as when they recite their potion ingredients in a grotesque parody of housewives making a stew:

Nose of Turk and Tartar's lips,
Finger of birth-strangled babe
Ditch-deliver'd by a drab,

Make the gruel thick and slab. (4.1)

But the witches do not exert any power over Macbeth's free will. They don't even technically lie to him, but rather mislead him through riddling language. They play on the desires and moral frailties that already exist in Macbeth, rather the way Iago targets Othello's weak points.

This is an important choice that Shakespeare makes about the nature of his antagonist and how it reflects on the protagonist. The witches are uncanny, but they cannot control Macbeth and his choices. It is Macbeth who takes his lethal steps.

Psychological Antagonism

Macbeth and his wife choose to break sacred bonds by killing a guest under their roof, and worse yet, this guest is the king to whom Macbeth has sworn loyalty. From the moment they decide to take this step, they will have no more peace.

They think their enemies are without. But the main threats come from within. Both he and Lady Macbeth become prey to hallucinations and compulsions. On his way to killing Duncan, Macbeth sees a dagger, just like his own, which develops spots of blood and "marshal'st me the way that I was going" (2.1.42).

At his banquet with the Scottish nobles, no one except Macbeth sees the ghost of Banquo, whose "gory locks" terrify him and who makes him behave erratically and incriminatingly.

In time, he becomes inured to his crime, while Lady Macbeth is increasingly disturbed. A Doctor and Gentlewoman witness Lady Macbeth sleepwalking as she compulsively washes her hands:

> LADY MACBETH Out, damn'd spot! out, I say! One—two—why then 'tis time to do't. Hell is murky. Fie, my lord, fie, a soldier, and afeard? What need we fear who knows it, when none can call our pow'r to accompt? Yet who would have thought the old man to have had so much blood in him? (5.1.35–40)

As the Doctor concedes, "This disease is beyond my practice." It is suggested later that she dies by suicide.

The psychological forces we witness in Lady Macbeth are what Sigmund Freud would come to call the subconscious. In *Macbeth*, as in *Lear*, Shakespeare formulates the notion that one's inner compulsions can serve as antagonists. Lady Macbeth, who encouraged her husband to commit the murder when he was fearful of the idea, now succumbs to her own inner fears.

In his essay on Lady Macbeth, Freud entertains the notion that she and Macbeth operate as a kind of symbiotic protagonist, even to the point of sharing psychological effects:

> the germs of fear which break out in Macbeth on the night of the murder do not develop further in *him* but in *her*. It is he who after the murder hears the cry in the house: "Sleep no more! Macbeth does murder sleep ..." and so "Macbeth shall sleep no more"; but we never hear that *he* slept no more, while the Queen, as we see, rises from her bed and, talking in her sleep, betrays her guilt. It is he who stands helpless with bloody hands, lamenting that "all great Neptune's ocean" will not wash them clean, while she comforts him: "A little water clears us of this deed"; but later it is she who washes her hands for a quarter of an hour and cannot get rid of the bloodstains: "All the perfumes of Arabia will not sweeten this little hand." Thus what he feared in his pangs of conscience is fulfilled in her; she becomes all remorse and he all defiance. Together they exhaust the possibilities of reaction to the crime, like two disunited parts of a single psychical individuality.... (Freud 323)

Just as Lady Macbeth can infect her husband's nature with her ambition, overcoming his initial reluctance to murder, so in time, she takes on aspects of his psychic suffering—losing sleep, feeling compelled to cleanse her hands.

Near the end, when she dies, Macbeth recognizes there is nothing left to live for. Life is no more than a walking shadow. As symbiotic protagonists, they share in each other's psychic collapse. They take turns encouraging each other to make the fatal steps, and in this sense, they serve as antagonists to each other, leading each other to their joint doom.

For both, Shakespeare depicts nuances in what happens when individuals disregard their conscience and do what they know is heinously wrong. One grows hardened and apathetic, the other disintegrates from within.

Shakespeare had shown Lear as a victim of his own inner compulsions—his unrestrained ego and his delirious imaginings of persecutors. In *Macbeth*, Shakespeare gives us an even more developed picture of a psychological force that serves to torment us: in this case, it is shared by two people, who together transgress humanity's taboos about murder and loyalty.

Freud points out the uncanny nature of the bond between this husband and wife. Shakespeare is showing one more way that we can be vulnerable to another, can fall prey to an antagonist force: this is in the close bond between a loving couple who can drag each other into the abyss.

Resolution in the Four Great Tragedies

In creating a protagonist, Shakespeare has the character's end in mind. The problems they face will be resolved in some way. For the most part, this is also the case with the antagonists.

When Shakespeare raises important questions, as he does in all of his tragedies, often through his antagonists, he resolves them as well. Sometimes this means simply acknowledging that some challenges are beyond our control and some mysteries beyond our understanding.

Hamlet

In *Hamlet*, the antagonist's end is straightforward and morally satisfying. Claudius dies at the hands of the person he wronged, Hamlet. Ironically, he is slain by the weapon he provided to Laertes to kill Hamlet, a poisoned rapier. Moreover, Claudius is struck down in the midst of his sins, as Hamlet wanted, so that Claudius is no more prepared for meeting his maker than was Claudius' victim, his brother. Claudius' accomplices, with their varying degrees of culpability, are dispatched—Rosencrantz and Guildenstern will be killed in England; and Polonius and Laertes are dead, also at Hamlet's hands.

The earlier prayer scene in which Claudius confesses that what he did was wrong provides a certain satisfaction to the audience: *he agrees with us on what is right and wrong.* When a villain refuses to acknowledge these moral norms, as we see in Iago, it strikes a dissonant note. But with this resolution in *Hamlet*, the world of Denmark will be rid of this fratricidal ruler, and the audience will have a sense that a more just, or at least, less tainted, world is arriving with Fortinbras.

As for the psychological antagonistic force—Hamlet's inner struggles—those, too, have been resolved through the protagonist's stoical embrace of fate:

> There is a special providence in the fall of a sparrow. If it be now, 'tis not to come; if it be not to come, it will be now; if it be not now, yet it will come. The readiness is all. Since no man of aught he leaves knows, what is 't to leave betimes? Let be. (5.1)

His questions and fears about the hereafter that plagued him are not answered; they cannot be. But Hamlet can let go of them now that he has learned to accept what is.

Othello

In Iago, Shakespeare is probing the nature of extreme malevolence. Iago is not so much inhuman as one of those rare humans whose motives and lack of conscience leave us aghast. They are a mystery. And that is how Shakespeare leaves Iago in the end.

Even when his deeds have been unmasked, he has no remorse. He cannot be brought to any kind of submission and refuses to justify his behavior. "Demand me nothing; what you know, you know: / From this time forth I never will speak word" (5.2). Othello searches for a sign as to why he would set out to entrap him. "I look down towards his feet; but that's a fable." If Othello could see the devil's hooves instead of feet, at least he would know Iago was diabolical, not a man. But he gets no satisfaction to this mystery.

In the final scene, we are told Iago will be imprisoned and tortured, so there is a sense of containment of this evil and of justice being meted out.

But more prominent is his glowering silence, his utter imperviousness to a normal sense of regret or guilt. With Iago's ending, we are not seeing an evildoer admit the error of his ways, or display even a twinge of remorse.

This casts a shadow over the ending. A malignancy like Iago cannot by cured or reasoned with. There is no way of reintegrating a person like this into a healthy society. And if Shakespeare had shown his ending otherwise, we'd have probably have found it unconvincing.

Instead, this sets up a sharper contrast with Othello, who does repent and delivers some of the most stirring final lines of any Shakespearean hero. The protagonist fully accepts responsibility and expresses remorse in detailed and vivid expressions, describing himself as

> one whose subdued eyes,
> Albeit unused to the melting mood,
> Drops tears as fast as the Arabian trees
> Their medicinable gum. (5.2)

He then inflicts on himself the ultimate punishment, killing himself.

Iago is shown as dominant during much of the play, but when the crimes are brought to light, Iago is made powerless and silent. This is the extent of the resolution that we get of this antagonist. He has succeeded in his goal of destroying the Moor, but Shakespeare shows he has no power over Othello's essential humanity, which is displayed poignantly at the end.

King Lear

The three main antagonist characters, Goneril, Regan, and Edmund, are killed near the end in poetically just ways. Edmund is vanquished in a duel with Edgar, the brother he maligned. Once stabbed, Edmund shows remorse and tries to revoke the order he gave to put Cordelia to death. His repentance goes some way toward restoring a sense of moral equilibrium at the end, even if it comes too late to save Cordelia.

The two elder sisters, however, die as viciously as they lived. Edmund has seduced each of the women with promises of marriage, and out of jealousy they turn against each other. Goneril poisons Regan in hopes of having Edmund to herself, and then kills herself from grief after he dies. Whereas the sisters were allies before, they end up mortal enemies.

The play shows all of the worst characters dying—even the minor ones such as Regan's husband Cornwall and Goneril's servant Oswald. Albany, who stayed out of the fray, is not sorry to hear of his wife Goneril's death. The daughters go to their graves unmourned.

King Lear does not, however, provide an ending with easy dramatic justice. The guilty die, but so do the good and innocent, such as Cordelia. Lear suffers a final, insupportable blow, even after having repented of his errors.

This ending was literally too much for some audiences to tolerate. Hence, for 150 years, a version of *King Lear* dominated the London stage showing a happy ending in which Lear and Cordelia live on.

Projected Antagonists

In the middle of the play, Lear wages a battle against his imaginary tormentors, which include the gods themselves. (Shakespeare, sensibly, set Lear in pre-Christian Britain, which allowed him to raise questions about the nature of divinity and not fall afoul of blasphemy laws.)

Lear implores the heavens to show justice. Gloucester, too, invokes the same theme when he claims, at his most desperate, that "As flies to wanton boys are we to th' gods, / They kill us for their sport" (4.1). It's a profound question that lingers over the play and gets to one of humanity's deepest mysteries. Why would the gods allow injustice to occur?

Does the storm represent a kind of sympathy between earth and heaven—a disorder on earth that is mirrored in the heavens? Or is it just a storm, and any causality is our projection, while the gods remain indifferent to our suffering?

Shakespeare does not directly answer this. Or rather, the fact that he does not answer this is his answer. He seems to be saying that the gods—the heavens, or that which creates and animates our world—are simply not within our control or ken. By their absence when we plead for their help, we cannot say evil has won out, or that the gods don't exist. We can only conclude that we cannot compel them to show themselves, not through entreaty nor through command. Even a king cannot make the gods show themselves. The gods that Lear tries to enlist, and then rages against, remain a true mystery.

The gods function as an antagonist because Lear demands of them something they will not do. The resolution to this antagonism must come from within Lear as well. And he does achieve this to a degree. He realizes his own culpability in not helping to relieve the suffering of others.

> O, I have ta'en
> Too little care of this. Take physic, pomp,
> Expose thyself to feel what wretches feel,
> That thou mayst shake the superflux to them,
> And show the heavens more just. (3.4)

Lear concludes it is incumbent on us to show justice, to do what we can to manifest what we would want the heavens to do. He acknowledges the heavens do not appear to show justice. But *we* can make them appear more just through our own actions.

Macbeth

At the end of *Macbeth*, one of the antagonists, Macduff, gets revenge for his family's murder by slaying the protagonist. Another antagonist, Malcolm, who is the son of the murdered king, ascends to the throne. With these events, the threat posed by Macbeth is eliminated and order is restored in Scotland. The antagonists are the ones who win in the end and gain some measure of justice.

But the witches, explicitly evil antagonists, are not accounted for in the ending. They are left uncontained. The last we hear of them is when Macbeth calls them "juggling fiends" upon discovering they misled him into believing he was invincible.

The threat the witches pose this world certainly isn't purged. How could it be? Burning witches was no solution (even if it was a practice Shakespeare's patron King James allowed for a time). The witches represent an eternal source of malevolence in the world, beyond the reach of mere humans. Shakespeare avoids giving an ending to these antagonists, presumably because there's no way of bringing this kind of evil to account.

On the other hand, the antagonistic forces that arose within Macbeth and Lady Macbeth—their guilt that becomes manifest in hallucinations and other kinds of mental illness—do reach some resolution. What they were willing to do for power is what ultimately undermines them. It is suggested that Lady Macbeth killed herself. For Macbeth, his "life is fallen into the sere"—he has no more enjoyment of life and is depleted. He will fight his last battle, losing against Macduff, but psychologically he has already lost.

Othello prompted Shakespeare to wonder "What kind of person is the most dangerous and hardest for others to defend against?" In *Macbeth*, Shakespeare turns this question inward, to the protagonists themselves. What happens to the person when they transgress moral boundaries? When they voluntarily reject their conscience and commit heinous crimes?

This is why Shakespeare chose to have the protagonist be the one committing the murders: the central problem is a psychological and moral one. In the figure of Macbeth, Shakespeare creates a character who is both the protagonist and his own worst antagonist. Both are purged from the world through his death.

Summary

A story depends on an antagonist to complete the protagonist's challenges and journey. Shakespeare shows, particularly in his great tragedies, how subtle and varied an antagonist can be. He creates his antagonists as forces against which the protagonist struggles, even setting their worldviews as dialectically opposed.

Through his quartet of tragedies, Shakespeare finds insightful new ways of conceiving of the threats a protagonist may face. In *Hamlet*, he begins with a single major antagonist whose motives are comprehensible, and a protagonist who struggles within himself to act. Shakespeare proceeds, in Iago, to single destructive individual whose nature in almost pure malevolence. Next, in *King Lear*, he conceives of a more widespread threat, a breakdown of familial and social bonds as well the existential fear that the gods do not intervene, or perhaps even notice, humans' sufferings. And he finishes Macbeth, which considers the threats and limitations of supernatural forces, and includes in his latter two works, perhaps most remarkably of all, the antagonism that arises within the psyches of his heroes Lear and Macbeth.

Without the antagonists we find in those plays, the great figures of Hamlet, Othello, King Lear, and Macbeth could not exist.

Takeaways for Writers

In the four great tragedies, Shakespeare reimagines the role and nature of the antagonist. The progression is from a rather straightforward single antagonist to a more complex set of antagonistic forces. Shakespeare varies and refracts the role of antagonist in his tragedies as follows:

- *Hamlet* has a single main antagonist; Claudius is relatable in the sense that he who knows he did wrong, but was unwilling and unable to do otherwise.
- *Othello* has a single main antagonist, the epitome of malevolence. He is defeated finally, but has no regrets because he has no conscience; his end is not easily resolved by the society left behind: there is no cure for someone like Iago, only containment.
- *King Lear* has many antagonists of various types; the antagonists die at the end, as do many of the sympathetic characters, including the protagonist. In both this play and in *Macbeth*, the antagonism is found pervasively within the social and familial realms, and even within.
- *Macbeth* has many antagonists of various types. Some of them are good characters who try to thwart the protagonist's violent and paranoid rule. The supernatural Weird Sisters seek to cause harm through deception, but cannot control the freewill of humans. The guilt Macbeth and Lady Macbeth experience because of their crimes destroy their mental equilibrium; it is their psyches that end up being the most formidable of all antagonists.

Extras

1. In this passage in *Hamlet*, **Claudius** is attempting to pray after being shocked by the Players' performance of a murder much like the one he committed:

O, my offense is rank, it smells to heaven,
It hath the primal eldest curse upon't,
A brother's murther. Pray can I not,

Though inclination be as sharp as will.
My stronger guilt defeats my strong intent,
And, like a man to double business bound,
I stand in pause where I shall first begin,
And both neglect. What if this cursed hand
Were thicker than itself with brother's blood,
Is there not rain enough in the sweet heavens
To wash it white as snow? Whereto serves mercy
But to confront the visage of offense?
And what's in prayer but this twofold force,
To be forestalled ere we come to fall,
Or pardon'd being down? then I'll look up.
My fault is past, but, O, what form of prayer
Can serve my turn? "Forgive me my foul murther"?
That cannot be, since I am still possess'd
Of those effects for which I did the murther:
My crown, mine own ambition, and my queen.
May one be pardon'd and retain th' offense?
In the corrupted currents of this world
Offense's gilded hand may [shove] by justice,
And oft 'tis seen the wicked prize itself
Buys out the law, but 'tis not so above:
There is no shuffling, there the action lies
In his true nature, and we ourselves compell'd,
Even to the teeth and forehead of our faults,
To give in evidence. What then? What rests?
Try what repentance can. What can it not?
Yet what can it, when one can not repent?
O wretched state! O bosom black as death!
O limed soul, that struggling to be free
Art more engag'd! Help, angels! Make assay,
Bow, stubborn knees, and heart, with strings of steel,
Be soft as sinews of the new-born babe! All may be well.
[He kneels.]   (3.3.36-98)

2. In this soliloquy from *Othello*, **Iago** is thinking through his plans for
    deceiving the protagonist. He mockingly denies he is a villain before

admitting he is like a devil, who puts on heavenly shows in order to entrap souls all the better.

And what's he then that says I play the villain,
When this advice is free I give, and honest,
Probal to thinking, and indeed the course
To win the Moor again? For 'tis most easy
Th' inclining Desdemona to subdue
In any honest suit; she's fram'd as fruitful
As the free elements. And then for her
To win the Moor, were't to renounce his baptism,
All seals and symbols of redeemed sin,
His soul is so enfetter'd to her love,
That she may make, unmake, do what she list,
Even as her appetite shall play the god
With his weak function. How am I then a villain,
To counsel Cassio to this parallel course,
Directly to his good? Divinity of hell!
When devils will the blackest sins put on,
They do suggest at first with heavenly shows,
As I do now; for whiles this honest fool
Plies Desdemona to repair his fortune,
And she for him pleads strongly to the Moor,
I'll pour this pestilence into his ear—
That she repeals him for her body's lust,
And by how much she strives to do him good,
She shall undo her credit with the Moor.
So will I turn her virtue into pitch,
And out of her own goodness make the net
That shall enmesh them all.   (2.3.336-62)

3.   In this passage from *King Lear*, **Lear** describes his acutely distressed state of mind, and fixates on the filial ingratitude of his daughters:

Thou think'st 'tis much that this contentious storm
Invades us to the skin; so 'tis to thee;
But where the greater malady is fix'd,

The lesser is scarce felt. Thou'dst shun a bear,
But if thy flight lay toward the roaring sea,
Thou'dst meet the bear i' th' mouth. When the mind's free,
The body's delicate; this tempest in my mind
Doth from my senses take all feeling else,
Save what beats there—filial ingratitude!
Is it not as this mouth should tear this hand
For lifting food to't? But I will punish home.
No, I will weep no more. In such a night
To shut me out? Pour on, I will endure.
In such a night as this? O Regan, Goneril!
Your old kind father, whose frank heart gave all—
O, that way madness lies, let me shun that!
No more of that. (3.4.6-22)

4.   In this soliloquy from *Macbeth,* which comes just as the protagonist is
     heading to Duncan's chamber to murder him, **Macbeth** describes the
     hallucinated dagger that seems to be leading him the way:

Is this a dagger which I see before me,
The handle toward my hand? Come, let me clutch thee:
I have thee not, and yet I see thee still.
Art thou not, fatal vision, sensible
To feeling as to sight? or art thou but
A dagger of the mind, a false creation,
Proceeding from the heat-oppressed brain?
I see thee yet, in form as palpable
As this which now I draw.
Thou marshal'st me the way that I was going,
And such an instrument I was to use.
Mine eyes are made the fools o' th' other senses,
Or else worth all the rest. I see thee still;
And on thy blade and dudgeon gouts of blood,
Which was not so before. There's no such thing:
It is the bloody business which informs
Thus to mine eyes. Now o'er the one half world
Nature seems dead, and wicked dreams abuse

The curtain'd sleep; witchcraft celebrates
Pale Hecat's off'rings; and wither'd Murther,
Alarum'd by his sentinel, the wolf,
Whose howl's his watch, thus with his stealthy pace,
With Tarquin's ravishing strides, towards his design
Moves like a ghost. Thou sure and firm-set earth,
Hear not my steps, which way they walk, for fear
The very stones prate of my whereabout,
And take the present horror from the time,
Which now suits with it. Whiles I threat, he lives:
Words to the heat of deeds too cold breath gives.
[A bell rings.]
I go, and it is done; the bell invites me.
Hear it not, Duncan, for it is a knell,
That summons thee to heaven or to hell.
[Exit.]   (2.133-64)

SHAKESPEARE RESOURCES

T here are abundant resources for those who wish to know Shakespeare's works better. The best method of all is to experience them directly, whether through live performance, film, or reading. There are also countless books, websites, and other resources that offer summaries and interpretations of the works, and critical and historical material to deepen your appreciation of Shakespeare's plays and poems. Sorting through it all to find what's meaningful for you will be the hard part.

Locating a Passage from Shakespeare and Making Sense of It

Sometimes you may want to refresh your memory about how a particular speech or scene in Shakespeare goes. If you can recall a few words of a passage, simply enter them in a search engine. Even if the wording is not quite accurate, you're likely to pull up the quotation you have in mind. You can also scroll through a site such as the Folger Shakespeare Library https://www.folger.edu/explore/shakespeares-works/ , and read their concise summaries of the plays and of individual scenes to prompt your memory.

Many online search results will offer not just the passage but interpretations of it as well. The value of this will be hit or miss. Some websites provide the original texts next to simple-English versions, which can be helpful in a pinch, but the simplified "translations" may be unreliable. Generally speaking, the best glossaries and interpretive notes on the plays will be found in scholarly editions of the works.

Individual and Complete Works

Shakespeare's works are, of course, widely available through libraries and bookstores, as well as online or as e-books, whether as individual works or in collections.

Everyone, even literary scholars, need help sometimes deciphering Shakespeare's meaning, whether it's his vocabulary, syntax, or historical references. It's definitely worth seeking out good editions that provide clear

263

explanatory notes. The Arden, Oxford, New Cambridge, and Norton Shakespeare series of individual editions are among the most highly regarded and generously annotated. Mass-market or student editions, such as the Signet Classic, Folger, Pelican, and New Penguin, with their sparser and more selective notes, can be very useful as well. Some are available, along with their annotations, in e-book versions.

Complete Works editions vary greatly in reliability. They are also a bit harder to manage because of their size (consider individual editions first). The Complete Works edition your college English professor assigned you is probably still just fine. But if you want to acquire a new one, take a little time to review the online descriptions and user comments about the editions you are considering. Well regarded, scholarly, and recently edited work include The Norton Shakespeare, The Riverside Shakespeare, Complete Works (Bevington), The Oxford Shakespeare, The New Oxford Shakespeare, The Arden Complete Works, The Complete Pelican Shakespeare, and The RSC Complete Works. Especially, be aware of whether the version is an outdated edition that has been repackaged. As older versions fall into the public domain, they are cheap to reproduce. If you pick up an antiquated copy with few notes or outdated glosses, then no matter how pretty it is on the outside, it will likely gather dust on your shelf.

Online Editions with Annotations

The daunting task of preparing a reliable and free version of Shakespeare's complete works online in an annotated and searchable format has not yet been completed. The Internet Shakespeare Editions project (https://internetshakespeare.uvic.ca/Library/plays.html) by the University of Victoria has made a good start, and as of this writing has completed a half a dozen titles (among them *As You Like It, Julius Caesar, Twelfth Night,* and *Henry IV, Part 1.*) The remaining plays are also offered there, minus notes, along with a wealth of historical and critical information.

The *New Oxford Shakespeare: Modern Critical Edition: The Complete Works* offers an e-book with explanatory notes and a searchable text. It's pricier than most of the other Complete Works you can buy for your e-reader, but also more useful. (It is also somewhat controversial for certain of its editorial choices, which include adding new works to the canon and attributing parts of the plays to authors other than Shakespeare.)

Less expensive, but still reliable versions for use on an e-reader include those based on the popular *Riverside Shakespeare.* Unfortunately, most of these will lack the excellent annotations found in the printed Riverside editions.

More awkward to use, but with searchable text and its excellent editorial information and notes, is the scanned version of early editions of the *Riverside Shakespeare.* These are available for free through the Internet Archive (https://archive.org/). The Internet Archive similarly has dozens of scholarly editions of individual works, most of them older, however.

Tips for Selecting E-Versions of the Plays

When purchasing an electronic edition of Shakespeare, whether the complete or individual works, be sure to view a sample of the page layout and notes. Some editions that purport to be "annotated" do not, in fact, provide notes, or else the notes are difficult to access. Skim through customer reviews as well. Some versions have been poorly converted into e-books and lack functionality.

In most instances, it's best to avoid texts that have long been out of copyright; they are cheap for publishers to reproduce but will not reflect the invaluable advances of recent textual and critical scholarship. As with many other online versions of the complete works, these texts usually lack good (or any) explanatory notes. Probably the biggest hurdle for readers of Shakespeare is trying to make sense of unusual words or references; this is why seeking out reputable editions with annotations is worth the effort.

Shakespeare Background and Criticism

Shakespeare has attracted legions of critics, and it can be overwhelming to wade through the vast body of criticism to find what's meaningful to you. Individual editions will include usually essays on the work and references to follow as your interests guide you.

The major Shakespeare institutions have put a wealth of interpretive resources online as well. Among these are:

- Shakespeare Birthplace Trust (https://www.shakespeare.org.uk/, especially their Discover Shakespeare collections https://collections.shakespeare.org.uk/)
- Folger Shakespeare Library (www.folger.edu/)
- Royal Shakespeare Company (www.rsc.org.uk/explore/)

The Internet Shakespeare Editions (https://internetshakespeare.uvic.ca/) provides a well curated collection of critical essays as well as links to online lectures, performances, interviews, recent discoveries, and other resources. The Shakespeare Resource Center (www.bardweb.net/index.html) similarly offers a wide range of materials on Shakespeare.

This list is just the start of fine and wide-ranging resources to help you deepen your understanding of Shakespeare. New insights on Shakespeare pop up in unexpected places. Skim through online and in bookstores to see what catches your eye.

Shakespeare in Performance and in Other Media

Perhaps the most rewarding resource of all is Shakespeare in performance. Viewing his works in or close to the medium in which he created them can be an ideal way to open up to Shakespeare's art. Attend local productions or head to Shakespeare festivals. Search for "best of" lists of Shakespeare on film, or find stage performances that are simulcast or recorded from theaters around the world. Some of the finest contemporary talents have been drawn to Shakespeare and are transforming them into a new media and new works of art altogether.

About the Author: Maggi Kramm, PhD

In its earliest version, the *Shakespeare for Writers* series began many years ago as a course I designed for students in the University of Minnesota's Compleat Scholars program. I am grateful to those students, as well as those who followed, for their insights and input on how Shakespeare can inspire writers.

In addition to teaching university courses on literature, Shakespeare, and writing, I have published theater criticism and essays for *American Theatre* and *Shakespeare Bulletin*.

In my doctoral dissertation, I placed Shakespeare's rarely performed *All's Well That Ends Well* in the context of the domestic dramas of the period.

I was exceptionally fortunate to have as my doctoral advisor and my own guide to Shakespeare Professor Tom Clayton, a brilliant Shakespearean and generous reader and mentor. I gratefully dedicate this first book of the series to him.

WORKS CITED

Aristotle. *Aristotle's Poetics.* Trans. S. H. Butcher, Hill and Wang, 1962. [Introduction by Francis Fergusson.]

Aristotle. From *The Poetics.* Poetry Foundation. Accessed online: https://www.poetryfoundation.org/articles/69372/from-poetics

Baldick, Chris. *The Concise Oxford Dictionary of Literary Terms:* [Defines over 1,000 Literary Terms from Absurd to Zeugma]. Oxford University Press, 2004.

Bandello, Matteo. "Timbreo and Fenicia" from his *Novelle* (1554). In *Tales for Shakespeare: Stories That Inspired the Plays,* Cambridge Scholars Publishing, 2020. 37-71.

Bandello, Matteo. The tragicall historye of Romeus and Iuliet written first in Italian by Bandell, and nowe in Englishe by Ar. Br. [Arthur Brooke]. In the digital collection Early English Books Online. Accessed online: https://name.umdl.umich.edu/A03435.0001.001

Brooke, Arthur, and Matteo Bandello. Brooke's "Romeus and Juliet," being the original of Shakespeare's *Romeo and Juliet.* ed by. J.J. Munro. New York: Duffield and Company; London: Chatto & Windus, 1908. In the digital collection of Shakespeare Navigators. https://shakespeare-navigators.ewu.edu/romeo/BrookeIndex.html

Cinthio, Giovanni Battista Giraldi. *Gli Heccatommithi,* Third Decade (1565). "Cinthio's Tale (Modern)." *Internet Shakespeare Editions.* University of Victoria. Accessed online: https://internetshakespeare.uvic.ca/doc/Cinthio_M/complete/index.html

Cleese, John. "How to Write the Perfect Farce." *The Guardian,* 17 Feb. 2017. Accessed online: www.theguardian.com/stage/2017/feb/17/john-cleese-farce-bang-bang-fawlty-towers-rat-manuel-feydeau

Field, Syd. Field, Syd. *Screenplay: The Foundations of Screenwriting*. Delta Trade Paperbacks, 2005. Accessed online: https://archive.org/details/screenplaythefoundationsofscreenwritingrevise dupdatedsydfield2005/

Freebury-Jones, Darren. Cited in Dalya Alberge, "Shakespeare Played Jealous Husband in 1598 Ben Jonson Drama, Scholar's Analysis Finds." *The Guardian*, 8 Apr. 2024. Accessed online: www.theguardian.com/culture/2024/apr/07/shakespeare-acted-in-a-1598-ben-jonson-play-scholars-analysis-finds.

Freud, S. "Some Character-Types Met with in Psycho-Analytic Work" (1916). *The Standard Edition of the Complete Psychological Works of Sigmund Freud* 14: 309-333. Accessed online: https://pep-web.org/browse/SE/volumes/14?preview=SE.014.0309A

Freytag, Gustav. *The Technique of Drama: Freytag's Technique of the drama: an exposition of dramatic composition and art.*. Ed. Elias J. MacEwan. Chicago: Scott, Foresman, 1900. 3rd ed. Accessed online: https://archive.org/details/freytagstechniqu00freyuoft/page/n3/mode/2up

Freytag, Gustav. *Die Technik des Dramas von Gustav Freytag*. Zehnte Auflage. [10th ed.] Leipzig, Verlag von S. Hirzel 1905. Accessed online: https://www.gutenberg.org/files/50616/50616-h/50616-h.htm

Hunt, Arnold. *The Art of Hearing: English Preachers and Their Audiences, 1590-1640*. Cambridge University Press, 2010.

Jonson, Ben. *Timber, or Discoveries* (1641). Published in *Discoveries Made Upon Men and Matter, by Ben Jonson*. Ed. Henry Morley. Cassel and Company, Limited, London, 1892. Accessed online: https://www.gutenberg.org/files/5134/5134-h/5134-h.htm

Marlowe, Christopher. *Tamburlaine, Parts I and II; Doctor Faustus, A- and B-Texts; The Jew of Malta; Edward II*. Edited by David M. Bevington and Eric Rasmussen, Oxford University Press, 1995.

Plutarch. *Shakespeare's Plutarch; the Lives of Julius Caesar, Brutus, Marcus Antonius, and Coriolanus in the Translation of Sir Thomas North*. Ed. T. J. B. Spencer.

Trans. Thomas North, Penguin Books, 1964. Accessed online: https://archive.org/details/shakespearesplut0000plut/page/338/mode/2up

Royal Shakespeare Company. *Macbeth*: Dates and Sources. Accessed online: https://www.rsc.org.uk/macbeth/about-the-play/dates-and-sources .

Shakespeare, William. *Antony and Cleopatra* from The Folger Shakespeare. Ed. Barbara Mowat and Paul Werstine. Folger Shakespeare Library. Accessed online: https://www.folger.edu/explore/shakespeares-works/antony-and-cleopatra/

Shakespeare, William, et al. *The Riverside Shakespeare.* Ed. G. Blakemore Evans: Houghton Mifflin, 1974.

Shapiro, James. *The Year of Lear: Shakespeare in 1606*. New York: Simon and Schuster, 2015.